THEORY Z

HOW AMERICAN BUSINESS CAN MEET THE JAPANESE CHALLENGE

WILLIAM G. OUCHI

AVON
PUBLISHERS OF BARD, CAMELOT, DISCUS AND FLARE BOOKS

AVON BOOKS
A division of
The Hearst Corporation
959 Eighth Avenue
New York, New York 10019

The Addison-Wesley Publishing Company, Inc. edition contains the
following Library of Congress Cataloging in Publication Data:

Ouchi, William
Theory Z.
  Bibliography.
  Includes index.
  1. Industrial management—Japan   2. Industrial
management   United States.   1. Title.
HD70J3088   658.3   81-8

First Avon Printing, January 1982

For Carol

ACKNOWLEDGMENTS

WHEN I began to study the managerial practices of Japanese companies in 1973, I was embarked on a scholarly attempt in which not many people were interested. The earliest funding for my attempts came from the National Commission on Productivity, which no longer exists. As my research progressed, the issue of Japanese quality and productivity became increasingly topical, and I was often called upon by American companies to share my research findings. Through discussions with many managers, I began to develop a fuller understanding of the changes that could be made in American companies, drawing upon but not mimicking the Japanese success. This initial research was done in collaboration with Richard Pascale. My understanding of the Japanese company I owe to the many managers who spent time with me, but two were of special importance. Akio Morita, co-founder of the Sony Corporation and a longtime friend, shared his broad understanding of business with me and gave me the run of his company. Joji Arai of the Japan Productivity Center in Washington, D.C., was most helpful in arranging contacts in Japan.

By this time, I had moved beyond the study of Japanese companies to the question that everyone was asking: can Japanese management methods be used successfully in the United States? Most businessmen doubted that they could be, and most scholars were and many still are convinced that it cannot be done. To a specialist in the Japanese society and culture, the differences between Japan and the United States are so great that a borrowing of social organization between them seems impossible. To a student of business organization, however, the underlying similarity in tasks between Japanese and American business suggests that some form of the essential characteristics of Japanese companies must be transferrable. The objective became to separate the culturally specific principles from those universally applicable to economic organization. I faced the greatest difficulty in finding support for my thesis. The director of the Alcoa Foundation, Charles Griswold, was the only one who saw some promise in my research and supported me financially. This he did in part on the advice of Arjay Miller, who was then dean of the Stanford University Graduate School of Business, where I was on the faculty. Dean Miller understood and supported my efforts with a constancy that I can never fully repay.

As I undertook a systematic study of Type Z companies in order to test the thesis that the Japanese approach could be found among some American companies, I talked with many business people. One of the most helpful was John Doyle of Hewlett-Packard, who was always skeptical of easy solutions and always insightful in understanding organization and management. Mel Lane and his brother Bill, of the Lane Publishing Company, allowed me to refine my research techniques by practicing on their Sunset Magazine and Books staff, so that I was able to look at a company that seemed to me to be of Type Z and to determine whether I could measure its key characteristics. Those statistics and measures do not appear in this book, but the insight provided by that work does come through, I hope.

By this time, the Japanese challenge was in full force, and Americans wanted to know what the American response was going to be. I was asked by literally dozens of publishers to write a book on this topic. All of them, however, wanted either a college textbook or a slick but, in my view, insubstantial quickie. I could not develop any enthusiasm for either, and thus did not begin to write this book until I was approached by Stuart Miller, an editor at Addison-Wesley, who asked whether I could write a book that would not promise simple-minded solutions but that would deal with the fundamental issues of Japanese management and American productivity. If I succeed in reaching a large audience of readers, then it is in part due to the thoughtful editing of Harriet Rubin and to Ann Dilworth and Warren Stone for having created the strategy so well explained by Stuart Miller. Pamela Pierson edited this final copy with skill.

Above all, this book recognizes that steel-pushing or fashion jeans-selling companies, mysterious hospitals, and bureaucratic post offices are social beings. This book, therefore, is about trust, subtlety, and intimacy. Without them, no social being can be successful. I learned about trust from my first pastor, Allen Hackett, who permitted his congregation to grow as individuals because he trusted in them. I learned about subtlety from my mother, my sister, and above all my father, who guided my development in unobtrusive ways. I learned about intimacy from my wife, who has shown me that through closeness both trust and subtlety develop.

This book addresses the practicalities of applying an understanding of Japanese management to the American setting. My exposure to the practical side of business has come from many sources. I learned about the personal challenges, pressures, and pleasures of managerial life through a long and special acquaintance with Charles W. Joiner, Jr., who was then a manager at the Chrysler Corporation. I learned about designing large organizations from James Farley and his partners at Booz, Allen and Hamilton, the largest management consulting firm in the United States, and from Oliver Williamson, an economist whose ideas are revolutionizing our approaches to organization design. My research involved hundreds of interviews and thousands of hours of collecting questionnaires and analyzing data. Again, although the numbers are not presented in this book, they were thoughtfully assembled and understood by my students: Mary Ann Maguire, Alfred Jaeger, Jerry Johnson, Alan Wilkins, Alice Kaplan, Raymond Price, David Gibson, Robert Kenmore, and Patricia Higgins.

I am grateful to Hewlett-Packard Corporation, Dayton-Hudson Corporation, Intel Corporation, Rockwell International Corporation, and Eli Lilly Corporation for permitting me to reproduce their statements of corporate philosophy. Their openness will benefit us all.

The final step of actually pulling the ideas together and committing them to paper began after I arrived at U.C.L.A. Dean Clay LaForce has created there an atmosphere of creativity and of support that has propelled me. My colleagues and students have helped me to clarify my thoughts and to see new points of view. I am grateful to all of them. Mostly, however, I am grateful to my wife Carol, and to our children Sarah, Jennifer, and Andrew. They provide the most primary of bonds that both support and restrain me, and without which I could not have passed through the many transitions that led to this book.

WILLIAM G. OUCHI
Santa Monica, California

CONTENTS

PART 1

LEARNING FROM JAPAN

INTRODUCTION

WHY WE NEED TO LEARN

NOT long ago, I arranged a luncheon for two of my Ph.D. students with the vice-president of one of the most respected and largest firms in the United States — a company that regularly appears on lists of the "ten best-managed companies." The luncheon provided an opportunity for these educators of the future to ask our guest questions for which his position and experience had given him a unique perspective. After a discussion ranging over many issues, the students summarized their interests in a single question: "What, in your opinion, is the key issue facing American business over the next decade?" His answer: "The key issue will not be technology or investment, not regulation or inflation. The key issue will be the way in which we respond to one fact — the Japanese know how to manage better than we do."

A case in point: A team of engineers and managers from the Buick Division of General Motors Corporation recently visited their dealer in Tokyo, who imports Buick automobiles and sells them to the Japanese. The operation appeared to be a massive repair facility, so they asked how he had built up such a large service business. He explained with some embarrassment that this was *not* a repair facility at all but rather a re-assembly operation where newly delivered cars were disassembled and rebuilt to Japanese standards. While many Japanese admire the American automobile, he noted, they would never accept the low quality with which they are put together.

Stories like this one abound. We know that productivity in Japan has increased at 400 percent the rate in the United States over the postwar years. More seriously, we know that productivity in the United States is now improving more slowly than in any European nation, including the much-maligned United Kingdom. While many observers have marvelled at the success of the Japanese, they have concluded that Japan is one country from which we cannot learn much. They feel Japanese techniques simply are not applicable to our situation.

But our story has a different sequel. The engineers and managers at Buick didn't assume that the Japanese success would work in Flint, Michigan, and they set out to invent their own version of it. They took the Buick Final Assembly Plant, which had dropped to one of the lowest levels of efficiency and quality in the whole corporation and with the cooperation of workers and their union redesigned the management of that plant in ways that resemble the Japanese approach to management. Within two years, Buick Final Assembly had risen to rank number one among all General Motors assembly plants in quality and efficiency. The ideas that shaped the remaking of General Motors' troubled Buick plant are the basis of what I call the Theory Z approach to management. Quite simply, it suggests that involved workers are the key to increased productivity.

As a nation, we have developed a sense of the value of technology and of a scientific approach to it, but we have meanwhile taken people for granted. Our government appropriates hundreds of millions of dollars for research on new techniques in electrical engineering, physics, and astronomy. It supports the development of complex economic ideas. But almost no funds go to develop our understanding of how to manage and organize people at work, and that is what we have to learn by studying the Japanese. The problem of productivity in the United States will not be solved with monetary policy nor through more investment in research and development. It will only be remedied when we learn how to manage people in such a way that they can work together more effectively. Theory Z offers several such ways. American workers perform just as hard as their Japanese counterparts. American managers want high performance just as much as the Japanese. Increased productivity will not come through harder work. Most employees work as hard as they can, and many work too hard for their own good in trying to catch up. Productivity, I believe, is a problem of social organization or, in business terms, managerial organization.

Productivity is a problem that can be worked out through coordinating individual efforts in a productive manner and of giving employees the incentives to do so by taking a cooperative, long-range view.

The first lesson of Theory Z is trust. Productivity and trust go hand in hand, strange as it may seem. To understand that assertion, observe the development of the British economy during this century. It is a history of mutual distrust between union, government, and management, a distrust that has paralyzed the economy and lowered the English standard of living to a dismal level. Karl Marx foresaw this distrust as the inevitable product of capitalism and the force that, in his view, would bring about the ultimate failure of capitalism.

But capitalism and trust need not be mutually exclusive. Thomas Lifson, a young scholar at the Harvard Business School, has studied in detail the Japanese general trading firms, those firms like Mitsui, Mitsubishi, and Sumitomo that maintain offices worldwide and have traditionally served as the sales force for Japanese-produced goods. Undoubtedly these trading companies have played a central role in the successful export strategy of Japanese industry. They have the capacity to move quickly into new markets, to strike deals where no American company can, and to coordinate far-flung operations. According to Lifson, the central feature of the trading firm is an extensive management system that maintains a sense of trust between employees in the trading company. Japanese employees, just like American counterparts, want to get ahead. They want to make deals beneficial to both their departments and themselves. They work in an environment of tremendous uncertainty, buying and selling copper ore, crude oil, wheat, and televisions. On a typical day, the central office of one of the major trading firms will receive 35,000 telex messages, each one with an offer to buy or to sell. Often, the firm's overall profitability will be maximized if an office takes a loss, which will be more than made up in another office so that the company benefits overall. The success of the trading company depends critically upon the willingness of individual offices and employees to make these sacrifices. That willingness exists because the Japanese trading firm uses managerial practices that foster trust through the knowledge that such sacrifices will always be repaid in the future. Equity will, in the end, be restored.

One American company that has a definite uniqueness but at

the same time closely resembles the Japanese management style is Hewlett-Packard, a major manufacturer of computers, precision instruments, and electronic components. A personnel specialist at Hewlett-Packard described a special assignment given to him by a vice-president, in which he was asked to develop a new procedure to be used company-wide. It provided an opportunity for him to look good, to have an impact, and to be recognized throughout the company. After one week on the project, he discovered that a very similar method had already been devised in an obscure office of the company but was not known to others. Like any of us, he had that brief moment of doubt, wondering whether to appear to invent a new procedure based on that which already existed. In the end, he went to the vice-president and told him that the problem had already been solved by someone else and needed only minor modifications to suit the corporate need. He knew that he could trust the vice-president to reward his honesty by finding him an equally challenging assignment and, more importantly, he knew that he could trust his fellow employees to be equally open and honest with him in the future. That is productivity.

The other important lesson that Theory Z translates from Japanese practice into American ways is subtlety. Relationships between people are always complex and changing. A foreman who knows his workers well can pinpoint personalities, decide who works well with whom, and thus put together work teams of maximal effectiveness. These subtleties can never be captured explicitly, and any bureaucratic rule will do violence to them. If the foreman is forced, either by a bureaucratic management or by an equally inflexible union contract to assign work teams strictly on the basis of seniority, then that subtlety is lost and productivity declines.

Consider the task of a machine operator in a Procter & Gamble toilet paper factory. The factory consists mainly of huge machines that put raw material through a series of steps, ending up with rolls of toilet paper. An error at one step of the process may not show up until three steps later, at which point a whole batch will be ruined: loss of productivity. Traditionally, these machine operators were supervised, as they are in virtually all of United States industry, by a foreman who directed their efforts and audited their performance. Even with an attentive foreman and willing machine operators, this system provided for precious little subtlety. Each machine operator had his or her own individual measure of performance — time away from the work station, scrap loss, and so on. If one worker suspected that a small adjustment at his station could produce a better flow two steps down, he had no incentive to go to talk to the other worker concerned. Indeed, his work report would reflect time away from his station, and he would be punished. No foreman, no matter how attentive, can simultaneously take into consideration all of the intricacies of finely balancing this complex production process, and if another foreman were added, the problem of coordinating them would arise. Instead, Procter & Gamble has in many of its plants created semi-autonomous work groups, much like those found in Japanese companies, in which workers govern their own workmanship. A group of those doing the work takes into account all the variables required to achieve great gains in productivity.

Productivity, trust, and subtlety are not isolated elements. Not only do trust and subtlety yield greater productivity through more effective coordination, trust and subtlety are inextricably linked to each other. While a department capable of subtlety has the great advantage of making use of important but inexplicit information, it has for that reason the great disadvantage of not being subject to outside review or audit. A decision made for subtle reasons is a decision that will not stand up to the crude scrutiny of an uninformed outsider. That outsider may be a higher-up manager who does not trust the supervisor or his work group, or it may be a government agency or union which does not trust the company. In either case, a lack of trust between parties will end up requiring that subtlety be thrown overboard in the face of the need for explicitly defensible decisions and actions.

There is a human side as well. How does a man or woman who is treated with distrust at work feel when they are at home? Conversely, is it a coincidence that Japan is not only an economic success but that its rates of alcoholism, drug abuse, and suicide are the lowest among industrial nations? Is it pure chance that a woman can walk alone in downtown Tokyo at midnight with no fear of bodily harm? Or is it that a society of people who are knitted together through many bonds come to develop a sense of mutual trust, grow to appreciate the subtlety in their interpersonal relationships, and thus can lead productive and balanced lives?

The common thread in Japanese life is intimacy. The caring,

the support, and the disciplined unselfishness which make life possible come through close social relations. The loss of closeness in modern life concerns many social observers. In American life, intimacy has traditionally been found in the family, the club, the neighborhood, the lifelong friendship, and the church. Yet all of these traditional sources of intimacy, or primary contact with others, are threatened by our present form of industrial life. Of those Americans who were born in the year 1900, twelve percent experienced a divorce. By comparison, of those born between 1940 and 1945, the best estimates are that forty percent will ultimately divorce, and among those who remarry, forty percent will divorce a second time. For younger Americans, the rate seems to be climbing. Much the same can be said of neighborhoods, clubs, churches, and friendships, all of which are casualties of our way of life. I recently conducted a survey among executives in the electronics industry. I asked these people if they had a close friend; one-half said they did not. Among those who had close friends, almost all reported only one such relationship. I asked them if they knew any of their neighbors intimately; again one-half said they did not know any of their neighbors very well.

Sociologists have long maintained that intimacy is an essential ingredient in a healthy society. Once intimacy in a society begins to disintegrate, the process feeds on itself. People who have not developed a sense of communal responsibility in one setting will lose their general sense of community. A society which loses its capacity for intimacy in one generation may be producing children who have a permanently diminished sense of community. In the end, we will be a dust heap of individuals without connections to one another, as the sociologist George Homans has put it.[1]

In the contemporary American mind, there is apparently the idea that intimacy should only be supplied from certain sources. The church, the family, and other traditional institutions are the only legitimate sources of intimacy. We resist the idea that there can or should be a close familiarity with people in the workplace. "Personal feelings have no place at work," is the common feeling. Yet we are faced with an anomaly. In the Japanese example, we find a successful industrial society in which intimacy occurs in the place of work as well as in other settings. The Japanese example forces us to reconsider our deeply-held beliefs about the proper sources of intimacy in society.

Americans may be a bit too narrowly focused in interpreting our economic and social life. The notion that productivity may be dependent upon trust, subtlety, and intimacy, for example, probably seems strange to most people. Perhaps we can open our minds to new insights and new alternatives by considering some unique models of organization. First among these is the Japanese model. Once we understand it, we can then compare our own forms of organization with it and determine what is wanting in our own setting. Second, let us consider some maverick American companies that have many Japanese-like characteristics to pinpoint the ways in which we can indeed learn from the Japanese. Finally, let us acknowledge that management style and organizational form are nothing more nor less than one aspect of the larger organization of a society. Our ultimate goal shall be to understand how the structure of society and the management of organizations can be coordinated.

1

WHAT WE CAN LEARN

A FEW years ago, while traveling in Japan on research, I visited a plant owned and operated by an American company. Unlike other Japanese plants with labor unions, this one had recently had a strike. The plant manager, an American, described the strike for me: "They warned us about six weeks in advance. On the day of the strike, a picket line with signs forced us to shut down for the day. But when I looked out my window at five o'clock, not only were the signs and handbills gone, but the workers were picking up all of the coffee cups and cigarette butts — leaving the grounds immaculate! The next day they made up the previous day's lost production with no overtime! I didn't understand the meaning of all this, so I asked one of the fellows I know to explain it."

"We had some grievances against the management," the worker answered. "The only way to let you know our seriousness was to go out. But this is our company, too, and we don't want to give you the idea that we are disloyal."

How do we explain this relationship between a company and its employees so radically different from that present in the West? Has the economic success of companies allowed them to buy the loyalty of their employees? Is it simply that East is East and West is West? Or was this one plant an anomaly not repeated elsewhere? These questions perplexed me enough to want to find the answers.

My inquiry actually began some thirteen years before that trip to Japan, as I sat in a class in freshman economics at Williams College. The instructor pointed out that since World War II, productivity in Japan had increased two to three times as fast as it had in the United States. This postwar miracle came about through the building of efficient plants and equipment, whereas we were burdened with old and inefficient capital stock. This, indeed, was the central explanation of Japan's economic success for many years.

More recently the productivity in Japan grows at a faster rate each year, while productivity in the United States now barely increases or even declines during some fiscal quarters. Over recent years, the United States has posted lower productivity improvements than France, England, or any other major European economy. The old plant and equipment argument has lost some of its force, since the Japanese capital stock has aged since the rush of post-war reconstruction, while we have continued to replace our oldest factories. The gap in age of plants and equipment between the two countries has narrowed while the gap in productivity continues to increase. We began to hear quite different explanations for the gap. Japan still attracts many workers from the country who bring their rural work ethic to the factories. They will work long hours at low pay. It's easier for the Japanese to make productivity gains because they can borrow technology from us whereas we must invent our own. Japan has somehow managed to maintain a work ethic while Americans have become soft, lazy, and feel entitled to the good life without earning it.

Some truth may lie in each of the preceding explanations, but none is completely satisfying. We cannot educate workers in old work values, we do not want to become second in technology so that we can borrow from elsewhere out of necessity, and we cannot dramatically change our national values if indeed they need repair. These explanations also fail to account for the variety of ways that companies are organized and managed in the two countries. This difference bears close examination. The straightforward description of the Japanese firm is of itself interesting due to the great success of the Japanese economy and the increasing importance of Japanese trade to the United States. More important, however, is the striking contrast that Japanese management provides to our own.

A visitor from the National Academy of Sciences in Poland asked me, as a specialist in organizations, to describe the unique aspects of the United States form of management. The question proved embarrassing. I realized that I had no organized view, no sense of what distinguishes the typical, much less the successful firm in our country. Indeed, I assumed that organizations everywhere respond to universal principles. Characteristically, our social scientists suspect any theory claiming that phenomena differ as a consequence of culture. This is a reaction to an earlier period when some scholars claimed simply that the differences were cultural and therefore not susceptible to scientific analysis, as though cultures were unique in a way that foreclosed scientific analysis genetically transmitted. In this reaction against nonscientific thought, we may have gone too far in believing no important differences exist between countries.

Perhaps humans respond in similar ways when presented with the same situation, but each culture presents its people with vastly different situations. So, although the same principles of behavior may hold true across cultures, the resultant social structures and patterns of behavior that evolve as a consequence of local conditions may vary greatly. My objective became to use the comparison between Japan and the United States both to identify those underlying features that apply in both cultures and to understand the differences in pattern that had emerged. The ultimate goal, of course, was to understand our own patterns of organization and management. The Japanese serve as the foil to contrast the unique features of our organizations and the forces in our society that shape them.

A colleague, Richard T. Pascale, and I designed a two-phase study to compare Japanese and American management. In the first phase, which was conducted during 1973 and 1974, Pascale and I visited the Japanese and American operations of more than twenty companies, each having a plant or an office in both countries. The second phase, which involved a more detailed collection of data, was carried on subsequently by Pascale and others and is not reported here. After the first phase of this study I turned my attention to those Theory Z companies, uniquely American, which are the focus of this book.

From the interviews in the first phase of the research emerged a clear picture of the underlying characteristics of both Japanese and American firms, but an unsuspected difference proved to be of central importance. The typical Japanese firm in the United States employs an approach to management distinctively different from the typical American firm. Rather than replicate the form developed in their native Japan, the firms modified their management to suit United States needs. Nonetheless, they retain a good deal of Japanese style and remain very different from most American firms. Most Japanese firms have been very successful in the United States. Besides success in financial and operating measures, they have also succeeded from the standpoint of their employees. All of the American employees, from managers to manual and clerical workers, would say, "This is the best place I've ever worked. They know what they're doing here, care about quality, and make me feel part of one big family."

On the other hand, a few American companies have attempted to take their uniquely American approach to management and transplant it in Japan. Without exception, every attempt has been a complete and total disaster. Why should this be? Why can't American firms successfully transport their management approach to Japan, when the Japanese can bring their form successfully to the United States? Particularly puzzling is the United States position as the industrial leader of the world, the greatest exporter of management and management education. Is the Japanese form in some respects more universal than the American form?

This is not to say that no American firms have succeeded in Japan. Clearly some have succeeded quite well. Two examples stand out. Much has been written about the McDonald's chain of fast food stores in Japan, which now number well over one hundred, including the world's largest volume McDonald's outlet (in the Ginza). McDonald's Japan is run by a Japanese entrepreneur with an entirely Japanese staff and style of management, although his stores conform to the food and service standards of McDonald's USA. Their arrangement with McDonald's USA headquarters is that the Americans can send management visitors to the Japanese operation at any time but those visitors may only stay a maximum of two weeks. McDonald's Japan, a great success, is run entirely Japanese style.

Perhaps a better known example is IBM in Japan. In Japan, as elsewhere overseas, IBM runs two separate organizations. The principal company, called IBM Japan, contains the manufacturing, distribution, service, and support functions of basically a complete company. IBM Japan, run entirely by the Japanese from president to janitor, has only an occasional visiting American. In another part of Tokyo, on one floor of an

office building, is the other company, IBM World Trade–
Japan, which is where the Americans are. When I visited them,
IBM World Trade–Japan had a total of twenty-one employees
including secretaries and clerks. Clearly, while the Americans
maintain liaison with IBM Japan, they make little if any attempt
to directly manage the enterprise. Indeed, one of the happiest
American managers I met in Japan was the production liaison at
World Trade. He had just convinced his superior in the United
States to eliminate his job, and he was going home. "They are
doing about as well in the manufacturing here as we do in the
States, in some cases better," he explained. "But even if they
were in deep trouble, I couldn't help them. I can't understand
how they work, and they can't understand how we work — it's
just too different."

No two companies anywhere have exceeded the business
success of IBM and McDonald's. Perhaps no companies are
better managed than these. Indeed, many scholars and managers carefully study these two companies with unusually successful formulae for organizing and managing. These firms, each
with a unique approach to management, make no attempt to
apply those techniques in Japan. Why? What have they learned
about the Japanese situation that has led them to conclude that
their success in Japan does not depend upon and perhaps even
excludes the export of their management system to that
country?

The problem of asymmetry in exporting management styles
or systems ordinarily would be explained by the formal
structure of organizations, but that approach proved fruitless in
this case. In both Japan and in the United States, expatriated
firms employ the same formal structure. The typical American
firm in Japan will have a few American expatriates in the top
managerial positions, with middle management and workers
being local Japanese. By the same token, the typical Japanese
firm in the United States will have a few expatriate Japanese in
top management, with middle and lower levels drawn from local
Americans. Thus no analysis of formal structure helps. Other
studies have confirmed this result, showing that the relationships between a company's size and its centralization, number of
divisions, and staff-line ratio is identical among United States
and Japanese firms.

Clearly, to discover what we can learn from Japan demands
an even closer examination of those complexities and subtleties

of Japanese management that have escaped earlier attempts. The next task, therefore, was to investigate the fundamental properties of the Japanese organization and to formulate a guide in comparing the Western firm.

Lifetime Employment

The most important characteristic of the Japanese organization is lifetime employment: Lifetime employment, more than being a single policy, is the rubric under which many facets of Japanese life and work are integrated.

Lifetime employment, although desired by workers and a goal of employers, is not universal in Japan. Not all firms can create the stability necessary for lifetime employment. Thus perhaps thirty-five percent of Japan's work force is under lifetime employment in large companies and government bureaus. These large organizations are the focus of our attention.

Lifetime employment means that a major firm or government bureau hires once a year, in the spring, when young people graduate from junior high, high school, and the university. A major firm which hires only "rookies" takes on a large inventory of new employees all at once, although it does not typically have work for all of them immediately. Promotions are entirely from within, and a person with one, five, or twenty years at one company will not be hired or even considered by another company. Once hired, the new employee is retained until mandatory retirement at age fifty-five. An employee will not be terminated for anything less than a major criminal offense, and termination is a harsh punishment, since the one who has been fired has no hope of finding employment in a comparable firm and instead must turn either to a minor firm that pays comparatively low wages and offers little security, or else must return to his hometown.

Upon reaching age fifty-five, all employees except the top few who are managing directors of the firm must retire. The company pays each retiree a lump sum separation amounting typically to five or six years' worth of salary. However, there is no pension or social security. Like other industrial nations, Japan over the past few decades has had vast improvements in diet, hygiene, and health care, so that life expectancy has risen steadily. Consequently people are retiring at age fifty-five with five years' worth of salary, but with the expectation of living another fifteen or twenty years in highly inflationary times. Clearly, a gap exists in personal finances, and filling that gap plays an important consideration in the organization of business and society.

In order to understand fully how this system functions, one must know something about the structure of industry in Japan. By World War II, the major firms in Japan were organized into a small number of groups called *Zaibatsu*. Each group consisted of twenty to thirty major firms, all clustered around a powerful bank. These major firms represented each of the important industrial sectors in the economy, so that a group would typically include a shipping company, a steel company, an insurance company, a trading company, and so forth.

Around each of the major firms, in turn, was a host of satellite companies, perhaps as many as a hundred or more in some cases. These satellite companies, small firms employing a family or perhaps one hundred persons, typically manufactured a subassembly or provided a service sold only to their one major customer. The satellites were not considered to be members of the group and did not enjoy the financial or other protections afforded to the major firms.

The relationship between satellites and major firms in Japan constitutes a bilateral monopoly, in which the satellite has only one customer for its product and the major firm has only one supplier for each of its inputs. Such a relationship can easily degenerate into one of mutual distrust and bickering where each side accuses the other of taking advantage and demands the protection of extensive contractual specificity and close auditing of performance. American firms rarely trust each other sufficiently to enter into such relationships. For example, in the United States semiconductor industry a major buyer of a new product commonly requires a "second source."

Semiconductor devices (such as RAMs, PROMs, and microprocessors) are among the most technologically advanced products in the world today. Companies manufacturing these devices must constantly invent new technologies and break new scientific ground. Usually when one company invents a new semiconductor piece, no one will be able to duplicate the design and manufacture it for perhaps two years. A new device may be so superior to anything else available that computer manufacturers will instantly want to incorporate this new element into their products. In such a case, the computer company says to the semiconductor company, "We will buy your new devices with the condition that you give your design to a competitor, who will become our second source." Only with this competitive protection will the buyer make plans for use of this device. Without such protection, buyers fear that the sole source may take unfair advantage of this monopoly position to raise prices, lower quality, or fail to meet promised delivery dates. Therefore, the companies will keep an arm's length relationship.

Similarly, in an American automobile assembly plant, a major United States automaker will maintain several alternative sources of supply. Likewise, each of those hundreds of firms that supply the major automakers in the United States will attempt to sell their products to several buyers. Both suppliers and purchasers distrust one another and purposely do not depend on one supply source or one customer. In a Japanese auto plant, however, the relationship between the major auto firm and its satellite suppliers is one of total cooperation. So close is the working relationship that the supplier will deliver parts right to workstations on the assembly line. Furthermore, the supplier will gladly deliver only a small amount of the part, perhaps enough to last for only three hours of production. Thus an assembly plant does not have to maintain a large inventory of parts and saves valuable space.

The bilateral monopolies result in great productivity as each side learns over time to coordinate smoothly with the other. Although the *Zaibatsu* were legally dissolved after the war, the relationships continue. This is due largely to the dependence of all companies in a closely-knit network of allied banks for their financing. The banks see to it that no one firm takes advantage of a trading partner, and so the spirit of the *Zaibatsu* survives.

The relationship between the *Zaibatsu* and the system of lifetime employment is an intimate once. Take, for example, Mr. Kagawa, a successful middle-level manager in a major life insurance company in Japan. Mr. Kagawa is now fifty-five and not of the managing director rank, and so must retire. His employer pays him a lump sum separation bonus of $120,000, six times his annual salary of $20,000. But that is not all — the company does not simply say "thank-you and good-bye." Rather, they send Mr. Kagawa off to the satellite firm that prints their forms, where he works in a part-time job for the next ten years. The combination of savings and part-time work allows Mr. Kagawa to live comfortably, although he has moved out of the mainstream to make room for younger people. His job security, however, is not as great as with his former employer, a major firm. Rather than paying taxes into a social security system, Japanese companies and employees in effect fund their own system of social security, one in which the government does not directly enter.

This same pattern applies to all major firms with close supplier relations, and the movement of personnel helps to cement the relationship between companies as well as promote a good working relationship between satellites and each major firm. The bank, at the center of each group, has even greater power to place retiring employees into any number of major firms or into their satellites. Consequently a career with a major bank is highly prized in Japan. Perhaps the ultimate goal, however, is a career at MITI, the Ministry of International Trade and Industry, which regulates all business in Japan. Only MITI can place retirees in a commercial bank.

Someone who begins a career in a satellite firm faces a less hopeful prospect. An aspiring young manager in such a firm will continually find higher positions occupied by retirees from major firms who have "dropped in" on his employer. More significantly, however, the employee in a satellite firm has nowhere to go at age fifty-five. He must take his lump sum payment and either open up a noodle shop of his own or move in with the family of his eldest son.

This system has led to a clear stratification among firms in Japan. Most people agree on which groups and firms within groups are the most desirable places to work. In the United States, by comparison, no general consensus exists among the workforce concerning preferred firms. In Japan an employee simply wants to work where there are the largest number of options at age fifty-five.

The stratification among firms has been paralleled by a similar stratification among educational institutions. One of the most sought after banks, until recently hired its new management trainees exclusively from the graduating class of the University of Tokyo, the premier institution of higher education. That bank has now liberalized its policy and hires a limited number of graduates of other universities, although its primary source continues to be the University of Tokyo. This system has produced tremendous pressure to gain admission to the Imperial Universities such as Tokyo. (Note: the universities are no longer officially imperial because Japan is not an empire, but they are commonly referred to in this way.) Just admission alone to an Imperial University virtually assures a young person of entry into one of the major firms or government agencies, so close are the ties between these institutions. Typically, each major firm and government agency is assigned a quota of graduates by each department in an Imperial University, and students are matched to employers upon their graduation. Both employers and students rely upon university placement officials to understand where the best fits are likely to occur. While the system has the disadvantage of foreclosing free choice, it allows the go between who knows both student and employer quite well to provide good matches. Employers who fail to live up to promises of opportunity or of development are penalized in future years, and students cannot misrepresent their talents to an unsuspecting prospective employer. Again, the system depends upon trust in the motives and skill of the placement system and its agents.

Not only is admission to the Imperial Universities and the elite private universities difficult, it is also contingent mostly upon performance by students in a national examination administered separately by each university. Because high school students typically take no optional coursework, all students have the same courses on their records, and all have learned from similar texts produced by one of the three textbook publishing houses. Universities thus have little to go by in arriving at admissions decisions save the entrance examination. The Imperial Universities are all state supported and tuition-free, so that rich and poor alike must compete equally. Therefore, the pressure trickles down to the secondary school level. There is fierce competition to enter the top high schools, which can give students the most rigorous preparation for the university entrance examinations. This translates into pressure to enter the top primary schools, which enhance the student's chances of getting into a top secondary school.

The final result was described to me by an old friend from Japan who was visiting one evening. He seemed somewhat subdued that evening, and I asked him what was on his mind. "Well," he said, "today is the day that my four-year-old son, who is back in Tokyo, is taking the entrance examination for a special kindergarten. I'm pretty sure that he won't get in." "That's ridiculous!" I replied. "I've met your children — they're

very bright and you have a terrific job, so of course he'll get in."
"No," my friend responded, "you don't understand. In this
special kindergarten, there are only thirty openings for more
than 500 applicants. Of those 500, more than half have been
going to a special summer school that does nothing but drill
those children for eight hours a day, six days a week, in how to
take the entrance exam for that one specific kindergarten.
Although I earn a pretty darn good wage, it's not nearly enough
to afford one of those special schools, because they charge a
tuition of $1,000 per week." Of course, such special summer and
after-school training does not end there but continues through
elementary, junior high, and high school, all to maximize the
chances of a high score on the ultimate university entrance
examinations.

While it may seem bizarre to us, we can understand that a
Japanese family of means can make no better investment in their
children's future than to buy them an education during the early
years. While money cannot assure entry into a publicly-funded
university, nevertheless, if a child has ability, then money can
buy the fullest development of that ability. An enhanced early
education will determine the university entrance, job choice,
and post-retirement life of this child. The child who gets off to a
less advantageous start can foresee entry into a minor university, a job in a satellite firm, and the choice at age fifty-five of
either opening up that noodle shop or business or moving in
with the children.

The resulting pressures on very young children concerns the
government, which now pressures for reforms in the entrance
policies at the state or public universities, but such change comes
slowly. Although not completely fair, the system is at least more
egalitarian than one where universities can use nonacademic
criteria to admit students whose families can give large gifts.

Lifetime employment is possible only as a consequence of a
unique social and economic structure not replicated in the
United States. Consider three major factors: first, every major
firm in Japan pays all of its employees a large share of their
compensation in the form of a bonus, typically paid each six
months. The bonus each year adds up to five to six months'
worth of salary for each employee, and since all receive the same
fraction of their salary, the amount is not contingent on
individual performance, but only on the performance of the
firm. This compensation method in part shifts the entrepreneur-

ial risks of business from the stockholders to the employees, who suffer through bad years and prosper in good years, unlike the case in the United States, where employees may enjoy salary increases although their firm suffers a decline in earnings. Bonuses give employees an incentive to feel a part of the firm and motivate them to cooperate in any way that they can. The lifetime employment system allows a firm to pay a small bonus in a bad year or even defer the payment of the entire bonus to a later year. Thus a firm can cut its payroll by perhaps thirty percent without laying anyone off. When good times return, an experienced and loyal workforce is ready to go. In a good year employees receive a larger than expected bonus in a lump and tend to save a large fraction of it. This effect, combined with tax incentives to save, has given Japan a rate of savings and of capital formation roughly four times that of the United States. Thus Japanese business can expand rapidly during prosperous times.

Second, every major firm in Japan has a large category of temporary employees who are mostly women. Even today, it is rare that a major Japanese firm will hire women into professional or managerial jobs. Working class women typically begin work in production and clerical jobs right out of high school. They are expected to work five or six years, get married, quit work, and raise a family. When the children enter school full time, the women often return to their original employer. Although they may work for the next twenty years, women are considered temporary employees and are immediately laid off in slack periods. On the other hand, Japanese firms have shown a great flexibility in scheduling working hours to accommodate women who have children to care for. At Sony plants, for example, regular production shifts begin at 8 AM, but other shifts work from 10 AM to 6 PM and from 10 AM to 3 PM in order to accommodate women with other responsibilities. The central fact remains, however, that women serve as a "buffer" to protect the job stability of men.

Third, consider for a moment the problem facing the satellite firms. They exist largely at the pleasure and at the mercy of the major firms, and they have little hope of ever growing into major competitors. Because a small number of firms dominate the major industries, and because the Japanese government encourages the creation of large firms and of tightly-knit *Zaibatsu*, small firms can grow only in new markets such as in consumer electronics over the past few decades. More typically, small firms cannot obtain licenses to import the raw materials necessary for manufacture in major industries, and they exist instead as suppliers to the major firms. The major firms contract out to them those services most susceptible to fluctuation, with the result that during a recession, these small firms will sharply contract or go out of business.

The combination of bonus payments, temporary employment, and satellite firms provides a substantial buffer against uncertainty that makes stable, lifetime employment a reality for the male employees of major firms. This structure distributes social costs in a way quite different from the United States and, to some extent, in ways that we would find to be unacceptable. That is why we must adapt only those aspects of Japanese management that suit our needs. However, the other facets of lifetime employment — such as trust, loyalty to a firm, and commitment to a job over most of one's productive years — are the foundation of Theory Z, as we shall later see.

Evaluation and Promotion

Part of the complex of intertwined features of the Japanese organization are approaches to evaluation and promotion. Imagine a young man named Sugao, a graduate from the University of Tokyo who has accepted a position at the fictitious Mitsubeni Bank, one of the major banks. For ten years, Sugao will receive exactly the same increases in pay and exactly the same promotions as the other fifteen young men who have entered with him. Only after ten years will anyone make a formal evaluation of Sugao or his peers; not until then will one person receive a larger promotion than another.

The very slowness of this evaluation process discourages the playing of certain kinds of short-term corporate games, although it does not entirely rule out such behavior. Sugao lacks an incentive to initiate projects or to press for decisions that may look good in the short run but may be unacceptable for the longer run. He also has no reason to advance his career at someone else's expense: Sugao knows that he will not be evaluated until the long run, and he knows that anyone unfairly treated will still be at the bank, due to the lifetime employment policy. While this process at times seems painfully slow to aspiring young managers in Japanese firms, it promotes a very open attitude towards cooperation, performance, and evaluation, since the system makes it highly likely that true performance will indeed come out in the wash.

The physical layout of the typical Japanese office supports this attitude towards performance evaluation. Consider the physical layout of the marketing division of one of the major Japanese automobile companies. The work space is one huge room with no internal walls or partitions of any sort. Row upon row of long tables fill the room with the staff for South America sales at one table, for European sales at another, and so forth. The section chief sits at the head of each table, and the division general manager has a desk at the head of the room, much like a school teacher. Around each table the staff and their secretaries sit side by side, with telephones and order books piled in the center of each table. With a constant hubbub of talk, both serious and playful, everyone notices just what each person is up to.

Imagine the situation of Mr. Fujioka, the division manager, who spends virtually all of his time in this room with his staff. It is inconceivable that one of his section chiefs can put out a special quarterly or annual review to impress him with his group's performance. Everyone knows what goes on. Each knows whose counsel is truly valued and whose is ignored.

This very public way of life can be intolerable to anyone whose values and goals do not conform, and it can be oppressive even to the Japanese. At five o'clock on a workday the secretaries and clerks in a Japanese office soon begin to drift away, heading for home. Managers usually stay put, perhaps with an order book open and a novel cradled inside, but not intending to deceive their boss or co-workers. The intimacy is far too close for any such attempts at deception to succeed, and attempts are rare. At perhaps six o'clock the boss makes the rounds and shoos everyone away, telling them to go home to their families. Most nights, however, the men will head for a bookstore or perhaps a *pachinko* parlor where they will spend the next hour, browsing through books or watching the steel game ball as it makes the sound from which it derives its name: *"pa-pa-pa-chin-chin-ko."* At about 7:30 PM they head for the trains. Because land is very dear in Japan, people tend to have quite long commutes, so that many will trudge up their front steps at 9 PM. The neighbors notice the late arrival, assume that he must be very valuable at work to stay so late, and his family's honor is safe in the neighborhood.

A student of mine from Japan told me the story of his good friend who worked at just such a major bank and had been kept exceptionally late at work for a period of months in order to complete a major project. When the project was complete, the section chief sent the staff home early every day for a week. After two days of coming home in the afternoon, the young man was confronted by his mother, with whom he lived. "Please," she asked him, "go to a bar, go play *pachinko,* but don't come home so early. The neighbors are stopping me on the sidewalk to ask whether you are having troubles at work, and it is embarrassing to have to explain to everyone." Again, it is not a system that we wish to emulate, but one we wish to understand and from which we can learn.

The slowness of formal evaluation and promotion seems wholly unacceptable to many Americans, not only because Americans desire rapid feedback and advancement, but also because the system seems to prevent the early assignment of the most capable people to important jobs. Many Americans returning from negotiations in Japan have remarked, however, that formal titles and actual responsibility seem often not to be matched in Japanese companies. Indeed, it is often the case that while a senior employee may hold the title of department manager, it will be an untitled person many years his junior who will carry lead responsibility for seeing that things happen. It is this de-coupling of formal titles from actual responsibilities that avoids a potential hazard of the slow evaluation and promotion. Those most able easily and quickly receive responsibility, but the irreversible step of promotion only comes when they have more completely proven themselves. In addition major contributors to success in the past are assured the security of title and higher wages despite the threat of young employees. This fact, observed by everyone, causes employees to be more willing to wait their turn.

But how is it that a young person will willingly take on more responsibility and more pressure without commensurate reward? The answer has to do with membership in working groups. Every employee, from top to bottom, is simultaneously a member of as many as eight or a dozen work groups, each with a different task. These groups work very closely together, and although their membership changes periodically, all know that throughout a career, each person will continue to function in many such groups. American social science research over the past few decades has demonstrated quite convincingly that our group memberships have more influence on our attitudes, motivation, and behavior than does any other social phenomenon. What we care about most is what our peers think about us. A person who is part of a group whose members feel a close kinship is subject to very powerful influence. Failure to adhere to the norms of the group can bring loss of group support, approval, and ultimately the group can throw the offender out of the membership. To someone who feels closely integrated with any small group, these are severe penalties. More than hierarchical control, pay, or promotion, it is our group memberships that influence our behavior. There are daily examples of the tremendous power group membership can exert upon people to the extent of changing their religious beliefs, their attitudes towards work, and even their self-image. Many of the most successful techniques for the rehabilitation of alcoholics, drug addicts, and those seriously overweight rely upon the integration of the individual into a cohesive treatment group, which can then exert tremendous force on the individual.

The Japanese organization takes in only young people who are still in the formative stages of life, subjects them to multiple group memberships, and so inculcates in them the kind of devotion to co-workers that one sees in the United States Marines. It is not external evaluations or rewards that matter in such a setting, it is the intimate, subtle, and complex evaluation by one's peers — people who cannot be fooled — which is paramount. This central fact underlies much of the success of many organizations, not only in Japan but elsewhere.

Non-specialized Career Paths

A frequently overlooked but very important feature of Japanese organizations is their development of individual careers. Recall Sugao, our young university graduate who has just joined the Mitsubeni Bank for a lifetime. Sugao will enter in a management training position, spending perhaps a year just meeting people and learning his way around while working on various assignments. Then he will be sent out to a branch to learn bank operations, including working with tellers and managing the flow of information, paper, and people. From there he will be brought back into headquarters to learn commercial banking, the process of loaning large sums to major firms with whom the bank maintains relations. Then back out to yet another branch where he will be in the retail lending department, learning to make automobile loans and other small consumer loans to individuals. From there he may come back again to headquarters, this time to a position in the personnel department, an essential and important activity with which he must be familiar. At about this time, ten years will have passed and Sugao will gain his first major promotion, perhaps becoming a section chief. In this capacity he will move again to another branch, perhaps in charge of new business, a job in which he will aggressively call on potential customers and attempt to get their business. He may then move back to headquarters, this time in the international division where he will help to coordinate the banking needs of Japanese firms who have operations in the United States or in France.

By the time he reaches the peak of his career, Sugao will be an expert in taking every function, every specialty, and every office of the Mitsubeni Bank and knitting them together into one, integrated whole. Compare this to an advertisement that appeared not long ago for one of the major United States banks, an ad that could have represented virtually any American bank. It said, in huge type across a full page in the *Wall Street Journal,* "BANK WITH US. WHY? EXPERTISE." Below the large type were photos of three senior officers of the bank. "Meet Fred," it read. "For thirty years Fred has done nothing but make commercial loans to forest products companies in the Pacific Northwest. He's an expert."

The typical Japanese bank will not have an expert with Fred's detailed knowledge of the needs, the people, and the problems of one industry. That is a weakness of the Japanese system of lifelong job rotation. However, when it comes time to achieve coordination across functions, say for the purpose of bridging the gap between commercial lending and operations in order to computerize some commercial lending information, then the Japanese form has great advantages. In addition, if for some reason the bank's business with the forest products industry in the Pacific Northwest declines sharply, then Fred and his staff may be out of a job, since there is little else in the bank that they are qualified to do. Knowing this, Fred will be careful to maintain his contacts in other banks as protection against that day and thus will be somewhat less committed to his present employer than he could be.

In the Japanese case virtually every department will have in it someone who knows the people, the problems, and the procedures of any other area within the organization. When coordination is necessary, both sides will be able to understand and cooperate with the other. Perhaps more important is the fact that every employee knows that he will continue through his career to move between functions, offices, and geographical locations. The person from another department who is asking for assistance today may be the person who will be his co-worker or even superior tomorrow. Thus there is not only the ability but also the incentive for taking a broad, organization-wide point of view and for cooperating with everyone.

One of the major Japanese banks in California has developed an interesting procedure for dealing with American banks. On those occasions when they are cooperating with an American bank on a project and have a request or question, they proceed as follows: " We make one telephone call to the American bank. If we do not get an answer on that one call, we write a letter to the president to explain our needs and ask that our letter be referred to the appropriate person. American banks are so highly specialized that if you get the wrong person on the first call, that person probably won't even know who you should call. We have at times spent the whole day on the telephone without making any progress."

Compare the Japanese career paths with those of the typical Western firm. Here Fred will spend his whole career in manufacturing, Mary will rise only within the sales division, Otto will always be in engineering, and Bob will always be an accountant. Jean-Louis Bouchet, a French scholar and former student of mine, has studied the career paths of the top officers in fifty of the largest American firms over a span of thirty years. In doing this research, Bouchet wanted to discover how many functions these top officers had worked in over their careers. Remembering that these people are at the peak of both their companies and their own careers with the broadest experience that anyone is likely to get, Bouchet found that on the average they had worked in less than two different functions. If they were in charge of either finance or personnel in their company, they had typically never worked in any other specialty. When people spend their entire careers within one specialty, they tend to develop subgoals devoted to that specialty rather than to the whole firm and they have neither the knowledge of the people nor of the problems to enable them to effectively help other specialists within their own organization.

This process of lifelong job rotation holds true for all employees in many Japanese firms. An electrical engineer may go from circuit design to fabrication to assembly, a technician may work on a different machine or in a different division every few years, and all managers will rotate through all areas of the business. Recent research conducted by management scholars at M.I.T., Columbia University, and elsewhere strongly suggests that workers at all levels who continually face new jobs will be more vital, more productive, and more satisfied with their work than those who stay in one job, even though the changes in job do not include a promotion but are entirely lateral. The United States economy over the past three decades has grown so rapidly that many companies have found that their expansion created many promotional opportunities and so have not considered the possibilities of nonpromotional job changes. As we face the prospect of a relatively slow-growth economy over the next few decades, we may find useful alternatives in the Japanese example.

A young manager in a major Japanese manufacturing company related a revealing story to me. "Our company has a joint venture with an American firm," he began, "and I was sent to the United States as a liaison for a period of two years. I found the experience very rewarding and the American managers very skillful. However, there was one thing about Americans that puzzled me a great deal — cocktail parties. Almost every American manager says that he hates cocktail parties. You stand around for hours drinking too much and talking to people you don't want to talk to, they say. I simply could not understand why they would go to these parties if they hated them so much. Then I understood. Americans never know when they might need to find a new job. Their company might have a decline in the need for their specialty, and then they will have to leave. As a result, Americans have to keep their contacts up. They have to stay in touch with people in other companies who are also in their same specialty, people who can help them to get a new job when they need it. In Japan we know that we won't have to go looking for a new job, so we don't need cocktail parties!"

In the United States we conduct our careers between organizations but within a single specialty. In Japan people conduct careers between specialties but within a single organization. This is a fundamental difference in the way that our two nations have dealt with the problem of industrialization. In the United States companies specialize their jobs and individuals specialize their careers. As a result a semiconductor specialist, a portfolio manager, or a personnel manager can be moved from company A to company B and within five days all can be working effectively. Full productivity takes longer but contributions begin right away. In Japan it is difficult to take a worker from one company, move that person to another company, and expect him ever to be fully productive. Japanese do not specialize only in a technical field; they also specialize in an organization, in learning how to make a specific, unique business operate as well as it possibly can.

One effect of lifelong job rotation is employer incentives to develop the skills and the commitment of their employees. In the United States employers are reluctant to invest in training employees in new technical skills, because a skilled employee can easily find another employer, taking along that investment. In the semiconductor and aerospace industries, some companies "raid" the most skilled engineers and supervisors from their competitors. Although the raider must pay a higher wage to attract a highly-skilled person, the cost is lower than in-house training, since in-service training is a time-consuming and costly venture. Consequently companies in the United States do much less training than they could, and our economy as a whole suffers.

A Japanese company committed to lifetime employment will go to great lengths to build loyalty among its employees by ensuring fair and humane treatment. In the United States, by comparison, an alienated, disgruntled employee can be laid off during the next downswing in the business cycle and thus represents only a short-term burden to the employer. The problem is purely one of incentives. People committed to long-term relationships with one another have strong commitments to behave responsibly and equitably towards one another.

In every Japanese company I ended my visit by interviewing one or more of the managing directors, the top executives in the firm. I would always inquire of them, "Please tell me, of the managing directors, who is most influential?" The response would always be a variation of one theme, "We manage as a group; we are equals." "I understand," I would probe, "but is one of you somewhat more equal, more powerful than the others?" In every case, the final reply surprised me: "Well, ordinarily, the most senior and the most respected managing director is in charge of personnel." This situation could not be more different than the case in American organizations. Personnel rarely is a powerful function in a United States organization and is often among the weakest. The difference does not have to do simply with a commitment to the importance of "people management" in Japan. It is deeper than that.

The Japanese understand that even a manager of good intentions can do no more than respond to the objectives that seem to him right and proper. Inevitably, managers in large organizations develop "local objectives," that further the performance of their local operation but that could lead them away in directions not best for the firm as a whole. In the case of selecting people for job transfers and promotions, the problem of local objectives is crystallized. Typically, the decision on whether or not to move a young engineer or manager to a new position is influenced most heavily by a consultation between the candidate and an immediate superior. Typically, the candidate has been performing well and is being considered for a new challenge. This will often turn out to be a very similar position in the same department or division. After all, this person's skills are needed for the success of the department. A raise and a promotion recognize and reward performance. This inescapable but "local" reasoning leads invariably to a narrow specialization of talents. The outcome results from a process of reasonable people of good intentions doing what seems right. The Japanese, understanding the power of local objectives, have removed the job assignment decision from local managers and have put all such decisions under the purview of the personnel department. To enforce broader corporate objectives in the face of local objections, personnel becomes the most potent force within the organization, capable of overruling even a division head who wants to keep the best talent right where it is. In this case, it appears "free choice" is abridged, since neither the candidate nor his boss can exercise their first choice. However, sometimes free will operates with the choosers not completely informed of the long-run implications of their choices. A structural solution brings to bear these more global concerns.

Clearly, such a system must contain strong safeguards against the abuse of such centralized power, or else the organization will ultimately decay and its employees will be mistreated.

The Japanese and the American approaches to career development have both succeeded. Each has its own peculiar strengths and weaknesses. The great strength of the American approach lies in the capacity to organize its specialized workers into a coordinated workforce. Each worker can perform a specialty in any work setting and thus can move from one city to another and from one employer to another with ease. This innovation, one of the great miracles of Western organization, made widespread industrial production possible. Industrial production can succeed only if technical experts can be brought together in a coordinated fashion. In our now highly mobile society, production would never advance rapidly if each company employed a unique set of skills and a different kind of worker. Every company would be spending so much time teaching its methods that productivity would be dismal. Given specialization and professionalization, however, workers can be nomads, committed to a lifetime to their profession but loyal to no one employer. Perhaps this system will prove to be stronger than the Japanese system over the long run, but there is at least one reason to doubt that.

The weakness of the American form is that workers can never be intimately integrated with one another. They can achieve a loose coupling of effort; they can coordinate so long as there is no call for understanding of anything beyond their own specialty. If the right specialties can be put together, like Lincoln Logs or Tinkertoys, then the structure will work. But if the production process requires that each specialist modify goals and talents or develop a unique set of skills, then our prefabricated approach to organization will not succeed. When the underlying production process demands integration of effort at an intimate and custom-crafted level, the employees must be asked to give up their local objectives and narrow professional point of view to learn new skills, to take on new goals. That kind of organization has worked on a few occasions when the task was so important individuals willingly gave up their individual goals to a need for closer integration. The Apollo project to put an astronaut on the moon was perhaps the outstanding example, but other exciting enterprises such as building the first aircraft and the first computers also yielded such organizations.

It is often said that NASA, IBM, and Boeing could build unique organizations in which people hand-crafted their careers to fit the needs of the company. Perhaps the excitement and challenge of the task induced talented workers to put aside their normal protections of specialization and of professionalization. The point is that such organizational forms can succeed in the United States and that nontraditional forms of organization may be necessary for particularly complex tasks. Industrialization may inexorably push toward closer integration, more difficult and ambiguous challenges, and thus a need for those unique organizations such as NASA and IBM to become the norm. But every task will not be as exciting nor as rewarding as putting an astronaut in space, and we cannot expect workers as a whole to give up the security of job mobility that goes with specialization, because the task is of such great importance. Instead, American industry will have to discover how to offer workers the proper incentives to develop unique skills without being penalized in the form of having lower job mobility. We probably do not want to adopt the Japanese career path entirely. However, some significant movement in the direction of company-centered rather than skill-centered careers could yield many benefits for both employee and employer in the United States.

Lifetime employment, performance evaluation, and career paths touch only part of the working conditions that encourage Japanese employees to achieve tremendous productivity. No less important than these, the managerial functions of each organization — from decision making to attitudes and values — create the backdrop for efficient operations. The workings of the Japanese corporation will be investigated next.

2

THE WORKINGS OF A JAPANESE CORPORATION

THE basic mechanisms of management control in a Japanese company are so subtle, implicit, and internal that they often appear to an outsider not to exist. That conclusion is a mistake. The mechanisms are thorough, highly disciplined and demanding, yet very flexible. Their essence could not be more different from methods of managerial control in Western organizations.

A visit to the United States headquarters of one of the major Japanese banks provided some interesting insights. As expected, the top officers were Japanese expatriates, the middle managers and other employees local Americans (many were Japanese-American). In this case, however, the bank had two vice-presidents who were local Americans, hired away from other banking institutions. Studying this peculiarity brought me an important insight to the managerial control system in a Japanese company. In this hybrid setting the basic differences between Japanese and American approaches clashed, thus illuminating those deeper characteristics not readily apparent among Japanese companies in Japan.

In an interview with the American vice-presidents, I asked how they felt about working for this Japanese bank. "They treat us well, let us in on the decision making, and pay us well. We're satisfied." "You're very fortunate," I continued, "but tell me, if there were something that you could change about this Japanese bank, what would it be?" The response was quick and clearly one that was very much on their minds: "These Japanese just don't understand objectives, and it drives us nuts!"

Next I interviewed the president of this bank, an expatriate Japanese who was on temporary assignment from Tokyo headquarters to run the United States operation, and asked about the two American vice-presidents. "They're hard working, loyal, and professional. We think they're terrific," came the reply. When asked if he would like to change them in any way, the president replied, "These Americans just don't seem to be able to understand objectives."

With each side accusing the other of inability to understand objectives, there was a clear need for further interviewing and for clarification. A second round of interviews probed further into the issue. First the American vice-presidents: "We have a non-stop running battle with the president. We simply cannot get him to specify a performance target for us. We have all the necessary reports and numbers, but we can't get specific targets from him. He won't tell us how large a dollar increase in loan volume or what percent decrease in operating costs he expects us to achieve over the next month, quarter, or even year. How can we know whether we're performing well without specific targets to shoot for?" A point well taken, for every major American company and government bureau devotes a large fraction of its time to the setting of specific, measurable performance targets. Every American business school teaches its students to take global, fuzzy corporate goals and boil them down to measurable performance targets. Management by objective (MBO), program planning and evaluation, and cost-benefit analysis are among the basic tools of control in modern American management.

When I returned to reinterview the Japanese president, he explained, "If only I could get these Americans to understand our philosophy of banking. To understand what the business means to us — how we feel we should deal with our customers and our employees. What our relationship should be to the local communities we serve. How we should deal with our competitors, and what our role should be in the world at large. If they could get that under their skin, then they could figure out for themselves what an appropriate objective would be for any situation, no matter how unusual or new, and I would never have to tell them, never have to give them a target."

This example illustrates that the basic mechanism of control in a Japanese company is embodied in a philosophy of management. This philosophy, an implicit theory of the firm, describes the objectives and the procedures to move towards them. These objectives represent the values of the owners, employees, customers, and government regulators. The movement towards objectives is defined by a set of beliefs about what kinds of solutions tend to work well in the industry or in the firm; such beliefs concern, for example, who should make decisions about what kinds of new products the company should or should not consider.

Those who grasp the essence of this philosophy of values and beliefs (or ends and means) can deduce from the general statement an almost limitless number of specific rules or targets to suit changing conditions. Moreover, these specific rules or targets will be consistent between individuals. Two individuals who both understand the underlying theory will derive the same specific rule to deal with a particular situation. Thus the theory provides both control over the ways people respond to problems and coordination between them, so solutions will mesh with one another. This theory, implicit rather than explicit, cannot be set down completely in so many sentences. Rather, the theory is communicated through a common culture shared by key managers and, to some extent, all employees.

The organizational culture consists of a set of symbols, ceremonies, and myths that communicate the underlying values and beliefs of that organization to its employees. These rituals put flesh on what would otherwise be sparse and abstract ideas, bringing them to life in a way that has meaning and impact for a new employee. For example, telling employees that the company is committed to coordinated and unselfish cooperation sounds fine but also produces skepticism about the commitment of others and creates ambiguity over just how a principle might apply in specific situations. When, on the other hand, the value of cooperation is expressed through the ritual of *ringi*, a collective decision making in which a document passes from manager to manager for their official seal of approval, then the neophyte experiences the philosophy of cooperation in a very concrete way. Slowly individual preferences give way to collective consensus. This tangible evidence shows true commitment to what might otherwise be an abstract and ignored value.

Recent research by Professor Alan Wilkins of Brigham Young University indicates that some American organizations have a rich inventory of stories that are told and retold from generation to generation. A value embodied in a specific story rather than stated more abstractly is more believable and better remembered, according to this research. These stories, which form a "corporate memory," may be based on real or partly real events, but they nonetheless form an important part of the culture of an organization.

An organizational culture develops when employees have a broad array of common experiences as touchstones through which to communicate with a great deal of subtlety. In the Japanese company, because managers have passed through many and the same functions over the years, they can refer to a large array of common experiences, tell stories, and remember symbolic events that remind each of them of their common commitment to certain values and beliefs. Moreover, this commonality provides them with a shorthand form of communication. Because the underlying premises or theoretical position from which each person proceeds is held in common with the others, each can assume certain responses or agreements without actually taking the time to negotiate them. Thus the common culture creates a general backdrop of coordination that greatly facilitates decision making and planning over specific issues.

Decision Making

Probably the best known feature of Japanese organizations is their participative approach to decision making. In the typical American organization the department head, division manager, and president typically each feel that "the buck stops here" — that they alone should take the responsibility for making decisions. Recently, some organizations have adopted explicitly participative modes of decision making in which all of the members of a department reach consensus on what decision to adopt. Decision making by consensus has been the subject of a great deal of research in Europe and the United States over the past twenty years, and the evidence strongly suggests that a consensus approach yields more creative decisions and more effective implementation than does individual decision making.[1]

Western style participative decision making is by now a fairly standardized process. Typically, a small group of not more than eight or ten people will gather around a table, discuss the problem and suggest alternative solutions. During this process, the group should have one or more leaders skilled at managing relationships between people so that underlying disagreements can be dealt with constructively. The group can be said to have achieved a consensus when it finally agrees upon a single alternative and each member of the group can honestly say to each other member three things:

1. I believe that you understand my point of view.

2. I believe that I understand your point of view.

3. Whether or not I prefer this decision, I will support it, because it was arrived at in an open and fair manner.

At least a few managers instinctively follow this approach in every company, government office, and church meeting, but the vast majority do not. Some companies have officially instituted this consensual approach throughout, because of its superiority in many cases to individual decision making. However, what occurs in a Japanese organization is a great deal more far reaching and subtle than even this participative approach.

When an important decision needs to be made in a Japanese organization, everyone who will feel its impact is involved in making it. In the case of a decision where to put a new plant, whether to change a production process, or some other major event, that will often mean sixty to eighty people directly involved in making the decision. A team of three will be assigned the duty of talking to all sixty to eighty people and, each time a significant modification arises, contacting all the people involved again. The team will repeat this process until a true consensus has been achieved. Making a decision this way takes a very long time, but once a decision is reached, everyone affected by it will be likely to support it. Understanding and support may supersede the actual content of the decision, since the five or six competing alternatives may be equally good or bad. What is important is not the decision itself but rather how committed and informed people are. The "best" decisions can be bungled just as "worst" decisions can work just fine.

A friend in one of the major Japanese banks described their process. "When a major decision is to be made, a written proposal lays out one 'best' alternative for consideration. The task of writing the proposal goes to the youngest and newest member of the department involved. Of course, the president or vice-president knows the acceptable alternatives, and the young person tries like heck to figure out what those are. He talks to everyone, soliciting their opinions, paying special attention to those who know the top man best. In so doing he is seeking a common ground. Fortunately, the young person cannot completely figure out from others what the boss wants, and must add his own thoughts. This is how variety enters the decision process in a Japanese company. The company relies so heavily on socializing employees with a common set of values and beliefs that all experienced employees would be likely to come up with similar ideas. Too much homogeneity would lead to a loss of vitality and change, so the youngest person gets the assignment."

Frequently, according to my informant, this young person will in the process make a number of errors. He will suggest things that are technically impossible or politically unacceptable, and will leave things out. Experienced managers never over-direct the young man, never sit him down and tell him what the proposal should say. Even though errors consume time, effort, and expense, many will turn out to be good ideas. Letting a young person make one error of his own is believed to be worth more than one hundred lectures in his education as a manager and worker.

Ultimately, a formal proposal is written and then circulated from the bottom of the organization to the top. At each stage, the manager in question signifies his agreement by affixing his seal to the document. At the end of this *ringi* process, the proposal is literally covered with the stamps of approval of sixty to eighty people.

American managers are fond of chiding the Japanese by observing that, "If you're going to Japan to make a sale or close a deal and you think it will take two days, allow two weeks and if you're lucky you'll get a 'maybe.' It takes the Japanese forever to make a decision." True enough, but Japanese businesspeople who have experience dealing in the United States will often say, "Americans are quick to sign a contract or make a decision. But try to get them to implement it — it takes them forever!"

Remember that this apparently cumbersome decision process takes place within the framework of an underlying agreement on philosophy, values, and beliefs. These form the basis for common decision premises that make it possible to include a very large number of people in each decision. If, as in some Western organizations, each of the sixty people had a fundamentally different view of goals and procedures, then the participative process would fail. Because the Japanese only debate the suitability of a particular alternative to reach the agreed-upon values, the process can be broadly participatory yet efficient. In Western-style consensual processes, by comparison, often underlying values and beliefs need to be worked out, and for that reason decision making teams are deliberately kept small.

Another key feature of decision making in Japan is the intentional ambiguity of who is responsible for what decisions. In the United States we have job descriptions and negotiations between employees for the purpose of setting crystal clear boundaries on where my decision authority ends and yours begins. Americans expect others to behave just as we do. Many are the unhappy and frustrated American businessmen or lawyers returning from Japan with the complaint that, "If only they would tell me who is really in charge, we could make some progress." The complaint displays a lack of understanding that, in Japan, no one individual carries responsibility for a particular turf. Rather, a group or team of employees assumes joint responsibility for a set of tasks. While we wonder at their comfortableness in not knowing who is responsible for what, they know quite clearly that each of them is completely responsible for all tasks, and they share that responsibility jointly. Obviously this approach sometimes lets things "fall through the cracks" because everyone may think that someone else has a task under control. When working well, however, this approach leads to a naturally participative decision making and problem solving process. But there is another important reason for the collective assignment of decision responsibility.

Many Americans object to the idea of lifetime employment because they fear the consequences of keeping on an ineffective worker. Won't that create bottlenecks and inefficiency? Clearly the Japanese have somehow solved that problem or they couldn't have achieved their great economic success. A partial answer comes from the collective assignment of decision responsibility. In a typical American firm, Jim is assigned sole responsibility for purchasing decisions for office supplies, Mary has sole responsibility for purchasing maintenance services and Fred is solely responsible for purchasing office machines. If

Fred develops serious problems of a personal nature, or if he becomes ill or has some other problem that seriously impedes his ability to function at work, a bottleneck will develop. Office machine orders will not be properly processed or perhaps will not be processed at all. The whole company will suffer, and Fred will have to be let go.

In a Japanese company, by comparison, Mitsuo, Yoshito, and Nori will comprise a team collectively responsible for purchasing office supplies, maintenance services, and office machines. Each of them participates in all significant decisions in purchasing any of those goods or services. If Nori is unable to work, it is perfectly natural and efficient for Mitsuo and Yoshito to take up his share of the load. When Nori returns to work again, he can step right back in and do his share. This does mean that Mitsuo and Yoshito probably will have to work harder than usual for perhaps six months or a year, and they may also have to draw on Masao, who used to work in purchasing but has now been transferred to the computer section. This flow of people can be accomplished only if Mitsuo and Yoshito are confident that the organization has a memory and know that their extra efforts now will be repaid later. Fairness and equity will be achieved over the long run. It also depends upon the practice of job rotation, so that short-run labor needs can be filled internally without having to hire and fire people as such needs come and go. As with all other characteristics of the Japanese management system, decision making is embedded in a complex of parts that hang together and rely upon trust and subtlety developed through intimacy.

Collective Values

Perhaps the most difficult aspect of the Japanese for Westerners to comprehend is the strong orientation to collective values, particularly a collective sense of responsibility. Let me illustrate with an anecdote about a visit to a new factory in Japan owned and operated by an American electronics company. The American company, a particularly creative firm, frequently attracts attention within the business community for its novel approaches to planning, organizational design, and management systems. As a consequence of this corporate style, the parent company determined to make a thorough study of Japanese workers and to design a plant that would combine the best of East and West. In their study they discovered that Japanese firms almost never make use of individual work incentives, such as piecework or even individual performance appraisal tied to salary increases. They concluded that rewarding individual achievement and individual ability is always a good thing.

In the final assembly area of their new plant long lines of young Japanese women wired together electronic products on a piece-rate system: the more you wired, the more you got paid. About two months after opening, the head foreladies approached the plant manager. "Honorable plant manager," they said humbly as they bowed, "we are embarrassed to be so forward, but we must speak to you because all of the girls have threatened to quit work this Friday." (To have this happen, of course, would be a great disaster for all concerned.) "Why," they wanted to know, "can't our plant have the same compensation system as other Japanese companies? When you hire a new girl, her starting wage should be fixed by her age. An eighteen-year-old should be paid more than a sixteen-year-old. Every year on her birthday, she should receive an automatic increase in pay. The idea that any one of us can be more productive than another must be wrong, because none of us in final assembly could make a thing unless all of the other people in the plant had done their jobs right first. To single one person out as being more productive is wrong and is also personally humiliating to us." The company changed its compensation system to the Japanese model.

Another American company in Japan had installed a suggestion system much as we have in the United States. Individual workers were encouraged to place suggestions to improve productivity into special boxes. For an accepted idea the individual received a bonus amounting to some fraction of the productivity savings realized from his or her suggestion. After a period of six months, not a single suggestion had been submitted. The American managers were puzzled. They had heard many stories of the inventiveness, the commitment, and the loyalty of Japanese workers, yet not one suggestion to improve productivity had appeared.

The managers approached some of the workers and asked why the suggestion system had not been used. The answer: "No one can come up with a work improvement idea alone. We work together, and any ideas that one of us may have are actually developed by watching others and talking to others. If one of us was singled out for being responsible for such an idea, it would embarrass all of us." The company changed to a group suggestion system, in which workers collectively submitted suggestions. Bonuses were paid to groups which would save bonus money until the end of the year for a party at a restaurant or, if there was enough money, for family vacations together. The suggestions and productivity improvements rained down on the plant.

One can interpret these examples in two quite different ways. Perhaps the Japanese commitment to collective values is an anachronism that does not fit with modern industrialism but brings economic success despite that collectivism. Collectivism seems to be inimical to the kind of maverick creativity exemplified in Benjamin Franklin, Thomas Edison, and John D. Rockefeller. Collectivism does not seem to provide the individual incentive to excel which has made a great success of American enterprise. Entirely apart from its economic effects, collectivism implies a loss of individuality, a loss of the freedom to be different, to hold fundamentally different values from others.

The second interpretation of the examples is that the Japanese collectivism is economically efficient. It causes people to work well together and to encourage one another to better efforts. Industrial life requires interdependence of one person on another. But a less obvious but far-reaching implication of the Japanese collectivism for economic performance has to do with accountability.

In the Japanese mind, collectivism is neither a corporate or individual goal to strive for nor a slogan to pursue. Rather, the nature of things operates so that nothing of consequence occurs as a result of individual effort. Everything important in life happens as a result of teamwork or collective effort. Therefore, to attempt to assign individual credit or blame to results is unfounded. A Japanese professor of accounting, a brilliant scholar trained at Carnegie-Mellon University who teaches now in Tokyo, remarked that the status of accounting systems in Japanese industry is primitive compared to those in the United States. Profit centers, transfer prices, and computerized information systems are barely known even in the largest Japanese companies, whereas they are a commonplace in even small

United States organizations. Though not at all surprised at the difference in accounting systems, I was not at all sure that the Japanese were primitive. In fact, I thought their system a good deal more efficient than ours.

Most American companies have basically two accounting systems. One system summarizes the overall financial state to inform stockholders, bankers, and other outsiders. That system is not of interest here. The other system, called the managerial or cost accounting system, exists for an entirely different reason. It measures in detail all of the particulars of transactions between departments, divisions, and key individuals in the organization, for the purpose of untangling the interdependencies between people. When, for example, two departments share one truck for deliveries, the cost accounting system charges each department for part of the cost of maintaining the truck and driver, so that at the end of the year, the performance of each department can be individually assessed, and the better department's manager can receive a larger raise. Of course, all of this information processing costs money, and furthermore may lead to arguments between the departments over whether the costs charged to each are fair.

In a Japanese company a short-run assessment of individual performance is not wanted, so the company can save the considerable expense of collecting and processing all of that information. Companies still keep track of which department uses a truck how often and for what purposes, but like-minded people can interpret some simple numbers for themselves and adjust their behavior accordingly. Those insisting upon clear and precise measurement for the purpose of advancing individual interests must have an elaborate information system. Industrial life, however, is essentially integrated and interdependent. No one builds an automobile alone, no one carries through a banking transaction alone. In a sense the Japanese value of collectivism fits naturally into an industrial setting, whereas the Western individualism provides constant conflicts. The image that comes to mind is of Chaplin's silent film "Modern Times" in which the apparently insignificant hero played by Chaplin successfully fights against the unfeeling machinery of industry. Modern industrial life can be aggravating, even hostile, or natural: all depends on the fit between our culture and our technology.

Wholistic Concern for People

Anthropologist Thomas Rohlen has described in detail the process of inducting young trainees into a Japanese bank.[2] Training culminates in a formal ceremony held in the company auditorium. The bank president stands at the podium, the training director at his side. The young trainees sit in the front rows with their mothers, fathers, and siblings behind them. The president welcomes the new members into the bank family, challenging them to live up to the expectations of their trainers and leaders. He speaks also to the parents, accepting from them the challenge of providing for their children not only honest work, but also accepting the obligation to see to their complete physical, intellectual, and moral development. A representative of the parents next takes the podium, thanking the bank for offering this opportunity to their offspring and reaffirming the charge to the trainees to be as loyal to their new family as they are to their blood family. Finally, a representative of the trainees rises to speak, thanking both parents and bank for their support and pledging to work hard to meet their expectations.

Most Western organizations practice an attitude of "partial inclusion," an understanding between employee and employer that the connection between them involves only those activities directly connected with the completion of a specific job. Many Western social scientists have argued that partial inclusion maintains the emotional health in individuals. Being partially included in a number of organizations makes moving from one social domain to another easy, and tensions that have built up in one setting can be released in another. The Japanese organization, by contrast, forms inclusive relationships. A set of mechanisms provide for the social support and emotional release necessary for emotional equilibrium. One such mechanism is the capacity of group members to "change hats" and alter the nature of their relationships to one another for a short time in order to provide this social release and balance. Consider one example: At one American-owned plant in Japan, a golfing day with the manager became a twice yearly tradition. A train ride of four hours each way, plus golf, consumed an entire day for this important event. The American plant manager, to prepare for the outing, made a list of critical issues of strategy and management that he felt were on the minds of his subordinates. As the group approached the first tee, he produced his list and set out the agenda for the next eighteen holes. His subordinates were discouraged and disappointed by this, and the day proceeded in a desultory fashion.

A Japanese manager interpreted the story for me. A Japanese company, he pointed out, is a quite formal and at times even an authoritarian setting. Rarely will an employee disagree openly with a superior or voice complaints. When people anticipate a lifetime of working together, they cannot afford to let deep rifts develop. Thus a stylized pattern of interaction develops. Conflict and refusal would disturb the harmony that must underlie the work relationship. On the other hand, no company can remain healthy with suppressed disagreement, conflict, and complaint. A symbolic change of roles in which different patterns of behavior are acceptable provides one outlet. In the golf outing, for example, the implication was that boss and subordinates were competing as equals. With the physical setting away from the place of work, the acceptable patterns of behavior are also meant to be far removed from the daily norm. At these times subordinates can feel free to ask questions and to raise objections suppressed in the office and expect the boss to respond sympathetically. In a similar manner, office parties with drinks and dinner permit the subordinates to adopt the guise of mild inebriation to tell the boss off and give opinions unspeakable under ordinary conditions. Thus the organization provides the group with a change of venue necessary to healthy social relations.

The wholistic orientation of Japanese organizations stems from both historical accident and underlying social and cultural forces. According to one commonly held view, the historical accident is that industrialism rushed into Japan after having been held out for decades by a feudal political system. Companies were forced to build plants near to the villages where they could recruit workers. With no long and gradual urbanization as Europe had, Japan found itself with a sparsely-distributed rural population faced with the onrush of industrialization. Each plant sent recruiters to village homes asking mothers and fathers to send their offspring to work in the plant twenty or thirty miles away. Village parents who loved their children would simply not release them to go to live and work in a strange place. The companies had to build dormitories, to provide a healthy diet, and to assure parents that their children would receive the moral, intellectual, physical, and domestic training that would prepare them for life. In the case of young women, the company arranged for training in domestic skills needed by a young wife. No partial inclusion, no tentative, tenuous link between company and employee was possible in this setting. Rather, it was a complete and whole relationship which formed between employee and employer.[3]

Some Japan experts argue that the underlying social patterns developed under feudalism prepared the Japanese for dependent relationship on a paternalistic force to meet their needs and to give their loyalty in return. If such an attitude had existed, it surely would have supported the wholistic work relationship.

When economic and social life are integrated into a single whole, then relationships between individuals become intimate. Rather than a connection through a single work relationship, individuals interconnect through multiple bonds. This one closely-knit relationship makes it impossible to escape the frustrations and tensions by spending time with another, completely unrelated group. Intimacy of this sort discourages selfish or dishonest action in the group, since abused relationships cannot be left behind. People who live in a company dormitory, play on a company baseball team, work together in five different committees, and know the situation will continue for the rest of their lives will develop a unique relationship. Values and beliefs become mutually compatible over a wide range of work and non-work related issues. Each person's true level of effort and of performance stands out, and the close relationship brings about a high level of subtlety in understanding of each other's needs and plans. This mixture of supports and restraints promotes mutual trust, since compatible goals and complete openness remove the fears of or desires for deception. Thus intimacy, trust, and understanding grow where individuals are linked to one another through multiple bonds in a wholistic relationship.

Social scientists have long noted that wholistic relationships develop in "total institutions," but have regarded these as anomalies limited to prisons, mental hospitals, religious orders, and military units. Amitai Etzioni of Columbia University asserts that a wholistic network comprises an effective means of social control, one in which individuals can be free but also capable of a peaceful co-existence.[4] But Etzioni, like others, has also contended that this form of social control is fundamentally incompatible with modern industrial society, because industrialism inevitably leads to a high degree of specialization of labor, frequent moving between employers, and consequently only a partial inclusion in the group. The Japanese show clear evidence that wholism in industrial life is possible. The final question must address whether wholism and intimacy in industrial life are desirable. In grasping just how we Americans really differ from the Japanese lies the key to what we can learn from them.

3

COMPARING JAPANESE AND AMERICAN COMPANIES

A MODEL is an abstraction from reality. It is a bare-bones attempt to lay out the important and distinctive features of a thing so that we can readily apprehend its uniqueness. The preceding chapters laid out a model of the Japanese organization that describes what is distinctive and unique about the type. While this approach enables us to describe a complex phenomenon, it has the drawback of over-simplification. Real organizations in Japan display these features in varying degrees. No one organization will contain each and every characteristic mentioned in pure form. On the other hand, virtually all managers of large enterprises in Japan seek to achieve, as nearly as possible, these underlying characteristics.

My purpose in describing the model Japanese organization was to use it as a foil against which to compare and better understand the American model. Thus we will end up with two abstractions from reality, each describing some set of underlying tendencies which capture the not-always-realized essence of an organizational form. When we do this, what we find is that the American model is the opposite of the Japanese model in every important respect.

The Contrast

Japanese Organizations *vs. American Organizations*

Lifetime Employment
Slow Evaluation and
   Promotion

Short-term Employment
Rapid Evaluation and
   Promotion

Non-Specialized Career Paths	Specialized Career Paths
Implicit Control Mechanisms	Explicit Control Mechanisms
Collective Decision Making	Individual Decision Making
Collective Responsibility	Individual Responsibility
Wholistic Concern	Segmented Concern

Not only the parts of the American model, but also the ways in which the parts fit together to form a working system need consideration. Employment is typically short-term in American companies. In manufacturing and clerical occupations, companies often have an annual turnover of fifty percent and even ninety percent in some years. A company may spend fifteen days training new employees then have them work for two to six months before they quit. Even at executive levels, turnovers of twenty-five percent per year are not unknown, so that the group of vice-presidents who must coordinate the overall operations of the company constantly changes and shifts. Studies by Professor Robert Cole of the University of Michigan have shown that turnover rates in American companies are four to eight times as high as for all Japanese companies, where resignations and layoffs are virtually unknown among the large Japanese firms.

Rapid employee turnover necessitates speedy evaluation and promotion. A constant need to replace managers places new employees not yet attuned to the subtleties of the organization in influential positions. This process of rapid evaluation and promotion often creates a hysterical attitude among managers who feel that three years without a significant promotion means they have failed. In recent years the huge influx of M.B.A. (Master of Business Administration) degree holders into industry has fueled the hysteria. In 1980 roughly 45,000 newly-minted M.B.A.'s entered American industry, up from 4,000 two decades before. Graduate Schools of Business tend to foster the attitude that everyone in their program will, by virtue of their superior ability and training, quickly rise to the top of American industry. The graduates tend to be very impatient, changing employers if they are not rapidly promoted. Indeed, studies by some of the leading graduate schools of business show that their M.B.A. graduates on the average work for three employers during their first ten years after graduation.

This rapid movement of people leads to an interesting

paradox. The young, aspiring manager wants to move quickly to an influential position, one in which he or she can have an impact on decisions and events. In a company slow to evaluate and promote before knowing skills and abilities of its employees well, these people will become impatient. Often they will seek out a really fast-paced company whose reputation quickly identifies talent and gives promotions regardless of age or time in grade. They soon discover what Einstein long ago knew — that motion is relative. Although this young person now receives promotions once a year, so are all the others, and the sense of standing still rather than moving ahead — that is, faster than others — returns. In this case, however, there is a further disappointment. Having achieved higher echelons of the organization, the manager now expects to influence events and decisions but finds this impossible. In a company with rapid advancement and turnover, people learn to operate without depending on or consulting others. No one else is likely to know or care about their problems or be around long enough to follow through with collaborative responsibilities. People and departments become sealed off from one another. In order to accomplish anything, each must stick to those things which they can do alone. In such a situation, broad influence over decisions and events is impossible, frustrating a manager. Some move on to yet another hopeful setting. The story, of course, does not have a happy ending.

One American firm has developed a unique and successful means of dealing with this problem. The Jewel Tea Company of Chicago is a large owner of grocery, drug, and other retail stores. One of my students, a young woman, went to work for Jewel after receiving her M.B.A. degree. She returned to campus for a visit six months later and related the following story:

"During the Christmas holiday, all of my classmates in the Chicago area had a small reunion to compare notes on our first jobs. Everyone bragged about the importance and complexity of their assignments. One fellow said that he was designing a world-wide computer network for a multi-billion dollar company, another described how he bought and sold tens of millions of dollars of bonds every day. When it was my turn, everyone asked what I was doing at Jewel. I was embarrassed somewhat to explain that after spending four months working in the stockroom of an Osco Drug store in Chicago, I had just been promoted to assistant in charge of fuzzy stuffed animals. I oversee a rack of toys five feet long and five feet high!" At the same time, however, this young woman is assigned a "sponsor," a high-ranking executive of the company who has lunch with her regularly, inquires into her well-being, and lets her know that although she is learning the ropes from the bottom up, she is being appreciated from the very top.

More typically, however, American firms respond to turn-over with rapid evaluation and promotion. Moreover, the typical career path is highly specialized. At operator levels, a company with employee turnover of fifty percent must train half of its workforce anew each year. To accomplish this feat, jobs must be divided into little pieces, each simple enough to be learned within a few days. Of course, these simple jobs become unbearably boring so that a worker with any options will quit at the first opportunity. The cycle renews itself.

At professional and managerial levels, the specialization is even greater. Managers who do not know one another person-ally depend upon others to be "professional," that is, to respond in standard ways to problems. An electrical engineer with a graduate degree is expected to respond to problems in pretty much the same way that a predecessor did. Knowing this, managers can make plans which involve some input from the electrical engineer without fearing a nonstandard, incompatible response. Thus, standardization replaces intimacy as the coor-dination mechanism. From the standpoint of the electrical engineer, the goal is to become highly specialized and well known within the specialty across the nation. A lifelong career with a current employer cannot be counted on. To maintain marketability to other companies, a high level of specialized skills that can fit in to any company must be maintained. A person who meets the needs of only one organization risks eventual unemployment. American organizations coordinate the efforts of highly specialized individuals in a gross way through the meshing of specialties. As a consequence few employees are capable of or committed to achieving integration and coordination.

We thus are left with a set of individuals of widely differing talents, skills, and objectives. Such people are in an important way strangers to one another. The division manager who came up through manufacturing does not understand the subtleties of the personnel job or the accounting job, and thus can neither direct nor evaluate people in those functions except as an amateur. The warehouse manager does not understand the nature of the work performed by the computer programmers, and thus can coordinate with them only in a distant and formal manner. Nothing can be left to an unspoken mutual understanding or to the imagination, since both probably will differ. Thus mechanisms of control become explicit and formal, losing all of the subtlety and complexity that can exist in cooperative life.

I had the opportunity to work with a large American company which manufactures and sells electronic products. These products are "stand-alone" in the sense that each one comes in a box, requires no other attachments, and is typically sold by one salesman working alone. The company, very successful for many years, prided itself on the individual aggressiveness and entrepreneurial spirit of its salesmen. As time passed, the nature of the business evolved towards systems of products. Now a customer typically did not purchase a "stand-alone" product, but rather bought a system of products which fit together into a working whole. Each part differed sufficiently from the others in technology so that no one person could understand all parts of the system; thus salesmen from all product divisions had to work together to make a sale. Thus it became critical that the salesmen integrate their efforts in presenting a unified system to the customer. Unfortunately, the control system was still one that encouraged each salesman to stand alone. Because the turnover among salesmen and managers was high, managers could not assess the long-run performance of salesmen in subtle ways and instead relied upon explicit measures of sales volume to determine raises and bonuses. The sales managers, themselves unfamiliar with all of the aspects of a system and the other salesmen as well, hesitated to depend on subjective measures of contributions and instead relied heavily upon measures of individual sales volume. The salesmen, realizing they were actually being evaluated only on the number of products sold, paid little attention to instructing or coordinating with others. They understood full well that such behavior was in the end self-destructive, but the enmeshing control system did not permit them to behave cooperatively. The company suffered great disorganization and losses in this new operation.

In similar ways, all of the characteristics of the American form of organization intertwine and mutually support one another. The parts comprise a system which closely resembles a form first described by the sociologist Max Weber as the bureaucratic organization.[1] The term *bureaucracy* has come to have pejorative meaning, but it was originally intended to describe an organizational system which is a marvel of efficiency. Why do contemporary scholars almost universally regard the bureaucratic form as inefficient, and all of us who deal with bureaucracies see them as inflexible, insensitive, and inefficient?

The answer may have to do with the social context of organizations. Weber lived and worked seventy-five years ago in central Europe, in what was then Prussia. In that setting, companies and government bureaus rarely employed more than a few hundred people. Cities typially held a few thousand inhabitants. Many members of the same family worked together in one business or one government bureau. Bonds of kinship, of friendship, of religion, as well as employment held them together. Indeed Weber observed that the principal source of inefficiency in administration stemmed from nepotism and favoritism: The social bonds were so numerous and intimate that "rational" or impersonal decision making was uncommon. In this setting, Weber proposed that the ideal form of organization would separate people from one another, forcing them to be technically specialized and formally directed and evaluated in order to maintain an impersonal attitude in dealing with one another. To Weber, the organization needed to press against the non-rational forces of social intimacy and balance effective work with fair treatment on the basis of skill and efficiency rather than on politics or friendship.

Since Weber's time, Western organizations and particularly United States organizations have maintained the bureaucratic form as their distinctive feature. But the social context has changed. Rather than having a closely-knit society of people who know one another so well that they can barely view each other objectively, we now have our bureaucratic organizations in a setting in which people barely know or care about one another. Rather than striking a balance between social intimacy and objectivity, we now have an objective but automated society as well as work organizations. The balance of forces has been replaced with a quite asymmetrical push towards formality, automatism, and individualism. Organizations can be effective economically and satisfying emotionally only by maintaining a delicate balance between intimacy on the one hand and objectivity and explicitness on the other.

The social and historical context in which organizations evolve is inevitably a primary determinant of how they take shape. These contexts account for yet another important difference in Japanese and American organizations—their quite different roots.

A Difference of Tradition

The *shinkansen* or "bullet train" speeds across the rural areas of Japan giving a quick view of cluster after cluster of farmhouses surrounded by rice paddies. This particular pattern did not develop purely by chance, but as a consequence of the technology peculiar to the growing of rice, the staple of the Japanese diet. The growing of rice requires the construction and maintenance of an irrigation system, something that takes many hands to build. More importantly, the planting and the harvesting of rice can only be done efficiently with the cooperation of twenty or more people. The "bottom line" is that a single family working alone cannot produce enough rice to survive, but a dozen families working together can produce a surplus. Thus the Japanese have had to develop the capacity to work together in harmony, no matter what the forces of disagreement or social disintegration, in order to survive.

Japan is a nation built entirely on the tips of giant, suboceanic volcanoes. Little of the land is flat and suitable for agriculture. Terraced hillsides make use of every available square foot of arable land. Small homes built very close together further conserve the land. Japan also suffers from natural disasters such as earthquakes and hurricanes. Traditionally homes are made of light construction materials, so a house falling down during a disaster will not crush its occupants and also could be quickly and inexpensively rebuilt. During the feudal period until the Meiji restoration of 1868, each feudal lord sought to restrain his subjects from moving from one village to the next for fear that a neighboring lord might amass enough peasants with which to produce a large agricultural surplus, hire an army and pose a threat. Apparently bridges were not commonly built across rivers and streams until the late nineteenth century, since bridges increased mobility between villages.

Taken all together, this characteristic style of living paints the picture of a nation of people who are homogenous with respect to race, history, language, religion, and culture. For centuries and generations these people have lived in the same village next door to the same neighbors. Living in close proximity and in dwellings which gave very little privacy, the Japanese survived through their capacity to work together in harmony. In this situation, it was inevitable that the one most central social value which emerged, the one value without which the society could not continue, was that an individual does not matter.

To the Western soul this is a chilling picture of society. Subordinating individual tastes to the harmony of the group and knowing that individual needs can never take precedence over the interests of all is repellent to the Western citizen. But a frequent theme of Western philosophers and sociologists is that individual freedom exists only when people willingly subordinate their self-interests to the social interest. A society composed entirely of self-interested individuals is a society in which each person is at war with the other, a society which has no freedom. This issue, constantly at the heart of understanding society, comes up in every century, and in every society, whether the writer be Plato, Hobbes, or B. F. Skinner. The question of understanding which contemporary institutions lie at the heart of the conflict between automatism and totalitarianism remains. In some ages, the kinship group, the central social institution, mediated between these opposing forces to preserve the balance in which freedom was realized; in other times the church or the government was most critical. Perhaps our present age puts the work organization as the central institution.

In order to complete the comparison of Japanese and American living situations, consider a flight over the United States. Looking out of the window high over the state of Kansas, we see a pattern of a single farmhouse surrounded by fields, followed by another single homestead surrounded by fields. In the early 1800s in the state of Kansas there were no automobiles. Your nearest neighbor was perhaps two miles distant; the winters were long, and the snow was deep. Inevitably, the central social values were self-reliance and independence. Those were the realities of that place and age that children had to learn to value.

The key to the industrial revolution was discovering that non-human forms of energy substituted for human forms could increase the wealth of a nation beyond anyone's wildest dreams.

But there was a catch. To realize this great wealth, non-human energy needed huge complexes called factories with hundreds, even thousands of workers collected into one factory. Moreover, several factories in one central place made the generation of energy more efficient. Almost overnight, the Western world was transformed from a rural and agricultural country to an urban and industrial state. Our technological advance seems to no longer fit our social structure: in a sense, the Japanese can better cope with modern industrialism. While Americans still busily protect our rather extreme form of individualism, the Japanese hold their individualism in check and emphasize cooperation.

In fact, modern industrial production and industrial life are better suited to cooperation than to individualism as we practice it. Giving up our individuality is no solution. Rather, the solution must be to achieve a more complete understanding of the close connection between work organizations and society. New organizational designs reflect this view. This ecological view of organizations is currently very much in fashion among social scientists who study organizations. This ecological viewpoint, borrowed from the biological model, suggests an internal form of an organization, just like the inside of a rose or an elephant is nothing more or less than an adaptive response to a particular ecological setting.[2] The argument suggests that the Japanese (Type J) form represents an adaptation to conditions of homogeneity, stability, and collectivism — a form where individual behaviors mesh intimately together. By comparison, the American (Type A) form represents a natural adaptation to conditions of heterogeneity, mobility, and individualism — a form where people link tenuously to one another and rarely achieve intimacy.

A strict use of the ecological model implies slow changes within a species rather than within a single organism. For example, an individual elephant, once born, cannot grow a fifth leg if five legs are needed. The species either adapts and survives or fails to adapt and becomes extinct. The adaptation process favors those organisms who change to fit the environmental conditions. The new characteristics of the survivors become standard. If Western society has systematically been selecting in favor of Type A organizations, just as Weber argued it would, then how do we explain the success of Japanese-owned and operated businesses in the United States? How is it that these

Type *J* organizations, although modified from the pure Japanese form, have maintained much of their Japanese character while flourishing in this setting which has produced the Type *A* as the dominant form?

The problem turns out to be more difficult even than that. At a midpoint in research comparing Japanese with American companies, I was describing my preliminary results to a group of executives at IBM. One of the IBM vice-presidents spoke up, "Do you realize that this form that you have been describing as Japanese is exactly what IBM is? Let me point out that IBM has developed to this form in its own way — we have not copied the Japanese!" Although this man's reaction was an opinion with which other IBM employees might strongly disagree, I was stunned at the thought that what I had conceived of as a culturally-bound form of organization, the Type *J*, might in fact not be culturally specific at all. Types of *A* and *J* may be general types, capable of surviving in a variety of environments, with Type *A* generally better suited to those conditions found most often in the United States and Western Europe, and the Type *J* more suited to the conditions generally prevailing in Japan. Perhaps some variability exists in the social conditions within the West, or perhaps social conditions in the West are in a state of transition. In particular, it might be that a form of the Type *J* organization, not identical but similar to the pure Japanese form, has properties that suit it well to the Western condition.

The Comparisons

In order to test this possibility, I arranged for the interviewing of managers from a great variety of industries. Each manager saw a list of the seven characteristics of the Japanese type, but with no indication that these were related to anything Japanese. Each manager was asked to name any American companies that had these characteristics. Initially, I wanted to identify one or two companies that someone felt fit this type for a study in greater depth. Surprisingly managers named the same companies repeatedly: IBM, Procter & Gamble, Hewlett-Packard, Eastman Kodak, the U.S. military. These organizations, all commonly thought to be among the best managed in the world, were identified by our respondents as having the same characteristics as Japanese companies!

During this period, I had invited as a guest speaker in one of

my classes a partner in a management consulting firm engaged
in executive search, the process by which he represents a major
company in attempting to locate and hire people to fill special
needs at the executive level. He described to my class the process
used in locating qualified top executives, often from a small set
of "feeder" companies. These "feeder" companies are known in
industry for developing an uncommonly high fraction of their
young people into very skilled and successful general managers.
Typically, if a search firm can induce a manager in one of the
"feeders" to leave, he will fill the bill specified by the company
that is looking for a qualified executive. In other words, a young
person beginning a career would do very well to find a position
in one of these companies, which somehow manage to develop
talent and are known for doing so. My students could hardly
wait for the question-and-answer period, and the first question
was, "Tell us the names of these 'feeder' companies." His list:
IBM, Hewlett-Packard, Eastman Kodak Company, Procter &
Gamble, and three or four others.

I will never forget that moment. Obviously the so-called
Japanese form of organization was a general type, not limited to
Japan. The difference between types was more than cosmetic.
The substantial difference involved the development of subtle
management skills in people. The problem was to discover how
such firms accomplished this task, to learn why they succeeded
in the United States, and to understand the similarities to and
differences from the Japanese type.

These organizations, which have developed naturally in the
United States but have many characteristics similar to firms
in Japan, I refer to as Type Z organizations. This choice of la-
bel is an intentional reference to the distinction made earlier between "Theory X" and "Theory Y" management by Douglas
McGregor, and my argument is related to his.[3]

Douglas McGregor was for many years a very distinguished
professor at the Alfred P. Sloan School of Industrial Administration at the Massachusetts Institute of Technology (M.I.T.).
He argued that much that is important about a manager can be
understood by knowing that manager's underlying assumptions
about human nature. McGregor felt that these assumptions
were primarily of two kinds, which he labelled "Theory X" and
"Theory Y" assumptions. A Theory X manager assumes that
people are fundamentally lazy, irresponsible, and need constantly to be watched. A Theory Y manager assumes that people

are fundamentally hard-working, responsible, and need only to be supported and encouraged.

In my framework, Western organizations are regarded as being primarily of the types A and Z (Type J is the term reserved for the form found in Japan). Just as most managers are not purely described by assumptions X and Y, organizations are rarely purely of the form A or Z. Nevertheless, understanding Types A and Z may be helpful in characterizing the underlying tendencies of organizations. Once I realized this difference between types, I set out to find out what made the existing Z organizations unique in their success.

4

THE Z ORGANIZATION

Eᴀᴄʜ Type Z company has its own distinctiveness — the United States military has a flavor quite different from IBM or Eastman Kodak. Yet all display features that strongly resemble Japanese firms. Like their Japanese counterparts, Type Z companies tend to have long-term employment, often for a lifetime, although the lifetime relationship is not formally stated. The long-term relationship often stems from the intricate nature of the business; commonly, it requires lots of learning-by-doing. Companies, therefore, want to retain employees, having invested in their training to perform well in that one unique setting. Employees tend to stay with the company, since many of their skills are specific to that one firm with the result that they could not readily find equally remunerative nor challenging work elsewhere. These task characteristics that produce the life-long employment relationship also produce a relatively slow process of evaluation and promotion. Here we observe one important adaptation of the Japanese form. Type Z companies do not wait ten years to evaluate and promote: any Western firm that did so would not retain many of its talented employees. Thus such firms frequently provide the sorts of explicit performance interviews that are commonplace. However, promotions are slower in coming than at Type A companies.

Career paths in Type Z companies display much of the "wandering around" across functions and offices that typifies the Japanese firm. This effectively produces more company-specific skills that work toward intimate coordination between steps in the design, manufacturing, and distribution process. An employee who engages in such "non-professional" development takes the risk that the end skills will be largely non-marketable to other companies. Therefore, long-term employment ties into career development in a critical way.

Typically Type Z companies are replete with the paraphernalia of modern information and accounting systems, formal planning, management by objectives, and all of the other formal, explicit mechanisms of control characterizing the Type A. Yet in Z companies these mechanisms are tended to carefully for their information, but rarely dominate in major decisions. By contrast, managers in big companies, hospitals, and government agencies often complain about feeling powerless to exercise their judgement in the face of quantitative analysis, computer models, and numbers, numbers, numbers. Western management seems to be characterized for the most part by an ethos which roughly runs as follows: rational is better than non-rational, objective is more nearly rational than subjective, quantitative is more objective than non-quantitative, and thus quantitative analysis is preferred over judgements based on wisdom, experience, and subtlety. Some observers, such as Professor Harold Leavitt of Stanford University, have written that the penchant for the explicit and the measurable has gone well beyond reasonable limits, and that a return to the subtle and the subjective is in order.[1]

In a Type Z company, the explicit and the implicit seem to exist in a state of balance. While decisions weigh the complete analysis of facts, they are also shaped by serious attention to questions of whether or not this decision is "suitable," whether it "fits" the company. A company that isolates sub-specialities is hardly capable of achieving such fine-grained forms of understanding. Perhaps the underlying cause is the loss of the ability for disparate departments within a single organization to communicate effectively with one another. They communicate in the sparse, inadequate language of numbers, because numbers are the only language all can understand in a reasonably symmetrical fashion. Let us consider one example.

A Matter of Company Style

One of the more dramatic new businesses to develop during the decade of the 1970s was the digital watch industry. At the outset, the digital or electronic watch presented a mystery to everyone in the business. The old, main-line watch firms such as Timex and Bulova were suspicious of the new semiconductor technology which replaced the mainspring and the tuning fork. The semiconductor firms that knew this technology supplied parts to other companies and did not know the business of selling goods to the individual consumer. I watched the reaction of two of these semiconductor firms to a new business opportunity: one of these firms previously identified as a quite pure example of Type A, the other a relatively pure example of Type Z. I was busily studying these two companies for reasons unrelated to the watch business as the story unfolded before me.

The digital watch seemed from the first to hold out the promise of a huge new industry. This new watch, which was more accurate, more reliable, and cheaper than the conventional timepiece, held the promise of replacing almost all timepieces in the Western world. Company A performed a careful analysis of the potential market, estimating the number of digital watches that could be sold at various prices, the cost of manufacturing and distributing these watches to retail outlets, and thus the potential profits to be earned by the firm. Company A, already a supplier of the central electronic component, possessed the necessary technical skill. The executives of the company knew that the business of selling consumer goods was unfamiliar to them, but they felt that they could develop the necessary knowledge. Following their analysis of the situation, they proceeded to go out and buy a company that manufactured watch cases, another that manufactured wrist bands for watches, and within weeks after their go-ahead decision, were in the watch business. Starting from zero, Company A rapidly gained a major share of the watch business and, eighteen months after the decision, was a major factor in the new industry and earned large profits on digital watches.

The executives of Company Z also recognized the opportunities in digital watches; they too manufactured the key electronic component that is the heart of the digital watch. Their analyses of the market promised very great rewards should they enter the business. But at Company Z, the numbers never dominate. The top executives at the firm asked whether this business really fit their "style." They saw the anticipated profits but wondered whether this would be a one-shot success or whether the company could continue to be an innovator and a leader in the watch business in the years to come. Most importantly, entering the watch business seemed to conflict with the company's philosophy. In Company Z, talking about the company philosophy is not considered soft-headed, wishful, or unrealistic. Rather, the company consists of a set of managers who see clearly that their capacity to achieve close cooperation depends in part on their agreeing on a central set of objectives and ways of doing business. These agreements comprise their philosophy of business, a broad statement that contemplates the proper relationship of the business to its employees, its owners, its customers, and to the public-at-large. This general statement must be interpreted to have meaning for any specific situation, and it is therefore important that managers be sufficiently familiar with the underlying corporate culture so that they can interpret the philosophy in ways which produce cooperation rather than conflict. One element of the philosophy concerns the kinds of products the company should manufacture, and that statement seemed clearly to exclude a product like the digital watch. On that basis, it seemed, the philosophy outweighed the financial analysis, and the watch project should have ended there.

But it didn't. A second major element of this corporation's philosophy had to do with preserving the freedom of employees to pursue projects they felt would be fruitful. In particular, the freedom of a unit manager to set goals and pursue them to their conclusion is cherished. In this case, a young general manager with a proven record of success wanted to take the company into the watch business. The top executives of the company disagreed with his judgement but were unwilling to sacrifice the manager's freedom. Two very central values conflicted in their implications for action. What was striking about this case was that values, not market share or profitability, lay at the heart of the conflict in Company Z.

Let me not seem to imply that Company Z is unconcerned with profitability. The record is clear. Company Z is among the fastest-growing, most profitable of major American firms. Every manager knows that projects survive only as long as they produce profits well above what other companies demand. But at Company Z, profits are regarded not as an end in itself nor as the method of "keeping score" in the competitive process. Rather, profits are the reward to the firm if it continues to provide true value to its customers, to help its employees to grow, and to behave responsibly as a corporate citizen. Many of us have heard these words and are by now cynical about that kind of a public face which frequently shields a far less attractive internal reality. One of the distinctive features of Company Z is that these values are not a sham, not cosmetic, but they are practiced as the standard by which decisions are made. Again, the process is not faultless. Some managers within the firm are skeptical about the wisdom of these values and about the firm's true commitment to them, but by and large, the culture is intact and operating effectively.

Why a philosophy of management when firms in a free enterprise economy are supposed to seek profits only? In a large organization, it is impossible to determine over the period of a few months or a year whether a business segment is profitable or not. Suppose that you become the manager in charge of a new division created to enter the digital watch market. You buy the electronics from another division, you share salespersons with other divisions, you draw on a central engineering staff to design and maintain both your product and your manufacturing process, you rely heavily on the good name of the company to promote your product, and you staff your new operation with skilled managers and technicians who are products of the company's training programs. How much should you be charged for each of these inputs to your business? No one can know. Someone, inevitably, will come up with some numbers, sometimes referred to as "transfer prices" and other times referred to as "magic numbers," and these numbers will be used to calculate your costs in order to subtract those from your sales revenues so that a profit can be measured. Everyone, however, knows that the stated profits are a very inexact measure of your true profits, and that your true profits are unknowable.

Suppose that your company is in fact run by a strict profitability standard. If you are being undercharged for the central engineering services, then you will use as much engineering as you can, thereby taking that service away from some other use in the company. If another division manager asks to borrow three of your experienced staff, you may deny this request or send three not very skilled persons instead, since another's success is not reflected in your profits. In many ways, large and small, the inexact measurement of value will result in an explicit, formal mechanism that yields low coordination, low productivity, and high frustration.

Organizational life is a life of interdependence, of relying upon others. It is also a life of ambiguity. Armen Alchian and Harold Demsetz, two distinguished economists at UCLA, have argued that where teamwork is involved the measurement of individual performance will inevitably be ambiguous. Knowing this, and understanding the extreme complexity of interdependence in their business, the top management of Company Z has determined that explicit measures not be the final arbiter of decision making. They feel that if most of the top managers agree on what the company ought to be trying to do and how, in general, it ought to go about that set of tasks, then they will be able to rely on their mutual trust and goodwill to reach decisions far superior to anything that a formal system of control could provide.

They furthermore understand that the informal, explicit mechanisms of control cannot succeed alone. They can develop only under the conditions of stable employment, slow evaluation and promotion, and low career specialization. Even with those aides, however, the subtle and the implicit must be supported with the crutch of formal control and analysis in a large, multi-product, multi-national, multi-technology organization in which a complete agreement on values and beliefs can never be fully realized.

In the end, Company Z authorized the general manager to enter a relatively small and specialized segment of the digital watch market. He had the opportunity to "grow" his new venture if it succeeded, but the initial venture was small enough that its failure would not jeopardize the health of the company overall. Three years after the initial decisions by both companies, the picture was quite different. Following a dramatic surge in sales and profits, Company A had encountered stiff competition from other firms who were more experienced than they in this industry. Eighteen months after their initial success, they had taken severe losses and had sold their watch business to a competitor. They were, once again, back to zero in watches. Company Z also experienced an early success with its more limited digital watch venture, and after the initial success they, too, experienced stiff competition and a decline in profits. Rather than sell off the business, however, they slowly de-emphasized it, continuing to service the watches that they already had sold and, perhaps, maintaining the skeletal business as a valuable lesson from which future managers could learn.

A Matter of Company Substance

In Type Z organizations, as we have seen, the decision-making process is typically a consensual, participative one. Social scientists have described this as a democratic (as opposed to autocratic or apathetic) process in which many people are drawn into the shaping of important decisions. This participative process is one of the mechanisms that provides for the broad dissemination of information and of values within the organization, and it also serves the symbolic role of signaling in an unmistakable way the cooperative intent of the firm. Many of the values central to a corporate culture are difficult to test or to display. Some do not come into play more than once every few years, when a crisis appears (for example, the commitment to long-term employment, which is tested only during a recession), while others, such as the commitment to behave unselfishly, are difficult to observe. These values and beliefs must be expressed in concrete ways if they are to be understood and believed by new employees, particularly since new employees arrive with the expectation that all companies are basically the same: they are not to be trusted, not to be believed. Consensual decision making both provides the direct values of information and value sharing and at the same time openly signals the commitment of the organization to those values. When people get together in one room to discuss a problem or to make a decision, that meeting is often noticed and even talked about: it is a highly visible form of commitment to working together. Typically, Type Z organizations devote a great deal of energy to developing the interpersonal skills necessary to effective group decision making, perhaps in part for this symbolic reason.

In Type Z companies, the decision making may be collective, but the ultimate responsibility for decision still resides in one individual. It is doubtful that Westerners could ever tolerate the collective form of responsibility that characterizes Japanese organizations. This maintenance of the sense of individual responsibility remains critical to Western society but it also creates much tension in the Type Z organization. When a group engages in consensual decision making, members are effectively being asked to place their fate to some extent in the hands of others. Not a common fate but a set of individual fates is being dealt with. Each person will come from the meeting with the responsibility for some individual targets set collectively by the group. The consensual process, as defined by Professor Edgar Schein of M.I.T., is one in which members of the group may be asked to accept responsibility for a decison that they do not prefer, but that the group, in an open and complete discussion, has settled upon.[2] This combination of collective decision making with individual responsibility demands an atmosphere of trust. Only under a strong assumption that all hold basically compatible goals and that no one is engaged in self-serving behavior will individuals accept personal responsibility for a group decision and make enthusiastic attempts to get the job done.

The wholistic orientation of Type Z companies is in many ways similar to that found in the Japanese form but with some important differences. The similarity has to do with orientation of superior to subordinates and of employees at all levels to their co-workers. Type Z companies generally show broad concern for the welfare of subordinates and of co-workers as a natural part of a working relationship. Relationships between people tend to be informal and to emphasize that whole people deal with one another at work, rather than just managers with workers and clerks with machinists. This wholistic orientation, a central feature of the organization, inevitably maintains a strong egalitarian atmosphere that is a feature of all Type Z organizations.

If people deal with one another in segmented ways, as one role to another rather than as one human being to another, then these dehumanized relationships easily become authoritarian. Feelings of superiority and inferiority prevail in relationships narrowly defined and constrained to "my" duties as department head and "your" duties as worker. That attitude, out of step in a democratic society, implies class distinctions. The subordinate will inevitably be alienated both from the superior who takes such an attitude and from the company that he or she represents. The superior is often relieved of some of the anxiety and stress that come with having to respond to the needs of others, whether those are superiors, subordinates, or peers. Most of us cannot block off the requests or complaints of superiors and peers, but if we become impersonal and formal and thus distant from the needs of subordinates, that gives one less thing to worry about. Of course we recognize that feeling as being improper, unfair, and unproductive, but short-term pressures will often beckon in that direction.

An organization that maintains a wholistic orientation and forces employees at all levels to deal with one another as complete human beings creates a condition in which depersonalization is impossible, autocracy is unlikely, and open communication, trust, and commitment are common. In one Type Z company with which I am familiar, each plant in the company holds a monthly "beer bust" at the end of a working day. Beer and snacks are consumed, neither in large quantities, and informal games and skits are frequently offered. Any manager who regularly fails to take part in the beer bust will fail to achieve success and continued promotion. Is this an example of "politics at work," of "it's who you know, not what you know," or is it simply a holdover from earlier days?

The beer bust, as I interpret it, is similar to the cocktails after work shared by bosses and subordinates in Japan. Both have the same group of people who work together each day now cast in different roles. The hierarchy of work, somewhat relaxed in this setting, gives people the opportunity to interact more as equals, or at least without the familiar hierarchical roles. Technicians can express their willingness to regard foremen as regular people rather than as superiors to be suspected. Managers show subordinates their acceptance of them as equals, as whole human beings. In this particular company with the beer bust, managers must be willing to engage in frivolous games and skits in which their obvious lack of skill and their embarrassment bring them down to earth both in their own eyes and in the eyes of their subordinates.

Very few of us are superior to our fellow workers in every way. As long as we cling to our organizational roles, we can maintain the fiction that we are indeed superior in every way. But if we engage these people in social intercourse, the fiction is dispelled. The natural force of organizational hierarchy promotes a segmented relationship and a hierarchical attitude. A wholistic relationship provides a counterbalance that encourages a more egalitarian attitude.

Egalitarianism is a central feature of Type Z organizations. Egalitarianism implies that each person can apply discretion and can work autonomously without close supervision, because they are to be trusted. Again, trust underscores the belief that goals correspond, that neither person is out to harm the other. This feature, perhaps more than any other, accounts for the high levels of commitment, of loyalty, and of productivity in Japanese firms and in Type Z organizations.

Let us return briefly to Douglas McGregor's "Theory X" and "Theory Y" assumptions about human nature. McGregor's work drew heavily on that of former student Chris Argyris of Harvard University.[3] Argyris argued that motivation in work will be maximal when each worker pursues individual goals and experiences psychological growth and independence. Close supervision diminishes motivation, retards psychological growth, and hampers personal independence and freedom. However, supervision can be supportive in "Theory Y" only when the supervisor trusts workers to use their discretion in a manner consistent with the goals of the organization. Thus the connection between an egalitarian style of management and mutual trust.

The central importance of trust is revealed in a study of utopian societies by Rosabeth Moss Kanter.[4] Kanter described the Amana (refrigerators), the Oneida (tableware), and other utopian communities that succeeded as commercial enterprises. In these communities one of the key values was egalitarianism—equality of influence and of power. Consistent with this value, all explicit forms of supervision and of direction were foregone. Now the problem was how to ensure a high level of discipline and hard work without hierarchical supervision and monitoring of production. The chief danger was of self-interest in the form of laziness, shirking, and selfishness at work. Such behavior could not readily be corrected without hierarchy, and other means had to be found to limit such tendencies. The answer was to develop a complete unity of goals between individuals and the community such that an autonomous individual would naturally seek to work hard, cooperate, and benefit the community. In order to accomplish this complete socialization, utopian communities engaged in a variety of practices that had the objective of developing common goals. Open sex or complete celibacy, the most dramatic of these, both have characterized all successful utopian communes in the United States. From Kanter's point of view, open sex and complete celibacy are functionally equivalent: each prevents the formation of loyalties to another individual and so preserves the loyalty of all to the community. Open sex allows no free choice of partners but rather a strict assignment of older men to younger women and older women to younger men. As soon as partners begin to show preference for one another in this system, they are reassigned. The example illustrates both the great difficulty of achieving complete goal integration in a Western society and the central importance of selfless goals in non-hierarchical organizations.

Type Z organizations, unlike utopian communities, do employ hierarchical modes of control, and thus do not rely entirely upon goal congruence among employees for order. Nevertheless, they do rely extensively upon symbolic means to promote an attitude of egalitarianism and of mutual trust, and they do so in part by encouraging a wholistic relation between employees. Self-direction replaces hierarchical direction to a great extent which enhances commitment, loyalty, and motivation.

Argyris challenged managers to integrate individuals into organizations, not to create alienating, hostile, and impersonally bureaucratic places of work. In a real sense, the Type Z organization comes close to realizing that ideal. It is a consent culture, a community of equals who cooperate with one another to reach common goals. Rather than relying exclusively upon hierarchy and monitoring to direct behavior, it relies also upon commitment and trust.

The Theory Behind the Theory Z Organization

The difference between a hierarchy — or bureaucracy — and Type Z is that Z organizations have achieved a high state of consistency in their internal culture. They are most aptly described as clans in that they are intimate associations of people engaged in economic activity but tied together through a variety of bonds.[5] *Clans* are distinct from *hierarchies,* and from *markets,* which are the other two fundamental social mechanisms through which transactions between individuals can be governed. In a market, there will be competitive bidding for, say, an engineer's services as well as for a weaver's baskets. Each will know the true value of their products according to the terms the market sets. In a bureaucracy, however, workers lack any clear sense of the value of their services. No competitive bidding sets the yearly wage for an engineering vice-president, for example. Since each job is unique, companies instead rely upon the hierarchy to evaluate performance and to estimate the amount that an employee is worth. The hierarchy succeeds only to the extent that we trust it to yield equitable outcomes, just as the marketplace succeeds only because we grant legitimacy to it. As long as the vice-president regards the president as a fair and well-informed person who will arrive at a fair appraisal of his performance, the contented employee will let the hierarchy operate unobstructed. However, mistrust will bring about prespecified contractual protections such as those written when selling some service to an outside firm. The writing and enforcement of that contract will vastly increase the costs of managing the vice-president.

More common is the example of the hourly employee who learns, over time, that the corporate hierarchy cannot be trusted to provide equitable treatment and insists upon union representation and contractual specification of rights. The employee pays additional costs in the form of union dues, the company pays additional costs in the form of more industrial relations staff, and everyone pays more costs in the form of less cooperation, less productivity, and less wealth to be shared. Thus the success of a hierarchy, or bureaucracy, can be costly. But whatever the financial cost, these protective mechanisms take over when individual contribution can be equitably assessed only through the somewhat more subtle form of bureaucratic surveillance.

By comparison clans succeed when teamwork and change render individual performance almost totally ambiguous. At these times long-term commitment, supported by agreement on goals and operating methods, is necessary to achieve an equitable balance. Individual performance and reward can be judged equitably only over a period of several years, thus relationships must be long-term and trust must be great.

In a market each individual is in effect asked to pursue selfish interests. Because the market mechanism will exactly measure the contribution of each person to the common good, each person can be compensated exactly for personal contributions. If one chooses not to contribute anything, then one is not compensated and equity is achieved.

In a clan, each individual is also effectively told to do just what that person wants. In this case, however, the socialization of all to a commn goal is so complete and the capacity of the system to measure the subtleties of contributions over the long run is so exact that individuals will naturally seek to do that which is in the common good. Thus the monk, the marine, or the Japanese auto worker who appears to have arrived at a selfless state is, in fact, achieving selfish ends quite thoroughly. Both of these governance mechanisms realize human potential and maximize human freedom because they do not constrain behavior.

Only the bureaucratic mechanism explicitly says to individuals, "Do not do what you want, do what we tell you to do because we pay you for it." The bureaucratic mechanism alone produces alienation, anomie, and a lowered sense of autonomy. This is the reason that the employees of Z companies report a higher sense of personal autonomy and freedom than do the employees of Type A companies. Feelings of autonomy and freedom make the employees in Japanese firms work with so much more enthusiasm than their counterparts in many Western firms.

In the sense that Z organizations are more like clans than markets or bureaucracies, they foster close interchange between work and social life. Consider this example: Chinese-American entrepreneurs appear in greater numbers than would be expected, based on their fraction of the population as a whole. For many years, the explanation offered by social scientists was that by contrast black Americans were systematically denied access to banks and other sources of capital necessary to start a small business, whereas Asian-Americans had better access to these capital markets. As a number of studies have shown, however, both blacks and Asians find the same difficulties in raising capital for businesses.[6] Yet Asian-Americans brought with them from their homelands the tradition of informal revolving-credit societies, the *Tanomoshi* for the Japanese-Americans and the *Hui* for the Chinese-Americans. A *Tanomoshi* or *Hui* typically consists of about one dozen individuals, each one wanting to own his own service station, a one-truck hauling service, or other such small businesses. Once each month, the group gathers at one member's home for dinner, and each person brings with him a prespecified sum of money, perhaps $1,000. The host of the evening keeps the whole sum — say, $12,000 — which he then uses to buy a second truck or open his service station. The group meets in this fashion for twelve successive months until each person has put in $12,000 and has taken out $12,000. In this manner, people who would have great difficulty saving the whole sum of $12,000 are able to raise capital.

The process on closer scrutiny has some unusual properties. First, the earlier recipients of the pot effectively pay a lower interest rate than do the later recipients. The first host has the use of $11,000 of other people's money for one month without interest, then $10,000 (as he adds his $1,000 to the second dinner), and so on. By comparison the last host has to put $11,000 dollars into the pot, money that he could have left in the bank to draw interest, before he receives his pot. Surely this is an inequitable process, yet it persists. The second interesting property is that no contracts are signed, no collateral is offered, even though the late borrowers willingly turn over large sums of money to others with no assurance that they will be paid. They have no evidence of even having made a loan that would stand up in a court of law, should there be a default.

Japanese-Americans' membership in a *Tanomoshi* is limited strictly by the geographical regions of birth in Japan, and by the region in Japan from which one's ancestors came. Among the Chinese-Americans, membership in a *Hui* is limited to those within the kinship network. Thus one can only be born into a *Tanomoshi* or a *Hui,* and one can never escape from the network of familiar, communal, social, religious, and economic ties that bind those groups together. If a member should fail to make good on his obligations, members of his family would certainly take up his obligation or else pay the very high price of having all branches of the family shut out of the economic and social network of the community. This ethnically-bound community thus obviates the need for contracts or collateral to protect a loan. But what about the unfair difference in the implicit interest rates paid by the early versus late borrowers? We can understand this phenomenon in two ways. First, we note that these short-run inequities are made up in the long run. Because each adult in these ethnic communities typically participates in a large number of *Huis* or *Tanomoshis* over his lifetime, at times simultaneously participating in two or more. Many opportunities arise to repay past debts by taking a later position in the chain. In addition, a debt incurred to one person may be repaid to that person's son or brother, who in turn has the capacity to repay the initial creditor through one of a thousand favors. What is critical is that there be a communal memory — much like that of the corporate memory in Theory *Z* — and that the community have a stable membership. The effects of this memory mechanism are far-reaching. Depending on his behavior as a borrower and lender, an individual may or may not be invited to participate in various other groups and may be included in or left out of religious and social activities that could affect the marital prospects of his children, the economic prospects of his business, and so on. In fact the more valuable his *Tanomoshi* membership, the higher the price he can command in the form of sought-after affiliations. Although the individuals in a *Hui* or *Tanomoshi* do not share complete goal congruence, they are at once largely committed to a congruent set of goals which have to do with maintaining the social structure of the community, and they are also subject to the long-run evaluation of an ethnically-bound marketplace.

These clans also work largely on the basis of trust. Marcel Mauss, a French anthropologist, has noted that the willingness to be in someone's debt is an important signal of trust.[7] For instance, in most societies it is considered rude to rush over to repay a neighbor for a favor just received. To do so implies lack of trust in that neighbor and a fear that the neighbor may abuse your obligation by asking in return something you find particularly difficult or distasteful. Thus, the leaving of many debts between people amounts to evidence of their trust of one another, and the evidence of trust in turn serves as the oil that lubricates future social transactions.

The point is that organizations are social organisms and, like any other social creations, are profoundly shaped by the social environment in which they exist. As we will see, the Type Z organization succeeds only under social conditions that support lifetime employment. The *Hui* and the *Tanomoshi* succeed in the United States only because the Chinese and Japanese immigrants found themselves living together in ethnic ghettoes.

Difficulties in Translation

Despite its remarkable properties, the clan form in industry possesses a few potentially disabling weaknesses. A clan always tends to develop xenophobia, a fear of outsiders. In the words of the president of one major Type Z company: "We simply can't bring in an outsider at top levels. We've tried it, but the others won't accept him. I consider that to be one of our biggest problems." In other ways, too, the Type Z resists deviance in all forms. Because the glue that holds it together is consistency of belief rather than application of hierarchy, it tends indiscriminately to reject all inconsistency. The trouble is that it is difficult, perhaps impossible, to discriminate in advance between a deviant idea that is useful and adaptive and one that is simply stupid and immoral. Companies such as IBM, General Motors, and Xerox, in which innovation is critical, typically segregate their researchers and those who come up with new product ideas, sometimes locating them on the opposite end of the continent from headquarters in order to shield them from the sometimes oppressive corporate culture. What happens, of course, is that those scientists indeed become deviant from the main-line culture, develop lots of different ideas, and then discover that the headquarters decision-makers reject their ideas as being too deviant.

In a Type Z organization, changing people's behavior by changing a measure of performance or by changing the profit calculation is an impossibility: The only way to influence behavior is to change the culture. A culture changes slowly because its values reach deeply and integrate into a consistent network of beliefs that tends to maintain the status quo. Therefore, a Type Z organization runs the risk of becoming an industrial dinosaur, unable to react quickly enough to a major shift in the environment. Where operating changes are involved, Type Z organizations tend to be unusually adaptive. A better way to accomplish some task can be adopted without having to rewrite a book of rules specifying job descriptions and without worrying about whether this change will hurt the current way of measuring our performance. This is one of the greatest strengths of the Japanese firm. Japanese companies in the United States are fast becoming legendary for their capacity to quickly adopt changes in procedure, unencumbered by bureaucratic paraphernalia. However, the coordination in this system is provided by adherence to an underlying set of values that are deeply held and closely followed. If adaptation required a change in those values, then Type Z organizations would be at a severe disadvantage. Consider one example.

I had the opportunity to work with a large retail company that had succeeded for many years in running profitable stores of medium size in small towns. The company had thoroughly cultivated the underlying value that each store manager was an independent entrepreneur who took orders from no one, including the company president. They were encouraged to take an aggressive, "can do" attitude towards their individual businesses, and their compensation was based entirely on the profitability of their one store. Each manager ordered goods from local distributors and ran his business quite successfully. Then the company one day determined that future growth would have to be not in small towns but in major metropolitan areas. They felt that their same discipline and entrepreneurial attitude would succeed as well in Boston as it had in Ely, Minnesota. The difference was that, in order to succeed in the highly competitive metropolitan markets, the company had to develop its own distribution network of warehouses, delivery trucks, and in some cases its own manufacturing plants in order to achieve low costs that could be passed along to potential customers. Now each store manager had to take a cooperative attitude above all else to coordinate this intricate system with the other managers on whom personal success depended. Everyone saw clearly the need for this change, but no one was able to make it. The old independent attitude, so deeply held and so widely supported by payment methods, training methods, corporate structure, and other values, was carried into the new integrated enterprise. The company has consistently lost money in these metropolitan markets, although it continues to succeed in the small towns, and the old culture survives.

Every Type Z organization that I know experiences some loss of professionalism.[8] Whether it is a financial analyst, a salesperson, a personnel specialist, or an engineer, a Type Z company manifests a lower level of professionalism. I systematically interviewed everyone at the level of vice-president and above at two high-technology companies, one a pure Type A and one a pure Type Z (or as nearly pure as possible). I also interviewed a random selection of employees in each company. At Company A, each person was introduced to me with pride as being, ". . . the top public relations man in the industry," or ". . . the most innovative electrical engineer, the holder of twenty patents on circuit design," or ". . . the personnel manager who set the pattern for industry in performance appraisal." At Company Z, by comparison, the emphasis was on how the individuals comprised a working team, with little mention of specialized skills, although great emphasis was placed on the company's practice of hiring only the most skilled and able young people and then developing them. The offices of Company A managers were typically filled with shelves of books and journals, and people would often offer me an article that they had written on their speciality. At Company Z people read fewer journals, wrote fewer articles, and attended fewer professional meetings.

At the extreme, Type Z companies will express the "not-invented-here" mentality: "We have most of the top people in the field right here, so why should I go talk to anyone else?" The trouble, of course, comes if the company starts to slip. They will not know it, since they have no external point of comparison.

With respect to sex and race, Type Z companies have a tendency to be sexist and racist. This is another paradox, because while Type Z companies typically work much harder and care much more about offering equality of opportunity to minorities, in some ways they have much greater obstacles to overcome than do Type A companies. As I visited the managers in the high-technology Type A, I was struck by the ethnic diversity among the upper levels of management: Spanish-Americans, Asian-Americans, Hungarian-Americans, and Anglo-Saxon-Americans. At Company A, new promotion opportunity is simply awarded to that candidate who has had the best "bottom line" for the past few periods. Whether that manager is obnoxious or strange, succeeds by abusing his employees or by encouraging them, doesn't matter. The only thing that counts is the bottom line, and thus a diverse group of people make it to the top. How well they are able to work with one another once at the top is another question.

At Company Z the cast of top managers is so homogeneous that one member of my research team characterized the dominant culture as "Boy Scout Macho." That is, the top management is wholesome, disciplined, hard-working, and honest, but unremittingly white, male, and middle class. Company Z has affirmative action goals at the top of its list and devotes great time and expense to recruiting, training, and developing women and ethnic minorities. Why is it nonetheless typical of "Boy Scout Macho"? Imagine that you are a general manager at Company Z. In your division you have an opening for a new manager in charge of marketing. Both a white male engineer and a female Mexican-American are completely qualified for the promotion. The difference between them is past experience. You have evaluated forty or fifty white male engineers in the past, you have worked with them day in and day out for twenty years, and you know how to calibrate them, how to read their subtle instincts, values, and beliefs. You are quite certain that you have correctly evaluated this white male engineer as being fully qualified for the job of marketing manager. But how about the female Mexican-American? How many of them have you evaluated or worked with at this level? She is probably the first. You cannot be sure that what you regard as initiative is truly that; you cannot be sure that the signs you see of ambition, of maturity, or of integrity are what they seem to be. It takes time and experience to learn to read subtleties in one who is culturally different, and because subtleties are everything in the Type Z organization, you cannot be confident that you have correctly appraised this candidate, and she is therefore at a considerable disadvantage, since no one in his right mind will choose an uncertainty over a certainty.

Probably no form of organization is more sexist or racist than the Japanese corporation. They do not intentionally shut out those who are different nor do they consider male Japanese to be superior. Their organizations simply operate as culturally homogeneous social systems that have very weak explicit or hierarchical monitoring properties and thus can withstand no internal cultural diversity. To the extent that women or ethnic minorities (caucasians or Koreans, for example) are culturally different, they cannot succeed in Japan. The Japanese firm in the United States has a considerably greater tolerance for heterogeneity and thus can operate successfully with white people and women in high positions, but the tendency toward sameness is still present. The Type Z organization is still more open to heterogeneity, but it too requires a high level of homogeneity. Perhaps the other extreme, the cultural opposite of the Japanese firm in Japan, is the United States federal bureaucracy.

In a sense the federal bureaucracy is a microcosm of our society. Here our values of equality of opportunity for all people are crystallized, if not always realized. Much the same is true of state and local government agencies, but let us consider the federal agencies for a moment. Equality of opportunity and of treatment is taken far more seriously in the federal agencies than in almost any private sector organizations. What this means is that the government must promulgate a series of bureaucratic rules that should ordinarily prevent, insofar as humanly possible, the application of capricious or unfair standards that will harm women and ethnic minorities. Unfortunately, this set of bureaucratic rules must be geared to catch the lowest common denominator. That is, they cannot leave any rule ambiguous, to be decided on the discretion of an individual manager, since that leaves open the possibility of the manager arriving at a discriminatory interpretation. Thus the bureaucratic rules are not only explicit and inflexible but also constraining and impersonal. This thoroughgoing bureaucratization rests on the assumption that bureaucrats cannot be trusted to share the society's egalitarian goals nor to enact an egalitarian form of organization. Thus they are directed not to use their discretion and judgement. If we place a priceless value on equality in our public institutions, then we will pay any price to keep them democratic.

The price that we pay, of course, is in inefficiency, inflexibility, indolence, and impersonality. All too often a federal bureau will fail to do that which makes sense because common sense does not fit the rules. All too often bureaucrats, trained not to allow personal values to intrude on decisions, will treat us, their customers, in an unfeeling manner. All too often the machinery of government will respond slowly and inefficiently with poor coordination between agencies, because they have learned not to trust one another, not to rely on subtlety, not to develop intimacy.

Social organizations are incompatible with formality, distance, and contractualism. They proceed smoothly only with intimacy, subtlety, and trust. But these conditions can develop only over a long period of cultural homogenization during which the people of a nation become accustomed to one another and come to espouse a common body of values and beliefs. In a nation as young and as heterogeneous as ours, that level of cultural agreement is yet some distance away. The United States is not Japan. We are not a homogeneous body of people. Our institutions cannot operate in a wholly synchronized manner. On the other hand, we cannot allow our institutions to become so thoroughly unfeeling and unthinking that they make work and social intercourse unbearable for all of us most of the time. We must find those organizational innovations which can permit a balance between freedom and integration, which go beyond our current interpretation of individualism.

PART 2

MAKING THEORY Z WORK

5

GOING FROM A TO Z
THE STEPS

CORPORATE giants and corner drugstores alike have found building an organization is not like building a house. It is more like building a marriage. An organization, constantly in the process of development, will degenerate without attention. But if the only glue that holds an organization together is a constant state of high excitement, then the romance is sure to wear off after a short period of time and the institution will fall apart. The development process is a slow one — it ordinarily takes years for the transition to occur. However, small and important improvements soon become apparent in people's work attitude and in their commitment to their jobs. The steps described here will guide anyone — employer or employee, CEO or chief office worker — in initiating a change to Theory Z. The steps represent the summary of my experience in applying Theory Z in several *Fortune* 500 companies. In all of them, the process, as described here, has the objective of developing the ability of the organization to coordinate *people,* not technology, to achieve productivity. In part, this involves developing people's skills, but in part it also involves the creation of new structures, incentives, and a new philosophy of management.

As of now, I do not have a complete theory of the change process. I cannot assure the reader that these steps, in the order suggested, will lead to the successful development of an effective organization. Management is too much an art and too little a science to submit to such regularity of description. However, some logic guided my arrangement of these steps into this sequence. The basis of this logic is simple: The objective is to achieve commitment of employees to the development of a less selfish, more cooperative approach to work. Before commitment can occur, however, there must be understanding. Understanding comes from the open expression of skepticism through a process of debate and of analysis. An incentive to dig into old assumptions and ask hard questions must be there as well as a sufficient level of trust so that individuals will speak candidly to peers, subordinates, and superiors. Above all, cooperation comes before any of these other things.

Throughout the change process, bear in mind that none of these steps will follow an exact 1-2-3 sequence. Many will overlap with one another, because the change to Theory Z, like Theory Z itself, is wholistic. The idea here is to provide a checklist of the many components of change and some guide for anticipating what comes next. Realize too that the target of change is not an individual but the whole organization.

The whole organization. No one begins by changing a whole organization all at once, especially when, in Theory Z terms, the "whole organization" consists not only of the corporation, but of its suppliers, customers, and community. Even if the chief executive officer promotes change, it necessarily begins with only a part of the whole. In other cases, managers in charge of a single division or department can initiate change. In one instance, the process of going from A to Z was initiated by a department manager who saw the critical need for a change in the rest of the corporation, if his department was to succeed. Through perseverance, he presented these ideas and a sense of urgency to a broad audience of other managers at his level. Ultimately their collective opinion caught the attention of the company president, who explicitly put his support behind a corporate-wide effort for change. In another case, a manager of an extraordinarily successful electronics firm recognized the "distant warning signals," as he put it, of a slow erosion of projected profits some five years away. It was more than enough to motivate him to seek change now.

That first small spark of desire to change typically comes from a key person who cares sufficiently about the organization to invest the time, energy, and risk in taking leadership. A manager who chooses to lead his department, division, or company in a new direction can produce sufficient trust and sufficient incentive for change to sustain the process for some period, perhaps a year. If, during his period, some signs of progress can be discerned by the followers, then the process of change will become nearly self-sustaining. But this is how it commonly begins:

Step One: Understand the Type *Z* Organization and Your Role

To begin, ask each of the managers involved to do some reading so that all are familiar with the underlying ideas of Theory *Z* represented here. The bibliography at the end of the book will suggest additional sources. Some people whom you ask to join in the reading will be skeptical of these ideas, just as others will embrace them. It is important at this and at later stages to present the reading and the ideas in a manner that invites the open display of skepticism. Invite discussion of ideas. Resist interpreting skepticism as foot-dragging, lack of cooperation, or the like; if you do, the skeptics will conceal their doubts and thus never go beyond them. And because in most companies the skeptics outnumber the true believers, their reservations must be openly debated for change to occur.

A second and more fundamental reason to invite skepticism has to do with the development of trust. Trust consists of the understanding that you and I share fundamentally compatible goals in the long run, and thus we have reason to trust one another. In the process of organizational change, the nature of these goals becomes ambiguous. The skeptic who is being asked to abandon his old managerial objectives does not know whether or not, in fact, he does share goals that are compatible with the new ideas. In such a case, a specific form of trust cannot be achieved, but a more generalized form of trust can. This is the trust that comes from knowing that, fundamentally, you and I desire a more effective working relationship together and that neither desires to harm the other. But how to believably establish this basis of trust? In my experience, the clearest evidence is complete openness and candor in a relationship. One who seeks to conceal nothing from me is one who, in all likelihood, does not seek to harm me. How is this best done?

Of the many ways in which openness can be encouraged, the only one that really matters is by setting an example. The leader who frankly disagrees with others and who goes out of his way to create an atmosphere where differing opinions are welcomed will produce change. Of course, this process will lead naturally to a key issue that emerges in all such developmental efforts — performance evaluation. Openness does not mean hostility, nor does it mean sweetness and light. Openness values a realistic appraisal of both problems and achievements. Ultimately subordinates will demand performance appraisal before they willingly attempt more cooperation and less self-protection. When a boss calls for frankness, the openness that subordinates care about most is forthrightness in discussing their performance, their pay, and their future prospects. This most basic form of candor precedes all others.

In this initial process of reading and discussion, the substance of the ideas of Type Z organization is important, but the *process* through which the discussion takes place is equally important. This process must reflect the egalitarianism, the openness, and the participativeness that are the ultimate objectives of the change. The leader, if the company has been largely of Type *A*, will have become accustomed to an authoritarian relationship to an extent that he is not likely to appreciate fully. Although the leader may perceive his own behavior as being quite open and egalitarian, research shows consistently that the subordinates will perceive him to be far less so. If you are taking this leadership role, be prepared for frank criticisms of your non-participative lapses. More important than criticism is your response to it. A consistently open and egalitarian response will begin to develop the underlying generalized trust.

One final admonition to those who intend to lead a process of organizational change. Perhaps the single most notable characteristic among those who have succeeded at going from *A* to *Z* has been an almost palpable character of integrity. By integrity I do not mean preaching morality to others; I mean an integrated response to problems, an integrated and consistent response to customers and employees, to superiors and subordinates, to problems in finance and in manufacturing. A person of integrity treats secretaries and executives with equal respect and approaches subordinates with the same understanding and values that characterizes his family relationships. A person with integrity can be counted upon to behave consistently even as organizational conditions change. Such a person can be trusted and can provide that key human capital from which others can draw in the process of change.

Step Two: Audit Your Company's Philosophy

A statement of your company's objectives — its philosophy — gives people a sense of values to work and to live by. It suggests ways to behave in the organization and a way for the organization to behave in response to its people, its clients, and the community it serves. A philosophy can provide answers to such questions as "Is this the right way to carry out a deal?" or "Am I doing *x* because profits are of paramount concern to the company — or are ideals of company image much more important?" If it seems unusual that a business should depend upon a philosophy of all things, reconsider: A philosphy clearly sets forth the company's motivating spirit for all to understand. Whether directly or indirectly, that philosophy determines how insiders and outsiders alike appraise, trust, and value the company and its products.

Though I describe in detail how companies construct such a philosophy in Chapter 6, I want to portray here some notion of when this step should occur in the process of going from *A* to *Z*. Usually it comes second, though it is a step of the first importance. Your group of managers must take stock of your company's current, actual, operating philosophy. Ask yourself, what is our business strategy, our goals in the marketplace, and the kind of value we place in people? The point here is not to define what your organization *should be,* but what it *is.* The reasons for this "audit" are many.

First, it is not possible to develop a philosophy out of thin air. It is necessary to understand your company's culture by analyzing the four or five key decisions the company has made in the past. Which have worked well? Which have failed? Where are the inconsistencies and omissions? Hold a series of meetings to identify these decisions and to discover what principles were consistently applied across many of those decisions. From this, the basis of a desired philosophy will begin to emerge.

The second reason a philosophy is important is that every organization develops inconsistencies over time between what is officially declared to be desirable by top managers and what those top managers actually do. Those inconsistencies between word and deed will be revealed through an audit, and the very openness and candor with which past inconsistencies are treated will be an important signal of the openness to be generally promoted. I would venture to guess that many of the inconsistencies of the greatest importance will have to do with decisions in promotion and hiring. A promotional decision is typically so complex that a distant observer can attribute any cause to explain it. An open discussion of the basis for specific key promotions in the past will help clarify the underlying basis on which individual performance is valued, provide openness, and promote the development of trust.

Third, the audit will reveal the connections between business strategy and management philosophy. Every company has a business strategy statement of some sort. Often, this statement refers purely to financial goals such as market share, sales growth, and measures of cost or of profitability. Other times, the strategy refers to development of technology, of managerial competence, and to other such broader objectives. Rarely are these statements of objectives linked explicitly to an understanding of the organization. The connection, however, is both critical and intimate.

In one instance, however, there was a wide discrepancy. Recall the case mentioned earlier of the young, bright manager who wanted to go into the digital watch business. A conflict arose between the company's proud philosophy of initiatives, its expression of go-out-and-do-what-you-want, and its statement of business objectives that said, in effect, "We don't expand into areas in which we have no prior expertise." This is an example of a company not being able to foresee everything. These two issues were clearly at odds. As a result, top managers sat down to do some serious soul-searching and decided it was more important to allow this manager to do what he wanted to do.

Many different techniques can be used to carry out this audit. One firm may choose to employ an outside consultant, while another holds a series of discussions among a team drawn from within. One may circulate a simple questionnaire to managers, soliciting their written views on the above questions, while another may prefer personal interviews. Depending upon the particulars of the situation, each of these approaches is viable.

Again, this process of identifying the current and future statements of philosophy is discussed in greater detail in Chapter 6. This step is one that should ordinarily be taken early on in the process of change, perhaps in the first month, but soon after a tentative decision to proceed with a general process of organizational analysis has been taken.

Step Three: Define the Desired Management Philosophy and Involve the Company Leader

Once a clear understanding of the prevailing practices is achieved, it usually becomes obvious which of the current beliefs are inappropriate, which are at odds with other practices, and where there are omissions. Precisely at this stage is the role of the formal leader or chief executive most critical.

Ultimately, a process of organizational change cannot succeed without the direct and personal support of the top person in the hierarchy.[1] That individual cannot be expected to support a statement of managerial philosophy which he or she finds to be wanting. At one company, the process of discussing Theory *Z* had developed an overwhelming sense of the importance of egalitarian participation. As a result, it became quite awkward for the top person to express disapproval of some key elements of the statement, since others had already reached a consensus on those elements. Sometimes this occurs when the group of managers is expected to disagree openly with the top executive. If such a group, with the encouragement of their leader, undertakes a participative approach to an audit, they will be just beginning to practice a new-to-them egalitarian relationship. The leader may be afraid of upsetting their tentative moves at confrontation and thus may withhold personal views on key issues. Consequently, the group discussing the issue will often reach a consensus, assuming the leader has given tacit consent. Unfortunately, the result will be public commitment to a position not personally supported, and that will produce a half-hearted and ultimately unsuccessful attempt at change.

On the other hand, say the person in charge does not want to share all decisions participatively with subordinates. Leaders may fear that a partial move to participation will result in inconsistent behavior that will be interpreted as an uncertain commitment to egalitariansim, causing the whole effort to fail. A few experts believe that subordinates will not be upset with sharing only some rather than all decisions, since sharing in some decisions most often represents an improvement over the current situation. The impression of inconsistency can be avoided if the most senior person involved in the process openly expresses, in advance, the intent to do just that. Certain decisions will be submitted to a fully consensual process of decision making, others partially by seeking information or suggestions while reserving the final decision to management. Finally, other decisions will be made privately, with others informed only after the fact.

Of course, the more fully the superior trusts the others to share this point of view, and the more completely it is in the best interests of all, the larger will be the fraction of all decisions that he can share with them. The more decisions that are shared, the greater will be the benefits of cooperation produced in the management team. Thus, the top manager has an incentive to develop, over time, a trusting relationship that permits a sharing of the decision-making authority with subordinates. Early on, however, no one expects that to happen, and an open recognition of that fact will permit the top person to intervene in the process of establishing the desired future statement of philosophy in a manner that is not disruptive.

Step Four: Implement the Philosophy by Creating Both Structures and Incentives

In a sense a company's formal reporting relationships — its system of who reports to whom — are crutches to prop up the occasional lapses in information and in cooperativeness that befall humans. My ideal of a completely efficient and perfectly integrated organization is one that has no organizational chart, no divisions, no visible structure at all. In a sense, a basketball team that plays well together fits this description, although on a small scale. The problem facing a basketball team is huge in its complexity, and the speed with which problems occur is great. Yet an effective team solves these problems with no formal reporting relationships and a minimum of specialization of positions and of tasks. Each person understands his task and its relationship to other tasks so well that the coordination is unspoken. In a less cooperative team, however, the players attempt to hog the ball, to take as many shots for themselves as possible, and in these attempts frequently move out of their defensive positions. The coach responds to this human frailty by asserting the hierarchical right to monitor each player closely, forcing them to stick to their job descriptions, to demur to authority, and to carry out bureaucratically prescribed plays and moves. Such a team can never perform with the same grace, the same satisfaction, nor the same productivity as can the one that operates as a clan.

Most organizations, though, need structure to guide them towards cooperation and subtlety, towards the long view when other conditions dictate the opposite. It is no disgrace for a group of twelve managers, each of whom earns more than $70,000 a year, to admit their frailties and to erect formal committees, reporting relationships and divisions of people and tasks that will support their long-run desire to learn how to work together.

Step Five: Develop Interpersonal Skills

Skills that involve dealing with clients, customers, even family, are the kinds of skills that people must learn to adapt to colleagues and co-workers. Interpersonal skills are central to the *Z* way of doing business, because working cooperatively and considerately is not just a means for soothing egos or getting your way. The stakes are much larger. Let me show you what I mean.

In a sense, a Type *Z* organization succeeds through the flexibility to modify its form as its needs change. Like the basketball team that speedily moves from one formation to another, a Type *Z* organization can rapidly meet the changing needs of customers and of technology. Formal reporting relationships are ambiguous in a Type *Z,* making varied responses possible. A job assignment is often unclear, how much authority over people or things is unclear, and the division between one department and another is also unclear. But because of the easily understood management philosophy, *Z* organizations have the capacity for the subtle and the complex. In such a setting, the number of corporate stripes on a manager's sleeve do not necessarily signal who is in charge. When a special committee meets *Z*-style to solve a problem, included will be four persons of equal official rank, three of subordiante rank who know more about the problem, and three of ambiguous rank and authority, who may be superior, equal or subordinate, but no one knows, exactly. In most cases, when rank is clearly specified, then everyone falls into well-understood patterns of interaction. Everyone knows when to defer, when to assert, and how to deal with disagreements. Of course, in that situation, the person who knows most may be ignored because of rank, but conflict is concealed and social intercourse appears to be smooth. In a Z company the complete opposite holds true.

Often, the skillful leader does more listening than talking. What matters most is the skill of observing the pattern of interaction in the group and knowing when to intervene. One case that I recall involved the skillful use of silence by the manager. Allowing a period of quiet every now and then instead of filling up space with talk enabled the real issue, which commonly lies just below the surface, to become apparent. Too often managers will talk around an issue, particularly in fledgling Z companies, just for the sake of filling that uncomfortable silence. "Letting the silence sit there until it's become so compelling it allows the real issue or conflict to surface," is the key, as one manager described it.

Nor does straight probing of co-workers suffice as an interpersonal skill. It does no good to ask employees to learn how to reach decisions and how to handle conflict in unstructured, nonhierarchical groups if the problems that matter most are not solvable. Once those primary steps to solving them have been taken, however, then formal training in participative decision making should begin. There exists a large number of competent consultants, professors, and counselors who are experienced at teaching these skills. The skills may be thought of as being of basically two types.

The first skill to be learned is the skill of *recognizing patterns of interaction* in decision-making and problem-solving groups. Just as one can learn in medical school to interpret an X ray meaningless to the untrained eye, so one can learn to "see" group interaction in quite a different way than that of the layperson. Learning to see when a group moves too quickly to a solution in order to avoid discussing the real problem, learning to observe how some members interfere in subtle ways with an open discussion, learning to note when the group drifts off course — all of these are acquired skills. One way to develop them is to try role playing outside of the context of a formal meeting. All participants need do is to exchange the roles: subordinates "play" supervisor, and vice versa, in order to develop an appreciation for the ways other people feel in different roles. Another possibility is the fish bowl exercise. One group observes behavior, takes notes, and then feeds back to the discussants their observations of who led, in what style, who interrupted, who contributed little, and so on. This gives everyone a clear idea of who needs to contribute more or in some cases less in order to achieve an egalitarian group balance. During a meeting, the same result can be achieved if everyone were asked to stop every forty-five minutes or hour and take five minutes to discuss the *process* taking place at the meeting, rather than its substance.

After learning to recognize patterns of group interaction, the second skill, of course, is learning to provide leadership in such a group, so that the group can quickly identify the important issues, get to the bottom of conflicts, and arrive at high-quality, creative solutions that have everyone's support. With practice, this skill can also be learned.

If the goal of these structural variations is to produce cooperation, then their form must force individuals to work together to share information, resources, and plans. One such typical structure is the committee composed of the seven or eight individuals who represent various departments involved, say, in planning a new product. If each of these individuals is a respected and influential member of his or her own department and can simultaneously continue to work in both the department *and* on the committee, then the committee will possess the information, the influence, and the energy to support a cooperative venture. Of course, the committee could also degenerate into a bickering focus of conflict. Which results occur depends on the general atmosphere of the firm. If these committees are presented as one part of a more general attempt to create cooperation, if changes in incentives, career paths, and evaluations are simultaneously taking place, then these structural crutches will be helpful. When a committee or a quality control circle is an isolated attempt at cooperation, it may become nothing more than the arena for multiple contests fought to no avail.

A second and newer but increasingly common structural crutch is the matrix form of organization. It is commonly used when two equally important but partially conflicting departments must cooperate on some task. Instead of appointing a committee, the manager in charge of the critical task was asked to report simultaneously to the two department heads who are in conflict. One such matrix involved the need to have plant managers and corporate engineers cooperate in allocating the engineers assigned to each plant to other tasks, as needed, in different locations. Both the plant manager and the corporate engineering office wanted exclusive control over the engineers. The matrix solution had the engineers in each plant report simultaneously to both the plant manager and the head of corporate engineering. These two would have to agree on job assignments, on the annual performance appraisal, and on any promotion recommendation for each engineer. Each head was in a matrix of reporting relationships. Of course, a matrix can resemble a jungle just as easily as it can resemble a finely woven cloth. Again, the outcome depends upon the surrounding organizational climate. In the case of the engineers, this structural crutch ultimately developed cooperation as the company moved towards a more complete Type Z form. The matrix as structural crutch has since been copied by a number of firms in the industry.

In addition to the subtle cultural influences, the explicit incentives facing each person must be designed. Incentives are the key for each manager and class of employee in the organization. What, in terms of the current philosophy, do you personally have to do to be a success? What does the manufacturing manager have to do? The sales manager? If short-term incentives spur you and co-workers on, then perhaps the sales manager can succeed only by maximizing sales volume today. This may mean demanding frequent changes in production runs for rush orders to a new customer, and, not incidentally, causing factory costs to rise and productivity to decline. The manufacturing manager, conversely, may be able to succeed only by minimizing per unit cost, causing a fight against all requests for changing the production schedule, even when it would mean winning an important new customer. How about the director of research, the foreman, the secretaries, and the clerks? At each step, the real incentives that currently face employees should be systematically assessed.

However, only the most critical of these faults can be corrected at this early stage. A clear case of inappropriate incentives facing top executives must be resolved before they can cooperate with one another in implementing later stages of this change. At lower levels, however, the changes from short- to long-run incentives and from individual to cooperative incentives cannot occur unless something else has been put in their place. One popular form of incentives is known as the Scanlon plan.

In a Scanlon Plan the company sets in advance of any change

a formula that specifies that if profits rise above a certain, prespecified amount, then a stated fraction of those profits will be paid out to the employees, with the remainder returned to the stockholders. The fraction paid to the employees may be twenty percent, fifty percent, or seventy percent of this additional gain. Of course, the questions of what constitutes a "fair" distribution cannot be settled in any objective manner. Ultimately, the question is how much the company must pay in order to hire and retain the kinds of employees who will actively involve themselves in a high level of effort to secure the success of the enterprise. But the salary paid to the employees should not be so much that the stockholders feel cheated and sell their stock. No one else would want to buy it at its former price, and the company will find itself unable to raise the capital necessary to build new plants. All of these matters must be considered in putting together such incentives to satisfy both employees and employer.

And not all the incentives need be monetary. The nature of the jobs, assignments, and task groups one is assigned to, and the time that senior managers devote to their staff members, can be more valuable than the raise offered elsewhere (which, if *Z* salaries are fair, probably isn't much beyond what people are already making). The *Z* companies are uniquely equipped to offer non-monetary incentives.

Step Six: Test Yourself and the System

I have always found it difficult to convince managers of the utility of the scientific method. When an organizational innovation is implemented, there must be some test to reveal whether it had the expected effect or not. The test need not be elaborate nor terribly expensive but must be capable of helping to convince the skeptic that his or her concerns were unfounded. On the other hand, the test serves to cool the enthusiasm of a true believer who is blind to the weaknesses of personal attempts at change. Before the top level of managers implement Theory *Z* management at lower levels, they must first test themselves to determine how much of the philosophy has taken hold.

The only form of testing inappropriate at the immediate outset is self-testing. A manager who has worked hard at being more cooperative and participative, who has intellectually embraced a new approach, is hardly a reliable first judge of personal progress. Instead, the initial process of testing might involve a brief questionnaire sent by each manager to direct subordinates who are asked to evaluate this person for participativeness, egalitarianism, and other changes that involve either personal managerial skills or changes in policy and structure. Of course, such an evaluation will be useful only if it contains candid reactions. An outside consultant or an obviously secure internal process of questionnaire distribution and collection will protect the anonymity of the respondents and insure honest responses.

Another form of testing invites someone not involved in the attempted change to visit the operation, interview some of the managers and their subordinates, and to write down impressions of the organizations. Preferably this "auditor" should not be informed about the extent or nature of the process until after the report is written. Knowing what has been attempted will necessarily color impressions.

Later, and in addition to these relatively formal tests, each manager can apply a personal test that I have found to be quite reliable. When the change to Type Z organization takes hold, each manager should begin to feel less harried and less pleased. Less harried because there should be fewer occasions where subordinates need help resolving disputes, fewer new projects that get into trouble through lack of information, fewer demands to create a specific policy or rule to decide an issue. In short, the managers end up by having more time to plan, to wander around, to reflect. Their jobs are not being passed down the line to subordinates who are busier and busier; rather, the time formerly consumed by fixing some lack of coordination and in settling disputes is now only partially filled by committees and meetings. The remainder of the time is available for going beyond remedial management to the building of a more effective organization.

The job of the manager does not become easier. With successful growth toward a Type Z organization, the managers will not only feel less harried but also less pleased. They will doubt their personal skill at management, question the coordinative skill of their subordinates, and feel unsure about being a manager. In the short run, a manager in an autocratic company has more pleasures. No one below you questions your word, everyone defers to you, and you feel both powerful and capable. In the long run, of course, each person defers with equal certainty to a boss, feeling powerless, and the capacity for a coordinated company is low. In a Type *Z* organization, however, subordinates regularly challenge and occasionally even ridicule superiors. Anyone who thinks that this is fun has not tried it, at least not from the manager's point of view. If this is happening to you with some regularity, proceed with confidence. Imagine the response of your newly-awakened subordinates when *their* subordinates give them the same treatment. Ultimately, the Type *Z* organization succeeds to the extent that the production workers listen to feedback from their customers and everyone in the organization truly participates in an egalitarian and integrated setting. This environmental setting demands more of managers, and perhaps that's why Japanese managers don't smile a lot.

Step Seven: Involve the Union

At some point, preferably well before any substantive changes in working conditions such as stabilizing employment (Step 8) or introducing slow evaluation and promotion (Step 9) are discussed, the new Type *Z* company will have to involve the union in its plans. Any company that has some or all of its employees represented by a collective bargaining unit, or union, will approach its union with great care. Dealing with the union is among the most emotionally-charged elements in a process of organizational development. "The union" has become among managers a code word representing poor quality, low productivity, worker apathy, absenteeism, work stoppages, and even employee theft. Sometimes, it seems as though unions invented these problems, to hear managers talk about them. Often, managers have fused into a single complaint their frustrations over inadequate employee relations and the existence of the union. Only if the management arrives at a clear understanding of how to distinguish these two realities and formulate a systematic philosophy of employee relations will it safely navigate the issue of working with a union.

Professor Richard Walton of Harvard University has crystallized this important issue: Unions do not necessarily stand for poor employee relations. Many United States unions grew up protecting the interests of employees who were being systematically abused by managements and have thus developed a contentious relationship with management. But Japanese companies are unionized with no apparent ill effect, although those unions constantly battle against attempted infiltration by the Communist party. Recent research by such as Professors James Medoff of Harvard and Kathryn Abraham of M.I.T. have done indicates that, on the whole, unionized companies in the United States have had higher productivity than have non-unionized companies.[1] Everyone is against poor productivity and poor employee relations, but everyone need not be against unions.

Remember that the Type Z organization relies to a great extent upon an egalitarian distribution of power for its success. One way to achieve this is through the creation of workers' councils as is done in West Germany, France, and Sweden. A second method provides systems of employee influence through Scanlon Plans or Type Z organization as outlined in the final stage (Step 13) below. Yet a third method creates distributed centers of power through the formation of unions. If the principles of egalitarianism and of equity are acceptable, then the principle of unionism must also be acceptable.

In many companies, however, the union has been forced into an adversarial position by an unfair and irresponsible management. Having no trust in the company, the union has resorted to extremes of bureaucracy. The union insists on detailed work rules to specify which classes of workers operate the machines, which repair the machines, and so on. This extensive rule-making protects employees from unfair demands by managers. The unintended consequence of this practice is a loss of flexibility. It is as though the players on the basketball team were told that one player may only take set shots, another must always bring the ball down court, and two others may only rebound. Although the actual distribution of tasks roughly does correspond to this kind of specialization on a basketball team, the effect on productivity would be disastrous if the shooter could never rebound, even if the ball fell into his hands. Our form of unionization has brought great costs in productivity. To counteract this, many Japanese companies opening manufacturing plants in the United States always first secure the best labor law firm available. Japanese companies already located here systematically warn others that the one thing in the United States that can ruin a company's productivity is an inflexible union contract. If that is so, then we can readily understand why our businesses, most of which must contend with these restrictive work agreements, have difficulty competing with the Japanese.

When the motives of the management conflict with a hostile union, the company can counteract to weaken the union. An increase in employee fringe benefits may work. Management may even try to decertify unionized plants, thereby throwing the union out. But in the long run, these approaches must fail.

A company that changes from an autocratic to a democratic style of management will and should win the trust of its employees who will have less need for union protection. Instead of sabotaging the union, a patient management will discover that the union eventually recognizes the need for more flexibility in work rules in order to provide higher productivity and job security. Indeed, in a healthy setting, the union provides the company with a ready-made conduit through which to communicate with employees, to organize them and explain benefit plans, and to integrate educational, social, and recreational activities. Winning over the employees *and* the union is necessary because in a Type *A* company where hourly employees mistrust the management, the attempt to push the union out will be perceived as a sign of bad faith. If the company believes in more worker participation, the employees will ask, then why not participate through the union? Or do they want to get rid of the union to take advantage of us in the future? On the other hand, the company, recalling past abuses, remembers local union officers elected in each plant who have specialized in baiting the management, fighting the management, and where possible, humiliating the management. In a sense, these union heads with specialized skills and narrow incentives stand for all that's inimical to a Type *Z* company. Given these veterans of wars past, the company argues, the hope of creating a new tie with employees is slim. Still, any attempt to drive out the union gives employees further proof of the duplicity of management.

For a workable situation with the union or any industrial relations specialists, both management and employees must be convinced of the value of different incentives broader than just protecting and fighting one another — incentives to sustain a productive working relationship. After all, unions and companies who fail to work for these changes lower productivity and otherwise bring about failure. These bureaucratized unions and companies will go out of business.

These provocative issues may prompt dissent. I do not expect all readers, whatever their persuasion, to entirely agree with me. The union-management relationship, complex to the point of confusion, is difficult to sort out since the issue is emotionally laden. Numerous discussions will be necessary within the company, within the union, and between the two.

One device to open lines of communication is the joint seminar between line managers of the company and top officials of the union. An initial meeting of a half-day might be used to set an agenda for future talks. At a three- or four-day meeting at a neutral site, individuals could meet one another in a more wholistic way, thus beginning to replace stereotypes with more accurate images of real people. The company needs to realize that the union members are their employees and that the union structure is potentially a contributor to the success of the company. Viewed in this light, the management may be able to justify to itself making a financial grant to the union, that union members can use in holding their own workshops and seminars. Unless the members of the union can internally engage in a thorough debate on these issues, express their skepticism, and develop some interpersonal skills, no amount of changing by the management will bridge the gap. The discussion process will go on for at least two or three years before the two sides are ready to take the kinds of steps outlined below, in the final stage. The process must begin as early as possible, therefore, but not before the management has fulfilled their responsibility to define and develop the underlying principles and strategies.

Step Eight: Stabilize Employment

Stability of employment comes in part as a direct outcome of policy. A great deal of voluntary termination by employees who have better alternatives can be overcome by providing them with a work environment that offers equity, challenge, and participation in decisions about their work. In Japan, where low unemployment makes finding workers quite difficult, firms have adopted the practice of widespread part-time employment. The Sony plant in Ichinomiya outside Tokyo, for example, operates shifts of four, six and eight hours, with varying starting times to fit schedules of women with young children who want to work while their children are at school. These variable shifts carry some scheduling costs, but such costs may be more than offset by an experienced and dedicated set of employees who stay with the firm for thirty or forty years.

Involuntary termination, or mass layoff and specific firing of employees, is largely a matter of company policy. Some companies will argue that layoffs are forced on them when the economy weakens and sales decline. To a basically noncompetitive company that is going out of business, layoffs become standard procedure when the economy declines. However, a company or economy suffering from short-run decline can avoid layoffs through a sharing of the misfortune. Shareholders can share in the loss by accepting less profits or even moderate losses for one year. In exchange, a highly committed and experienced team of employees will repay them in future years with large profits. Similarly, employees at all levels can share the burden by accepting shortened work weeks and paychecks, foregoing perquisites, and temporarily performing tasks they find distasteful. Twice in recent times, Hewlett-Packard has adopted the nine-day fortnight along with a hiring freeze, a travel freeze, and the elimination of perquisites. Each time, these steps kept employees on while other companies in the industry had layoffs. The result at Hewlett-Packard has been the lowest voluntary turnover rate, the most experienced workforce in the industry, and one of the highest rates of growth and profitability.

In a more basic sense, the fate of most firms ties into employment security. A company that enters frequently into unfamiliar technologies knowingly risks its investment in research, plants, and equipment. However, it also assumes a greater risk of failure almost never recognized. In entering this new business, a company typically moves some old employees into the new effort and hires from the outside as well, in order to bring expertise to this area. If the effort should fail, then the employees associated with the venture, except for a lucky few, are commonly turned out into the street. The cost of this layoff to the firm shows up in greater difficulty in hiring the most talented employees in the future, in the higher cost of voluntary turnover, and in the lower commitment of the employees who stay. If actual costs of these ventures were added up, fewer firms would undertake them. Should such a shift occur, the rate of innovation would not slow down, rather new ventures would be undertaken only by companies who already have some knowledge of the field.[2]

A pivotal factor in stabilizing employment is slow evaluation and promotion.

Step Nine: Decide on a System for Slow Evaluation and Promotion

Motion is relative. Young people are impatient. Despite the constancy of these two facts of life, slowing down the process of evaluation and promotion is vital to underscore to employees the importance of long-run performance. Then they will forget about the short run and instead do what basically makes sense for the short or long run — right?

That approach overlooks that the best people always have the most outside options and that impatient, young people may irrationally leave a more promising career with a Type Z company to join a Type A company. The solution to the problem is simple: promote them rapidly compared to the competition so that they won't leave, but promote them slowly compared to their peers so that they will develop a long-run view. Of course, there is a catch. This solution requires that a whole cohort of new bankers, managers, etc., who entered together (roughly during the same six months, usually in the spring) all be promoted rapidly. The best of them have no incentive to leave, since all are being promoted at the same rate internally. If everyone is going to be promoted, to evaluate any of them is unnecessary, except for your personal amusement. Over the long run, the high performers will emerge and will take the positions of greater responsibility while developing long-term values and cooperative attitudes. That is a considerable gain, perhaps worth the cost of having to relatively overpay the low performers in the group during the early years. A modified and perhaps superior overall method is to promote the entire cohort at a faster rate than the average person in the class merits, but not quite as fast as the most talented person deserves. In this case, fewer people will be overpaid during the early years, but a few will be underpaid and may leave for their better options. The overall result may be preferable.

No doubt someone who performs at a high level without recognition will, justifiably, feel frustrated and leave. But superior performance need not be acknowledged with higher pay during the early years in a career. People aged twenty-one who know they are above average in ability regularly enter a long period of below-average income in order to become physicians. Aha, you say, but they look on those early years as an investment in their future income that will more than offset their current loss. Indeed, that is so as it is among young lawyers, accountants, and managers in Japan. What is critical is that this young person realize that his or her superior performance is recognized and will indeed be well compensated for in the long run. In order to induce young employees to accept a slower process of formal evaluation and promotion, a system of nonmonetary forms of evaluation, such as frequent involvement with superiors on projects, including close instruction and guidance, must be provided. They commmunicate the expectation of greater income in the future without creating short-run incentives. In an extensive and thorough process of performance reviews set up by an organization, employees can receive feedback from more than one superior on their effectiveness during the past six months or year.

The slowing down of promotion will also be aided, at this point, by some of the other Type *Z* innovations that have been put in place. For one thing, as turnover declines and managers young and old move from assignment to assignment, each young person will develop quickly a wide circle of more experienced acquaintances. Some will naturally develop a mentoring relationship with that young person and will provide the kind of specific and believable feedback needed. The cooperative atmosphere provides many opportunities for new employees to participate in challenging and important assignments where senior managers can be observed in action. This kind of challenge comes only with promotion in a Type *A* company. After a few years, the more senior managers will specifically ask for the young person's help in one or another project that cuts across departmental lines, and these requests will serve to further bolster confidence in future rewards. Indeed, in a Type *Z* organization, the employees do not receive less information about performance and prospects; they receive more. At the same time, however, they know that the fundamental granting of hierarchical position and of future large differences in pay are based upon performance over a long run.

Step Ten: Broaden Career Path Development

Recently, as it has become increasingly clear that the United States' economy was entering a sustained period of slow growth, research has increasingly focused on the middle-aged, middle-level professional or manager who has limited prospects for further advancement. The results to date suggest that managers who continue to circulate across jobs within a company, but without hierarchical promotion, retain their enthusiasm, their effectiveness, and their satisfaction at a level almost as high as that of the "stars" who continue to move both around and up. By comparison, those who remain in the same position without vertical or horizontal movement quickly lose their interest, their enthusiasm, and their commitment. A number of large United States firms have, therefore, begun to develop systematic programs of job movement for all managerial, professional, and white-collar employees as a consequence of this research, much of it conducted at the schools of business at Columbia University, M.I.T., and the University of Southern California.

The approach to developing non-specialized career paths will vary widely by industry and to some extent by firm. In the insurance industry or the retail industry, the nature of jobs does not change radically from one year to the next. Such industries can develop a systematic process of advertising new positions widely and encourage employees to transfer to related jobs that permit them to learn something new. In rapidly-growing companies, this process occurs naturally: As new stores, offices, or factories open up, jobs must be filled by people who understand the company, and the best candidate comes from a related but not identical job.

In order to have the process of career circulation succeed, top-level managers need to set an example. If the top managers rotate every three to five years between jobs, so that the vice-president of personnel takes over international sales, and the vice-president of international sales takes over domestic manufacturing, then each of them will, over time, bring along managers at the next level down whose skills they need. Those managers will, in turn, want to bring along some that they know, and the process will naturally trickle down through the organization.

The most difficult move in this direction is the first one, especially in a company with a firm tradition of specialization throughout a career. Typically, the people in the computer department will argue, "You can bring a plant scheduler in here, and inside of one day our whole system will be down. They can barely add, let alone understand our computer system." The marketing people, in turn, will say, "If you let one of those computer jocks get close to any of our customers, we'll be out of business in a year." I can only say that in my experience firms tend to overestimate the value of specialization in many cases and to underestimate the importance of having people in each department who understand the other departments. When such a change is implemented after conditions of cooperation have been established to some extent, they lead to superior performance. New product introductions go off on schedule and without mishap, because design, manufacturing, and marketing are better coordinated. New information systems are introduced more rapidly and effectively when systems understand the plants and vice versa. After all, it's not as though the plant scheduler has never seen a computer print-out. Not only doesn't he need retraining in computers, he's been on the receiving end of the technology for years — and has been complaining about its failings. He will, hopefully, be able to make suggestions about how to improve the print-out for other schedulers — things the computer specialists wouldn't understand. Encouraging a better blend of related expertises benefits everyone.

A successful program of career circulation is based on a cadre of managers widely informed about the skills available in departments other than their own. Working together they can make appointments to benefit not only their department but the departments with whom they must coordinate. With the properties of the Type *Z* organization in place, this information will be widely distributed, and the incentive to cooperate emerges. Each of the elements of the Type *Z* organization relates to the others. In isolation, none will accomplish much. Together, they constitute a cooperative system.

Step Eleven: Preparing for Implementation at the First Level

All the stages of implementation to this point have focused on managerial and professional employees. Many suggestions will prompt managers to deal with first-level supervisors and with hourly or production and clerical employees in new ways, but the target group so far has been the middle and upper employee. Traditionally most United States firms have introduced changes in the lower ranks. But Theory Z advocates the opposite approach that has been taken by Japanese companies as well as some United States firms such as General Motors.

The reasons for starting at the top boil down to one central issue: A lower level employee or manager cannot participate unless those above provide the invitation to do so. If an organization begins by being rigidly hierarchical, evolutionary change must begin at the top of that hierarchy. The only change that can begin at the bottom in such an organization is revolution, and revolution was the solution that brought on the United States labor union movement in its currently antagonistic form.

The steps outlined above will typically take one to two years to achieve, and they will produce notable results of their own. The improved integration of efforts and willingness to cooperate will yield greater efficiency and productivity. Managers will less often be forced to respond to short-run objectives and disrupt the activities of plants and offices. First-level supervisors will less often be caught in contests for power and resources between competing middle managers. All of these improvements will be felt by the sales clerk, the machinist, the stewardess. Only after these results have begun to emerge should implementation at the first level of employees be contemplated.

The hourly employee and the first-line supervisor live a world apart from the professional and the manager in most organizations. The hospital orderly is as distant from the surgeon as the bank teller is from the commercial lending officer. In most American organizations, those employees who determine the basic productivity and quality of the products and services know little about the future plans or current performance of the company. Rarely are they asked for opinions. They receive different benefits packages, are paid hourly rather than monthly and, not surprisingly, don't stay for very long. As a consequence, these employees have little understanding of the company, little trust in the management, and little tolerance for a confused attempt to make a fundamental shift in the management style.

The first-line supervisor has, in many ways, the most difficult task of all. This supervisor must maintain enough goodwill among workers of short experience and low trust and commitment to meet his production quotas while at the same time keep sufficient credibility with superiors to exert influence in favor of the employees when needed. Both workers and managers expect the foreman to represent their interests to the other side, and both suspect the foreman of having sold out to the other side. As long as management and workers take opposing sides, the foreman will be in the middle. Until the management has developed some confidence in its own ability to achieve cooperation and trust, it cannot support the magnitude of change that will take place in the plant and the office.

If employees at the bottom of the corporate pyramid are to be included in a cooperative and trusting relationship that departs sharply from their current state, they will have to overcome the deepest sort of skepticism. This skepticism can be overcome only through great effort and only with the most consistent signals from above. The workers in the plants and in the field do not rub shoulders with the decision makers, do not look them in the eye. They can gauge their true intent only dimly, through the decisions and the policies handed down from afar. Although a more direct approach to communication with employees will help, there are simply never enough top managers to provide first-hand evidence of commitment to change to all of the workers. Instead, the policies and decisions affecting the hourly employee must consistently express openness, trust, and emphasis on the long run. In one company I know of, a group of workers and managers decided, in true participative fashion, that the arrangement of machines should be changed to make the flow of materials more efficient and productive in the long run. When the plan was announced, the workers felt justifiably proud and eager to start the new system. Immediately thereafter, however, an unexpected rush of orders postponed the change. Six months later, the plan was all but forgotten; in fact, the new arrangement never occurred, and the workers tended to disbelieve subsequent efforts to institute Theory *Z* at the first level. Their faith in the whole system, in fact, had been destroyed. Full implementation of Theory *Z* methods from that point on became impossible. Consistency is to be strived for. But only if the middle and upper managers and professionals have thoroughly worked through the preceding steps will such consistency be possible. Only then can the boundary between the two sides begin to blur, releasing the foreman from his precarious perch and permitting a new approach to management.

This step, then, truly involves patience. Rather than rushing to right old wrongs by bringing participative management to the plants and warehouses, the successful Z companies have taken the time first to establish understanding and true commitment at higher levels in the organizations. In this manner, a lasting program of change can begin in the plants and warehouses where quality and productivity are determined. Introduce this change by speaking with your behavior rather than with your voice. Introduce participation, and make sure to recognize results of any effort soon. As one disgruntled worker told his manager, "Your behavior is so loud I can't hear what you're saying."

Step Twelve: Seek Out Areas to Implement Participation

If equitable reward, job stability, and inter-departmental coordination have been achieved, then the commitment and the productivity of hourly employees will already have begun to rise. Although I know of no systematic way to test the proposition, I would guess that most of the poor productivity attributed by managers to workers in fact is the result of inputs not received, machinery not repaired, and designs poorly coordinated by uncooperative managers who are competing against one another. Nonetheless, significant gains in productivity have been achieved by companies such as Proctor & Gamble, Herman Miller, and General Motors, through the application of participative approaches at the office or shop floor level. Solicit suggestions from workers as a group rather than from a few anonymous suggestion boxes. And don't be fearful of implementing them. In one office, orders taken from customers were passed on to the distribution part of the company. These customers, however, consistently called at the busiest part of these office workers' day. Management's attitude had traditionally been grin-and-bear-it. But, under a Type Z approach, the employees decided to contact those customers, explain their problem, and try to understand the customers' needs. A system was arranged whereby the bottleneck of calls was soon avoided — all through employees', not management's, ideas.

These particular innovations are fully consistent with the principles of Theory Z, although each of them began some years ago, well before the ideas in this book had been conceived. Out of these successful experiences, some described in Chapter 7, have come new approaches to the arrangement of workers into semi-autonomous teams and to the design of plants and offices as sociotechnical systems to reflect both human and mechanical considerations.

Step Thirteen: Permit the Development of Wholistic Relationships

Wholistic relationships are a consequence rather than a cause of organizational integration. In part, they help to maintain the egalitarian nature of the organization by bringing superiors and subordinates together as temporary equals and thus demonstrate that the distance between them is neither great nor impassable. However, it would be a mistake for an organization to expect to attain the benefits of productivity and of social integration by dressing employees in uniforms, commissioning the writing of a company song, and sponsoring bowling leagues and picnics. These are the kinds of expressions of solidarity, of cohesiveness, that emerge from a group of employees who enjoy working together and who enjoy sharing their feelings of belonging. Any organization blessed with such an atmosphere will have a difficult time keeping it under wraps.

A wholistic relationship cannot be developed, but once the *Z* changes are underway, it has a chance to grow. Regular question and answer sessions among hourly employees will help. Talk to employees about how the company is working against competitors, about its successes and problems. Be prepared to ask as well as answer some tough questions. These work-related issues hold the key to wholistic relations and keep them free of any company paternalism.

Summary

These steps are intended as an approximate guide and as a focus for discussion, rather than as a cookbook for management development. A sequential logic underlies them despite the overlap found in going from *A* to *Z*. For example, successful changes from bureaucratic to participative organizations have, by and large, begun at the top and worked their way down the organization. But the precise ordering of steps need not be exactly as presented here. The process does take time. As a rough guide, allow approximately two years from the beginning of the process until it has percolated through the ranks of managers. By then, the majority of managers should have achieved some understanding of Type Z organization and have observed some believable signs that the top management is committed. Evidence of smoother coordination, faster reaction, and more effective planning should begin to appear. However, not every manager will understand, perhaps barely half will be committed, and only a start will have been made. Going from A to Z reaches down to touch every worker in every office and plant within perhaps ten to fifteen years. The large-scale successful developments are to date so small in number that it is not possible to gauge these estimates reliably. The process of participative management, once begun, is largely self-sustaining because it appeals to the basic values of all employees. And in fact the process promotes greater productivity and efficiency through better coordination and will flourish unless intentionally stopped by a disenchanted or threatened union or by top management.

6

GOING FROM A TO Z — BLUEPRINTS FOR A PHILOSOPHY

THE BEDROCK of any Z company is its philosophy. The thought of mixing practical business matters with pie-in-the-sky concerns may seem strange, but popular belief aside, philosophy and business are the most compatible of bedfellows. To the extent that practical, no-nonsense business decisions come from a consistent, integrated set of ideals, they are more likely to prove successful in the long run. A philosophy can help an organization to maintain its sense of uniqueness by stating explicitly what is and isn't important. It also offers efficiency in planning and coordination between people who share in this common culture. But more than a vague notion of company right-and-wrong, there needs to be a carefully thought-out philosophy, preferably one available to all employees in booklet form. Such companies as Hewlett-Packard, Dayton-Hudson, Rockwell, Eli Lilly, and Intel, among others, have already done so.

A philosophy is especially important to a Z company. Dependent as these companies are upon long-range thinking, their decisions must be carefully weighed. Because decision making is typically based on cooperation and participation, all employees need to be aware of the acceptable goals. Let me put it another way: A large organization is a bit like each of us. Just as we have beliefs, attitudes, objectives, and habits that make us unique, so an organization over time develops a distinctive personality — the culture of the organization as I have called it. Some individuals have consistent, integrated personalities, and others struggle with internal conflicts. Some individuals exhibit stability while others seem erratic. Most individuals hold in common some broadly accepted beliefs, while others do not. Organizations span a similar range of corporate cultures or personalities.

Even at their most integrated, however, organizations do not achieve the same level of internal consistency possible within a single individual. Organizations, comprised of unique individuals, must allow in their cultures for a considerable range of individual differences. Nonetheless, some organizations do have a self-conscious awareness of the underlying values and beliefs that they represent. With such an explicit awareness, an organization's philosophy can be its most useful tool in uniting the activities of employees through a common understanding of goals and values. A philosophy provides a standard of responses to problems, explains why certain behaviors will be rewarded, and accounts for the company image, which may even affect individual self-image.

So important in terms of building Z companies is applying the principles expressed in the philosophy to everyday working life so the cultural patterns of behavior and of interaction will grow. Moreover, this development of organizational culture can in part replace bureaucratic methods of giving orders and closely supervising workers, thus leading to both increased productivity and supportive relationships at work.

This chapter contains examples of statements of corporate philosophies. Other philosophies can be found in total in the appendix. Of course, a statement of philosophy not faithfully enacted becomes a meaningless statement. Therefore, the development of a consistent organizational philosophy must begin with an underlying set of values and beliefs that are internally consistent with each other as well as being externally consistent with the realities of the economic marketplace and the social environment. The following examples manifest both internal and external consistency but differ in their stage of development. Some mature statements have undergone changes and emendations in the test fire of a company's experiences.

Others represent early attempts that will be refined over time. Each statement describes a unique corporate personality, and all of them will be instructive to any organization, large or small, economic or social, that wants to clarify its underlying values and beliefs.

The Makings of a Philosophy

The process of making a philosophy and culture explicit, where no such statement already exists, may take any of several forms. One popular method uses the survey-feedback approach, in which one or two persons interview key managers one by one, later "feeding back" to the assembled group a summary of these individual views of the philosophy. That starting point should be followed by discussions of basic points of strategy and direction and of style and form. Ordinarily, this discussion will lead to a consensus on the elements of philosophy that must co-exist if the many components of the firm are to cohere in a single, logical structure. Then, if other employees are systematically allowed to debate this preliminary statement, to shape it further into a form most can accept, the resultant philosophy can in reality become the focus of the management system.

Another approach, appropriate when an organization has one or two founders or leaders, encourages key individuals to set down the principles that in their view have led to the organization's success. Again, if such a statement is ever to function effectively as the basis of control and of decision making, it must be widely debated and broadly accepted throughout the organization. Certainly other organizations can develop their own ways to begin the process of defining the organizational culture and philosophy.

A corporate philosophy must include (1) the objectives of the organization, (2) the operating procedures of the organization, and (3) the constraints placed on the organization by its social and economic environment. It thus specifies not only ends, but also means. In most cases these statements will not be complete. In some areas the ends are not fully specified while at other times the means are incomplete. These gaps can result from new developments in tasks that did not exist before, or they may arise from an unusual degree of ambiguity in some area of operations. However, a complete statement of philosophy will be stated in a general manner that provides each employee and manager with guidance, as in this statement of ends:

> *OBJECTIVE: To achieve sufficient profit to finance our company growth and to provide the resources we need to achieve our other corporate objectives.*

In our economic system, the profit we generate from our operations is the ultimate source of the funds we need to prosper and grow. It is the one absolutely essential measure of our corporate performance over the long term. Only if we continue to meet our profit objective can we achieve our other corporate objectives.

Our long-standing policy has been to reinvest most of our profits and to depend on this reinvestment, plus funds from employee stock purchases and other cash flow items, to finance our growth. This can be achieved if our return on net worth is roughly equal to our sales growth rate. We must strive to reach this goal every year without limiting our efforts to attain our other objectives.

—HEWLETT-PACKARD

The statement of objectives should include more than financial objectives such as the rate of growth and of profitability. It should also include less tangible objectives such as the rate of technological advance and the quality of service to customers. Often these areas are left unspecified by companies on the grounds that progress in such areas cannot be reliably measured, and thus setting an objective that managers are committed to reach is unfair. In a Type Z company, however, these apparently ambiguous objectives can be mutually understood in subtle and complex ways, and reliable judgements of progress can be reached among the more experienced managers. To do this the objectives should be further broken down into financial, technical, developmental, and other regions central to the success of the organization, no matter how ambiguous they may seem. If the ambiguous areas do not appear in a statement of objectives, then managers will naturally focus their efforts only on those more explicitly measurable objectives that are officially stated, and the unspoken objectives such as technological advance or customer service will languish and fail to be realized. Typically, these more ambiguous objectives can be reliably measured only after the long run, whereas the financial objectives can be measured monthly or even weekly. Thus, a complete statement of objectives is feasible only in a company that has the ability to realize trust, subtlety, and intimacy.

After pinpointing the ends or operating principles, the second part of the philosophy should set forth the means for the organization. Here the philosophy will prescribe, in a general way, how managers and workers share power, how decisions are made, how local communities should be dealt with, and so forth.

This statement of means guides the decisions and acts of employees and of managers when short-run pressures might lead them in other directions. For example, Dayton-Hudson's philosophy includes a section that spells out the areas for autonomy in operating companies as a protection to them against the natural tendency of top management to give unwanted and perhaps ill-advised direction to these subunits. In addition, complete statement describes the practices to be followed in the development and treatment of employees, particularly those employees at lower levels who are least able to defend themselves against abuses from the top. The following is another excerpt from Hewlett-Packard section "Our People":

OUR PEOPLE

Objective: To help HP people share in the company's success, which they make possible; to provide job security based on their performance; to recognize their individual achievements; and to insure the personal satisfaction that comes from a sense of accomplishment in their work.

We are proud of the people we have in our organization, their performance, and their attitude toward their jobs and toward the company. The company has been built around the individual, the personal dignity of each, and the recognition of personal achievement.

We feel that general policies and the attitude of managers toward their people are more important than specific details of the personnel program. Personnel relations will be good only if people have faith in the motives and integrity of their supervisors and of the company. Personnel relations will be poor if they do not.

The opportunity to share in the success of the company is evidenced by our above-average wage and salary level, our profit-sharing and stock purchase plans, and by other company benefits.

In a growing company there are apt to be more opportunities for advancement than there are qualified people to fill them. This is true at Hewlett-Packard; opportunities are plentiful and it is up to the individual, through personal growth and development, to take advantage of them.

We want people to enjoy their work at HP, and to be proud of their accomplishments. This means we must make sure that each person receives the recognition he or she needs and deserves. In the final analysis, people at all levels determine the character and strength of our company.

— HEWLETT-PACKARD

In developing the means section of a philosophy, identify the situations in which a manager might be inclined to reach an objective of higher sales or faster production by adopting methods such as abusing employees or forgetting technology development. These methods can be concealed in the short run but ultimately do great harm to the well-being of the organization. If objectives are forcefully stated and monitored but operating principles or means are not, then managers may tend to adopt whatever means they can to reach their objectives. It is essential that the philosophy specify not only the desired objectives, but also the means to reach those goals as well. A complete statement of philosophy builds in the subtle and the complex, so that these elements regularly come to the attention of managers and employees.

Finally, the philosophy must relate the organization to its wider environment. In Type Z companies, the philosophy describes the desired relationship of the company to its owners, its employees, its customers, and to the public at large, as the Dayton-Hudson philosophy below makes clear:

CORPORATE PURPOSES

The corporation has specific purposes with regard to serving each of its four constituents. These purposes and key objectives are as follows:

A. To serve as the consumers' purchasing agent in fulfilling their needs and expectations for merchandise and services.

B. To contribute to the personal and professional development of our employees.

C. To provide an attractive financial return to our shareholders.

D. To serve the community in which we operate.

Detailed specifics on how the company can serve each constituency follow, under the topic of communities, running from the decision to "observe the highest legal, ethical and moral standard" to promising to "contribute annually five percent of taxable income" to improve the communities of which the company is a part.

This statement on the company's role in the larger world may appear irrelevant, but it in fact defines the most fundamental principles from which all other parts of the philosophy flow. It is precisely this fundamental sense of what an organization is, what role it must play in a society and in an economy, which does not change. Clearly articulated goals such as these provide top management with the largest yardstick they can use in determining whether future changes in the objectives and means should be adopted. Thus a complete statement offers much more than a guideline on profits and their importance to the company. Beyond that stands the notion of the meaning of those profits to everyone. Hewlett-Packard expresses the idea that profits are the reward paid to the company by the public at large only if the company provides the public with real value. A manager must be able to show that his or her new product proposal offers a real and substantial new benefit to customers — not just that it will sell.

As the Hewlett-Packard philosophy explains, managers can not attempt to provide value to customers and then look at profits as a measure of their success. On the other hand, the statement also emphasizes that the company cannot exist without profits, and thus managers are warned not to undertake new projects that they find interesting or appealing but that will not earn a profit. Thus a manager has been directed by the statement of philosophy to pursue those aims that are of real value to a customer and that the customer values highly enough to provide the company with a profit. Hewlett-Packard's specific objective is "to provide products and services of the greatest possible value to our customers, thereby gaining and holding their respect and loyalty."

The task of developing a statement of philosophy, both internally consistent and complete, can be extremely difficult. To develop such a philosophy from scratch might be intellectually impossible. The task is simplified, however, when the philosophy comes from the experience of people who have consistently applied their sense of right from wrong to a series of business problems and who have worked through the practical implications of their beliefs.

Putting the Philosophy to Work

Such philosophies are still more commonly used in Japan than in the United States. In Japan the chief executive officer will typically write a book describing his own personal interpretation of the company's philosophy. Included will be an explanation of how the company and its employees can best serve the economy and the nation through their productive efforts. In addition, the obligations of managers to help employees become productive and to provide a future for them will be described.

In the United States such statements are comparatively rare. Alfred P. Sloan's *My Years with General Motors* is perhaps the outstanding exception, along with William Rogers' *THINK*, a biography of the Watsons and IBM. Somewhat more common in the United States is the company history. Some of these, such as the seventy-fifth anniversary history of the 3M Company, *Our Story So Far*, present elements of the corporate culture and history. Usually company histories focus instead on major product innovations and financial results, rather than on descriptions of goals and prescriptions for attaining them.

Although most companies in the United States do not have a complete statement of corporate philosophy, many have in mind (but not on paper) major portions of one. Some of the examples mentioned here and reproduced in the appendix began with just such a long gestation period, having been in existence in some form for forty years, while others are newly developed and composed within the past year.

United States firms tend to support the philosophy with a mixture of formal training programs and informal word-of-mouth to transmit their underlying values and practices to new employees. When these methods communicate the elements of the philosophy to new employees in a consistent manner, they permit a more subtle, complex, and long view to develop. However, the chief disadvantage of this system is the greater latitude for inconsistency and lack of attention to ideals that appear not well thought out if they are not presented in black and white. If an internally consistent, broad statement of corporate philosophy has been written down and widely distributed, all employees can refer to it in ambiguous situations. Decision then will reflect not only profitability in the short run but other long-range elements as well. Let me offer one example of such a use.

Recently, in speaking to a marketing manager, I asked whether his company's statement of philosophy actually had an impact on his everyday work or whether it was just a pie-in-the-sky statement. He said he frequently referred to it, as he reached into the top drawer of his desk for his copy. A while ago he had to determine price for a new product the company was about to introduce. Since the product was unlike anything else on the market, he had no point of comparison to know what price should be charged. The company could make only a small number of these new machines at first, so the cost of each one would be quite high. A high price would insure a profit right away. If the product succeeded and the company managed to take over most of the market, then increased production volumes would drive costs down quickly. The prevailing strategic theory in the industry argues that he should initially charge a low price, causing the company to lose money on each machine sold. At that price, however, no competitor could earn a profit either, so as sales rose and costs of production fell, the parent company could earn a large profit as a result of its dominant position in the market. This theory implies that the first company to get large production volumes could develop the lowest production cost and thus permanently retain an advantage over its rivals. Profits foregone in the short run, then, would be more than made up in the long run.

Thus, this manager's first inclination was to price at a loss. However, he felt something was amiss in this logic, and so he consulted his copy of the statement of management philosophy. The statement reminded him of two things: first, that the company's purpose was to produce new technologies, and second, that profitability is a reward customers pay to the company for supplying them with something of real value. That review of the philosophy clarified his decision: He should price at a level providing a profit now. If this new product didn't offer a real value to customers, if it didn't do something of great use to them, then the company shouldn't be making it. If it did provide that much value, then customers would be willing to pay the company a profit for it. More importantly, he concluded that pricing down encourages the development of mass products on the basis of intermediate profitability, rather than development of new technologies that might not become profitable for ten years. Such a strategy would, he felt, lead the company into making "me-too" products and putting efforts into building up production volumes, as the United States automakers had done, rather than anticipating the future and trying to understand what would best serve its customers, employees, and owners in the long run.

The point here is not that the marketing manager made the right or the wrong decision. Intelligent people would disagree on the point. Rather, because the company had an explicit statement of philosophy, that manager went through a subtle and complex analytical process in which he weighed many issues and arguments before coming to his final decision. Furthermore, he knew the manufacturing manager and the general manager of his division also were committed to this philosophy and would ask him these same questions regarding his pricing strategy. All of the managers involved, sharing a common set of values and a common language, could explore issues beyond those of short-run production volumes, costs, and profits.

For the non-managerial employee, a clear, widely-distributed statement of philosophy serves as a protection. Each employee will understand the company philosophy as it relates to employee rights and to employee participation in decision making. A foreman who abuses those rights or who fails to involve employees in decision making cannot claim to be doing what he or she was told or what is normal elsewhere in the company. Employees can evaluate managerial practices according to the common standard and can take their grievances to the personnel department or to another level of management. Because a shared philosophy exists, everyone speaks a common language. The more clearly the corporate culture is understood by all, the better the communication with one another in all matters.

More and more *Z* workers use company philosophies in their daily working lives. These documents do not gather cobwebs in forgotten corners, they are not simply handed out to new employees and then forgotten; they are living documents. In each case, the company emphasizes the meaning of this statement in its orientation programs for new employees — manual, clerical, and professional. Rarely does anyone reach managerial levels until he or she has been in the company for some time. Upper managers, in evaluating candidates for promotion, regularly give explicit consideration to the extent to which each candidate lives according to this statement.

The statements we will be looking at are sufficiently general that they can be applied to each of the activities of the company, from research to manufacturing, selling, and even to the mail clerk. As a consequence, the philosophy must be interpreted by each division and department, sometimes for each case. Commonly, each such unit of the company will produce its own explicit statement of what this more general philosophy means for its specific setting. These statements in turn must be widely discussed with corporate officers and with subordinates so that both consistency and understanding are achieved. I want to emphasize the seriousness with which these statements are taken in these companies. Only within the larger setting of cooperation, trust, and openness will a statement on a piece of paper be brought to life. While these statements are an integral part of a corporate culture and often the first step taken by an organization undergoing change, they ultimately make only part of the difference.

In my experience Type *Z* companies tend to be modest about their successes and down-to-earth in their attitude. Most of them would be embarrassed to be held up as examples for others to follow. Indeed, the statements referred to may not be among the clearest or the most complete that exist. In their corporate settings, however, they play an important role. Although not examples of perfection, these examples may stimulate the initiative and the creativity of other companies to develop their own statements and to devise the accompanying characteristics of the Type Z organization.

Refining the Living Document

Hewlett-Packard's is among the most mature and consistent of corporate philosophy statements. Revisions every few years attempt to ensure a contemporary attitude that addresses new issues and activities of the firm. That statement, well-known to all employees of Hewlett-Packard, while not universally adhered to, directs and influences operating decisions within the firm. The history behind the process provides an understanding of how their guide for operations came about.

In 1957 Hewlett-Packard, a small but flourishing company, had been in business for nearly twenty years, starting with two men making oscilloscopes in their garage. From this base, the company had grown into a small manufacturer of electronic instruments. Over this time, the owner-managers, Bill Hewlett and Dave Packard, had developed a distinctive approach to management where young engineers flourished and employees were productive, turnover was low, and the company prospered. With a continued pattern of rapid growth, many new employees came each year. It seemed to Bill and Dave that their basic principles of management had to be passed on to these new employees in a clear and systematic way. When the company consisted of two hundred employees, they knew each employee by name, often chatted with a worker in the plant, and could provide their own on-the-job guidance that produced a consistent approach to decisions and actions. As the company grew, however, they could no longer rely on this apprenticeship program to completely pass on the culture. So they sat down and put in writing the underlying principles that had guided them and which, they felt, had caused their company to succeed.

This corporate philosophy, therefore, was not created in a vacuum. Rather it reflects a pattern of decisions over a period of nearly twenty years. As Hewlett and Packard set these patterns in those formative years, they were simply responding to immediate problems with their own sense of what was appropriate. Each new problem called for an immediate response.

Remarkably, they acted consistently on one issue after another, so that after a period of years, a clear pattern had evolved. Through this process, their personal values about business were revealed to them and to others. Their behavior rather than their words defined the early pattern.

Perhaps because they were engineers, Hewlett and Packard had a taste for the abstract and the analytical. Thus when they described the pattern of decisions that had emerged, they put down no specific acts or problems but the underlying principles and values that produced a consistent corporate culture. One such underlying value was their determination not to be a "hire and fire" company. They understood the cost of maintaining this principle. To consistently follow this policy, they would have to turn down many lucrative government contracts since these contracts often meant hiring a large number of employees for a year or two and then laying them off when the contract ended. That underlying commitment to employees has guided the firm into its present businesses, which are quite different from those it might have naturally entered without a value of employment stability. They expressed this in a separate section on "Our People" which most recently has said:

> The objective of job security is illustrated by our policy of avoiding large ups and downs in our production schedules, which would require hiring people for short periods of time and laying them off later. We are interested that each employee carry a full load and be eager to remain with and grow with the company. This does not mean we are committed to an absolute tenure status, nor do we recognize seniority except where other factors are reasonably comparable.

The HP philosophy represents a mature corporate culture. In 1977, when HP reached a size of more than 40,000 employees, Bill Hewlett explained the importance of his company's philosophy. That statement recognizes that the company is unique in many ways:

> Any group of people who have worked together for some time, any organization of long standing, indeed, any state or national body over a period of time develops a philosophy, a series of traditions, a set of mores.

These, in total, are unique and they fully define the organization, setting it aside for better or worse from similar organizations.

A philosophy that is both internally consistent and in harmony with the larger values held by our society and our economy need not be either long or complex. The great strength of the HP philosophy lies in a set of principles so simple and clear and so "natural" to most people that they can be readily applied to all manner of issues.

The HP statement has all of the three elements required of a complete philosophy. The basic relationship between the company and its economic and social environment is spelled out in the sections on "Customers" and on "Citizenship." The basic ends or objectives of the firm come under "Profit," "Fields of Interest," and "Growth." The fundamental means or operating processes are covered in the sections on "Our People" and on "Management." However, each of the sections overlaps the others because each aspect integrates closely into one underlying spirit or culture. Thus the statement on profit expresses not only a goal but also an understanding of the firm's relationship to its broader economy and society, while the statement on growth sets not only a goal but an understanding that growth is and should be limited by the company's ability to train skillful managers who can execute the desired means.

These objectives are brought to life primarily through the consistent behavior of managers and of employees. When the company opens a new plant, it transfers to that plant not only experienced managers, but also experienced employees at all levels. This policy provides role models of employees who live the company's philosophy, so that new employees can learn by their example. Anyone who seriously violates the philosophy is likely to be chastised in a serious manner. A manager who takes advantage of a small supplier to the company, for example, will be sternly reprimanded by those at the very top of the company. In addition to this learning by example, the company takes a number of opportunities to have senior managers speak to new employees and at meetings to stimulate discussion and understanding of the philosophy.

No company perfectly executes one single point of view, and Hewlett-Packard provides no exception to this general statement. People interpret the philosophy in their own ways which sometimes lead to opposite conclusions. Some employees disagree with elements of the philosophy, and others do not even understand it very well. All, however, are exposed to the philosophy. The statement of philosophy at Hewlett-Packard is one with which almost no one could quarrel. It presents a set of values central to our society. The entire body of employees would agree on the statement of common values if they held a giant meeting for that purpose. Not restrictive or constraining, the HP philosophy does not require a mystical process of brainwashing neophytes into a strange corporate culture. Instead, it represents underlying principles natural to any stable society of people but which, unless explicitly stated, can be easily lost in the short run and bureaucratic world of business.

Making the Pieces Fit

Unlike Hewlett-Packard, Dayton-Hudson is a retail company consisting of Dayton's, Hudson's, Target, Mervyn's, and B. Dalton Bookseller, along with other divisions. Though its business is quite different from Hewlett-Packard's, its statement of philosophy is no less important and no less complete. Because Dayton-Hudson — one of the most respected and profitable retailers in the United States — has grown in part by acquiring other companies, it has had to work harder at being explicit about the underlying values to which each of the divisions should adhere. A company that grows by acquisition takes on new divisions that have themselves developed unique cultures and philosophies over time. In such a case all divisions must (1) be explicitly aware of the nature of each of the component sub-cultures and (2) agree on a larger statement of corporate philosophy specifying relationships to one another. Without such a philosophy, each division may attempt to pursue objectives incompatible with the others, resulting in lack of coordination.

Remarkable about the Dayton-Hudson statement is the clarity of its merchandising philosophy (see Appendix). Under a section entitled "Dominance," Dayton-Hudson suggests that a store not carry all lines of merchandise but offer more colors, styles, and types than any of its competitors in the lines that it does carry. "Quality" provides that the company will pay for its mistakes, take returns from customers without question, invest in training employees, and compete by providing better service rather than by offering the lowest price, if low price means cutting costs to the point where service suffers. A section on "Fashion" stipulates that the company wants to be known for having the latest merchandise, rather than being thought of as primarily a place to buy standard goods such as undershirts or sweat socks. "Value" means that stores will think of a customer's trip to the store as an investment by the customer of time and money. That customer's investment must be repaid by an efficient layout, sufficient stock, low price, and other conveniences that make that trip a good investment for the customer.

The statements of strategic mission, of corporate purposes, and of corporate objective are all consistent with this underlying merchandising philosophy. Many retail companies take a mystical view of merchandising and feel that great merchants are born rather than trained. To them, building an organization and a management is far less important than selecting those merchants who have the magic "touch" and firing those who don't. At Dayton-Hudson the atmosphere couldn't be more different. Their statement reflects a company that adheres to an explicit, thoughtful approach to management and that values cooperation between managers and employees.

As in the case of Hewlett-Packard, Dayton-Hudson offers a simple yet powerful underlying sense of what the company is about. Its corporate purpose is "To serve as the customer's purchasing agent. . . ." They try to serve society and the economy by providing real value to people. To do this they must understand what shoppers want, how to buy those goods at a low price, and how to make them available in a way that minimizes the time and confusion to the shopper. This may be the same objective held by all retailers, but few others express the objective in as clear a manner. And, in a retail company that does not explicitly recognize these underlying purposes, the heat of business often leads salesclerks astray. Often, no one trains new employees, no one takes accurate count of stock, and no one puts away things that have been tried on. The potential for disorder is greater, and after a while customers stop coming and business declines. A philosophy like D-H's tries to prevent that from happening by going beyond a simple measure of sales, profits, or gross margin. It provides a particular theory of how to run a retail store. If the managers systematically employ this theory of philosophy, they will end up by maximizing profits.

Using Self-criticism

The H-P and D-H philosophies developed slowly, building upon long reflection and review of each company's past experience. Their staffs worked from case after case, time after time, studying what made them successful and filing this information away in the backs of their minds. They met and discussed these features, heatedly sometimes, until their managers all agreed upon those points that would form their philosophies.

At Rockwell International's Automative Operations Group, a philosophy was built very differently. Rockwell is a large, mature company without two people like Hewlett or Packard who have lived with the company all its life. Rockwell had to involve many people to single out the key features for success. To develop their philosophy in this way required a unique tool called the "culture profile." Somewhat like a height, weight, and growth chart, it measures — in almost equally specific terms — a company's set of ideals and, more importantly, how *realistic* those ideals are.

A culture profile, in other words, summarizes the most important features, from information sharing to individual orientation and long-term employment, both as they presently exist and as they *should* exist in the eyes of the top management. Rockwell's profile does not deal with a whole corporation, but with the half of it that includes a set of plants and divisions which, together, would easily be large enough to rank within the "*Fortune* 500" of largest industrial firms in the United States. Rockwell's profile also has a dynamic nature: it shows where the group was five years ago, evaluates the progress made since then, and specifies the future directions of development. As an intermediate step to a complete statement of corporate philosophy, the culture profile provides a "working paper" towards a philosophy.

Putting this profile together was not entirely dispassionate, objective, and calm. Rockwell's top managers had attempted to do just what Hewlett and Packard did, to review their past major decisions and actions and to discover the underlying principles which guided them successfully. They tackled this process determined to be completely candid, to admit their mistakes, and to identify their underlying purposes, no matter how distasteful those might have been. After a small team developed the initial profile, they presented their work to a wider circle of managers.

The profile sparked rejection, denial, and criticism of the team. After considerable discussion, however, all admitted that the description was accurate, and all admired the clarity that the culture profile had provided. Thus while the auditing of a culture profile is almost inevitably painful in some respects, it can also be a major source of encouragement and of inspiration. A group of managers who have decided to trust one another enough to expose their deepest weaknesses is a group that can begin to move forward together.

Rockwell broke their profile down into five elements, one — short- vs. long-term environment — is reproduced here (others are in the Appendix). These elements represent a view of the culture felt, by and large, to be accurate. Not all members of the management accepted the way each element is interpreted, although general agreement was substantial. The very process of reaching a mutually agreed upon description of the managerial culture was itself a central part of the process of building a philosophy. Managers could sit down and discuss at length what they felt was going on, what they felt should be going on, and what they ought to do to change things. To identify one custom that ought to be changed in any company is easy. The difficulty comes in making the desired change, since each practice is linked to others. Only understanding the whole complex of managerial practices uncovers the underlying causes that can begin to bring change about.

"Environment" in the following table is classified under *Culture Category*. In the next column, Rockwell briefly summarizes how this particular value and its practice were typically used five years ago. Then comes *What We've Done* in the past five years to change those old practices in a desired direction. To formulate this, Rockwell managers looked at the past in order to develop a sense of perspective, so that present conditions can be better understood. Seeing how many attempts at change had succeeded proved helpful in realistically appraising just how difficult future change would be.

Culture profile

Culture Category	Where We Were Mid-70's	What We've Done	Where We Are 1 3 5 7 10 X	Future Direction
Short vs. long term Environment	Short term focus—monthly, quarterly and annual pbt—were central issues.	Improved strategic planning process	Organization still perceives many mixed signals	Need better balance between short and long
		Recruited planning talent at A.O.	Futures people eliminated from headcount	Reinforcement from top management that long term focus is key to business and individual growth
		Acquisitions in non-core businesses	College recruiting vastly reduced	A. T. Kearney study is good example. Many thought we would not proceed
		Introduction of quarterly business reviews	Quarterly reviews heavily weighted with a short term operational review	Increase R & D focus
		Promotions of non-manufacturing executives	No discernible movement to creating a real marketing organization	Create a true marketing department and hire the required people
		Commitment to new facilities	Little perceived response to competitive challenges.	Generate management commitment to bring in people needed for future growth
				Get strategic planning to become a daily process. Short term decisions made under umbrella of long term

This perspective also allowed the managers to see where they had inadvertently undertaken two or more separate actions contrary to each other, thus emphasizing to them the need for a coordinated and consistent development in the future. Finally, these steps made explicit the links between the various elements of the culture.

Then follows the "cold eye" glance at *Where We Are*. The X on this scale indicates Rockwell's score. To judge their success in long-term environments, be aware that a score of ten represents a complete achievement of the cultural elements. A score of one represents a complete absence of them. For additional clarity, under the score are listed brief phrases describing the kinds of acts and decisions that are typical of the organization at present. This column tends to be self-critical, perhaps more so than an outsider would consider appropriate. This self-criticism stems from a desire to identify areas for improvement. The willingness to expose weakness and fault signals that the managers willingly trust one another and will cooperate in the future. The final column on the right summarizes the steps that management feels should be taken in the future to realize the desired means and ends. These items are the focus of further discussions at lower levels of the organization, where middle managers suggest concrete steps that can be taken in their departments to bring about these changes.

Through this philosophical audit, Rockwell's top managers have let in a breath of fresh air. They have made it possible for managers and workers at all levels to make suggestions for better coordination never before brought up for fear that their ideas would be seen as unwelcome criticism. The managers have begun systematically to identify the key points, such as information sharing and individual orientation, that the organization must coordinate. They have acknowledged the kinds of performance measures and incentives that currently discourage cooperation. Their success inspired managers at lower levels to undertake similar audits of their own.

An audit like this cannot typically occur in a weak or flagging company. Only a management team sufficiently successful and secure can bear the criticism required and undertake change. A company in severe difficulty may cause more harm than good by undertaking this process. If a culture profile papers over the real problems, the outcome will serve only to demonstrate to all the impossibility of real openness and candor. If it raises conflicts that produce defensiveness and self-protective behavior, it will only exacerbate problems. In a fundamentally secure management team, however, this approach can lead to an open discussion that will foster increased trust and possibly improve the management's capacity to deal with complexity and with subtlety in the future.

Best of all, the culture profile will emphasize the intent of the management to improve cooperation. The profile will create expectations among employees at all levels that such change will be forthcoming. Once those expectations are met, then the organization will move toward its potential as a productive and satisfying entity. If management loses interest in the process, however, then employees at all levels will feel betrayed, and the organization may well be worse off than before. A culture profile is a philosophy with significant risks — and very high rewards.

And what if your company has the fortune to be more extraordinarily innovative, more heavily populated by individualists, and more economically successful than most? Intel is such a company. A manufacturer of semi-conductor devices, the most advanced and exotic of electronic products, Intel has recently grown in sales and profits at more than sixty percent per year. Does Intel therefore need a philosophy at all? The corporate executives indeed wanted to identify those underlying values and practices they felt had contributed to their success. A process of presenting and discussing these objectives and practices with managers throughout the company has begun. Their action makes clear that the development of a uniform corporate culture goes hand in hand with the development of individual autonomy, creativity, and responsibility.

Intel's statement of "Informal Culture" resulted from an audit similar to that undertaken by the Rockwell International group. The audit process involved a survey-feedback process. After finishing the surveys, the management team set up a task force of volunteers to draw up a more comprehensive statement. Their draft, discussed by the top dozen or so corporate executives, brought about a more thorough statement over a period of weeks.

Perhaps that explains why Intel's statement emphasizes a description of its *current* culture than of its future desired state, unlike the other philosophies. Intel, a young company, ranks among the "*Fortune* 500" and stands among the most successful and profitable of United States companies. A desire to maintain those elements that had made the company successful provoked Intel's philosophical statement. With the company doubling its employees every two to three years, the top management urgently needed to be able to pass on their values and objectives and keep them consistent throughout the firm.

But, what is maybe even more unique about Intel's statement is its heavy emphasis on means rather than ends, on the proper forms of action and behavior. Their written philosophy follows:

Work Ethic / Environment

It is a general objective of Intel to line up individual work assignments with career objectives. Further, we seek to create an environment that allows the employee to enjoy his/her work while achieving his/her goals.

We strive to provide an *opportunity for rapid development*. A necessity for this is a strong commitment to training.

o Intel is a *results oriented* company. The focus is on *substance* vs. form, *quality* vs. quantity.

o We believe in the principle that *hard work, high productivity* is something to be proud of. A high degree of discipline is to be expected and admired.

o The concept of assumed responsibility is accepted. (If a task needs to be done, assume you have the responsibility to get it done.)

o *Commitments are long term;* if career problems occur at some point, reassignment is a better alternative than termination.

o We desire to have *all employees involved and participative* in their relationship with Intel. We want the employees to care about their company. To aid in achieving this end, we stress good communications and attempt to organize the company in smallest possible groups to allow a sense of identity and closeness.

o There is an expectation of *ethical behavior* on the part of all employees.

INTEL TEAMS

- Teams are an integral part of the Intel work ethic/environment. Team performance is critical to the accomplishment of Intel objectives.
- Teams at Intel come in a variety of forms. There are (essentially) formally defined teams in many organizations of the Company (e.g., the Field Sales Force, Fab IV, etc.). There are special teams that are formed to solve major problems, many of which are interdivisional in nature. We frequently call this type of team a "task force."

  Although the above teams are important, probably most important to Intel are the "invisible" teams, not formally defined, not special formed, that rise to the occasion to solve team problems that occur on a continuing basis during normal operations. It is only through the efforts of these invisible teams that Intel achieves its aggressive objectives.
- *Team objectives* take *precedence* over *individual objectives*. The principle is applied in day to day operations and is fundamental. If changes in job assignments or organizational structure are necessary, they are made in a manner to optimize team results, rather than to maintain individual career paths.
- There is much emphasis on *"managing interfaces."* We operate in the world of matrix management and "multi bosses." In many situations responsibilities are ill defined and it is critical that the principle of assumed responsibility is applied. The alternative is to build large overhead operations, with much duplication of talents, to cover such situations.

As this material makes clear, Intel's complex business is one in which many different technologies and departments must accomplish an often intricate kind of cooperation. This cooperation comes only with a sense of collective responsibility accompanied by consensual decision making. The entire statement emphasizes the need to hold collective objectives above individual objectives and to avoid narrow competitiveness between individuals. Indeed, the greatest sin would be engaging in "political" behavior to advance one's self-interest at the expense of the whole. In exchange for this kind of dedication, the firm commits itself to stable employment, particularly among professionals and managers who may have worked hard on a project that turned out to be a blind alley. But, as introspective as Intel is on the subject of staff cooperation, it doesn't ignore issues of profitability or management style. Bracketing the above philosophy on work ethic and teams are notes on these more "mundane" matters.

The first section of Intel's philosophy sets out the basic objectives of profitability and of technological superiority (see Appendix). The delicate balance between these must be constantly worked at. Looking only at profits is not enough, because which new projects will ultimately become profitable is unpredictable. Thus the emphasis must be on invention and on technological superiority. On the other hand, scientists must not forget about profits and the need to meet delivery schedules, so these goals must be stressed as well. This statement quite clearly stresses the joint importance of both.

Intel's section on "management style" emerges from a company daily facing problems that no company has ever faced before. In order to cope with each new situation, everyone must be open. Openness means that managers must probe deeply into each other's affairs to identify conditions that need to be remedied. Intel is not a company making standard products with well-known characteristics and commonly understood difficulties. In the process of pushing back the frontiers of technology, Intel is in an industry that many feel will become the largest industry in the United States within a decade or two. No one knows what new dilemma may appear, and no formulism will solve even an identified problem. Therefore, all employees must be open to constant scrutiny that searches far and wide for the unknown problems and opportunities that may appear.

Intel's statement details the specifics of managerial practices, much more than others may need to do. These references form a guide to training and development in a process of maintaining a corporate culture in the face of rapid growth and technological change.

More recently, Intel has begun systematically to move its corporate culture down through the ranks of production employees. Participative decision making and collective responsibility are leading to the development of quality control circles at the plant level. Profit-sharing through employee bonus plans is one of many changes taking place. Guided in a consistent manner throughout the corporation, these changes reflect an understanding of the philosophy that motivates these developments.

Commitment to the organizational philosophy runs high at Intel. The professionals and managers have a sense of mission and of urgency. They believe that they are jointly engaged in developing one of the most important frontiers — electronics. Their efforts may well lead to changes in our society that will rival those brought on by the industrial revolution. A sense of common purpose and a desire for cooperation already exists, so the corporate philosophy aims at reaching an understanding of the means that all will use to reach their goals. Because of the rapid growth and the great disparity of geographical locations and of technical specialties in the company, that communality of understanding cannot be left to chance. Thus Intel explicitly states operating principles. This approach substitutes for controls that might otherwise come from an elaborate, bureaucratic system of production standards, budgets, and objectives. While those bureaucratic mechanisms do exist at Intel, everyone knows that situations change too fast for budgets drawn up ten months previous to have any meaning, or for standard production techniques to be realistic for products that no one has ever made before. In place of those bureaucratic devices, each person refers instead to a description of the underlying purpose and method agreed upon for guidance and for control. Consequently, employees do not feel encumbered by the need to respond to old and senseless rules and standards. Instead, they do what makes sense, guided by a definition of what that common sense is. Working in such a setting, everyone has the great pleasure of making progress, of accomplishing a great deal, and of working together as part of a team. The statement of philosophy contributes a great deal to the maintenance of this positive atmosphere.

Final Comments on Corporate Philosophy

A corporate philosophy states the goals and practices that a community of employees is trying to enact. That philosophy leads, over time, to the development of a host of smaller practices and modes of conduct that become a corporate

culture. In the early years of a young company, the elements of
the philosophy almost certainly exist in the values and predis-
positions of the founder, whether or not he or she acknowledges
them. As problems are encountered and solved, as directions are
taken or not taken, and as crises are overcome these philosophies take form through decisions. In this sense, an organizational philosophy underlies the moral philosophy of one or a
few individuals who have shaped a company through their
actions. Their sense of right from wrong, articulated in a
particular social and economic setting, visibly emerges over the
years as a culture and a philosophy.

Each of the philosophies noted in this chapter (and at greater
length in Appendix One) is unique in some respect. All,
however, share some elements. All reflect an understanding of
the underlying function or purpose of the company, and all
emphasize the necessity of cooperation for the fulfillment of that
purpose. After all, organizations exist only to enable individuals
to cooperate in some integrated activity. Thus, any statement of
organizational culture must emphasize the means through
which that cooperation may be achieved. If corporate philosophy is to provide for a consistent development of policy across
the whole range of corporate activity, its statement must specify
three things: (1) the relationship of the firm to its social and
economic environment, (2) the basic objectives or ends of the
firm, and (3) the essential means used to achieve those ends. Any
group of managers and of workers who commonly understand
these principles will be capable of putting into practice the kind
of common sense so elusive in modern organizational life.

7

WHO SUCCEEDS? SOME Z CASE HISTORIES

BY now we know why Z companies are successful, but still to be understood is why certain companies are successful at being Type Z. How, in other words, have firms put the steps in the previous chapters to use? Instead of one answer, I will present brief descriptions of four companies with whom I have worked in making the transition to Theory Z. All are "*Fortune* 500" companies, but their identities will not be revealed. In each case, particular attention will be given to their reason for wanting to make the change, the unique aspects of their transition, and the results of that attempt, insofar as they are known. Although various approaches to plant-level participation have been tried for some years — at Mead Paper, TRW, and General Foods, for example — these have not been corporate-wide developments. Changing one plant is quite a different proposition from revising the culture of a whole corporation. These broader changes of culture from A to Z have been undertaken only recently, and few examples of mature attempts at change exist. In addition to illustrating aspects of these four broad attempts, I will present the best-documented of the corporate-sponsored approach to change at the plant level, which is underway at General Motors. Of course, these case histories in no way constitute a scientific test of the utility of Theory Z. They are intended to give you a feel for the variety of approaches to change and a sense of the process itself.

Case History One: Change from the Top

This case involved a large division which was itself part of a larger corporation. The division distributed manufactured industrial and consumer goods and had warehouses and field offices across the United States and in many foreign countries. Relatively autonomous from other units of the corporation, this division had traditionally been permitted to operate considerably on its own. I was called in by the division head, a young "star" in the corporation who had been promoted to this job six months before. He had previously held a variety of posts in the company but was new to the division.

THE STIMULUS FOR CHANGE

The new manager had continued a monthly top-management "seminar" begun a year earlier by his predecessor. In this seminar, the top eight managers of the division met once each month to discuss a topic related to improvement of their operations. No short-term operating issues were to be discussed. The group met in a hotel near their headquarters, talked, had dinner together, and talked some more. Slowly, they discovered common themes ran through all of their managerial problems. The new general manager, who read widely, had just finished an article that I had written for a business journal, and felt that the Theory Z approach captured the essence of their discussions. The new manager wanted to improve the coordination in his division and to increase its already good profit margin. There was no specific problem to be solved, no special urgency, but rather a generalized sense that they could do better if they had a systematic approach to organization and management.

THE ACTION

We began with a series of discussions with the top group, during which Theory Z was completely explored. As a consequence of these discussions, the group drafted a statement of their philosophy of management, which hinged on "open communication and participative decision making, based on mutual trust and respect." The general manager, I felt, took pleasure in working out the intellectual and analytical problem of creating a consistent statement of philosophy. The other managers in the group participated cooperatively but without the same enthusiasm, so the effort clearly depended on the support of the new manager.

The next step involved the design of a five-day seminar to present these ideas to all managers in the division. The seminar included a discussion of Theory Z, a study of theories of organization generally, and exposure to both the concept and practice of participative decision-making. The seminar, the first such activity ever undertaken by the division, generated a lot of interest. The division had a long tradition of operating in an extreme Type A style. Warehouse managers expected weekly telephone calls from headquarters asking why index number twenty-three on page four of the weekly operating report had declined. Foremen were accustomed to coping with new computer systems designed and put into place to control their workflow without their involvement. Everyone assumed that their business, both competitive and complex, required a tight, centralized control, as unpleasant as that may be. Everyone, that is, except for the new manager who always asked, "Why do we do it that way?", "Does this make sense?", and "Why shouldn't we change this?" He systematically approached each problem by looking for the most sensible solution and then proceeding to wade through layers of bureaucracy and tradition to allow common sense to flourish.

By the time of the first seminar, a good deal of gossip had circulated among the managers. They expected that during the five-day seminar a new program would be "crammed down our throats." The atmosphere in that first seminar boiled to the point of hostility. One of the middle managers asked point blank why we thought this new program would work and why we had to force it on them. By the end of the seminar, a transformation in attitude had taken place. The top managers of the division had not only attended, but had participated in teaching the seminar. They had treated the field managers with respect and even with deference, for the first time ever. Again, the grapevine worked so fast that field managers throughout the United States had heard the story two or three times each by the following Friday. Repeating this seminar eight times exposed all managers to the same ideas so they could discuss these new ideas with one another. At this point, no field manager was asked for a commitment to change, but was just expected to consider some new ideas.

The seminar ended approximately eighteen months after my

first meeting with the top management group. During this period, the division initiated a process of career circulation, in particular moving computer specialists into field jobs, and field people into central computer operations, because the computer information system in this case was not only massive, but was a critical feature of the success of the division. Much work was put into the development of a two-day seminar that taught managers how to effectively provide performance feedback to their subordinates in a face-to-face situation. After taking this seminar each manager gave performance appraisals to his or her subordinates and then, in an anonymous questionnaire, the subordinates rated the manager on the manager's skill at giving feedback. An outside firm was retained to design and administer a questionnaire on the quality of working life which was systematically administered to all employees. Discussions with union leaders were initiated. Committees, formed to evaluate candidates for promotion, replaced the old process of one boss deciding single-handedly on who got promoted. The old practice of moving young "stars" to a new job every eight to fourteen months was stopped, and instead a wider range of managers was transferred after about three years in one position. Explicit procedures were developed to forecast workload in each plant and to shift work to under-utilized plants in order to avoid layoffs.

Within two years, managers throughout the division carried out their own Theory Z projects, making innovations in their departments and warehouses and trying out new approaches. Not all managers supported the change. Some remained skeptical. A few espoused the new approach but continued to work in the old ways. None were fired or forced out. By and large, however, the change was widespread at the end of the second year. It has continued to develop in the two years after that, when I ended my active involvement.

THE RESULT

Before the change, the division had been turning in operating results on key measures of about eighty-eight to ninety percent on items like quality, reliability, and delivery time. After two years of development work, these same measures ranged ninety-six to ninety-eight percent. Before the change, the division contributed approximately fifteen million dollars of profit each year to the corporation. During the third year after the change, it contributed sixty million dollars on the same sales volume.

Even before the numbers started to come in, however, work at the organizational development level seemed to be paying off. The top group of managers began to work much more cooperatively. Rather than having a guarded approach to one another, they became open and friendly, sharing their disappointments and aspirations. Finally, they surprised even themselves by allocating the scarce and precious time of computer programmers to help one another, rather than hoarding the time as had been the practice in the past. Secretaries, formerly somberly protecting their bosses from intruders and competitors, began to smile. New rules encouraged secretaries to go off and learn something interesting when their bosses were out of town, rather than sitting idly at a desk just to answer the telephones. Turnover dropped sharply, and absenteeism declined. The organization reached a robust, healthier state.

Case History Two: Passing on the Culture

The president of a high-technology company called me in. In fact, when he first called me, he had just been promoted to this position, although the change had not yet been publicly announced. A veteran of the company, one of its first employees, he was a scientist with great energy and confidence in his analytical abilities. The company itself has maintained above-average growth and profitability, and the ability of its top management team is held in high esteem. In many respects, the company is regarded as the unquestioned industry leader.

THE STIMULUS FOR CHANGE

The president had talked with a large number of academics and consultants, had read widely, and had concluded that the company needed to specify its underlying managerial philosophy. The company was indeed a huge success. Such rapid growth, however, had brought about a large body of managers who barely knew one another. Given the rapid growth, there was never time for all of the explicit planning and bargaining necessary. Past company success, the president felt, resulted from a core group of managers who shared a common vision of their business, a long-term commitment to one another, and what he described as a common managerial culture. The company prided itself not only on its technology, but also on its reliability in producing and delivering the goods on time. During the past year, two late deliveries to important customers embarrassed the company. The source of the problem seemed to rest on a misunderstanding of the culture.

THE ACTION

At our first meeting, the president bowled me over with his energy, his aggressiveness, and his quickness of mind. It later developed that everyone else had been similarly bowled over, and some of them had never gotten up again. We agreed on a complete process of interviews, during which I talked at length with all of the top managers of the corporation and with a few engineers. These interviews served as an audit of their current culture.

This was a company quite different from the company in the previous case history. Here the employees tended to be young, had master's or doctoral degrees, and displayed an openness to the point of unnecessarily contending over each and every idea and assertion. The atmosphere was full of excitement, of discovery, of bright people working hard to cross new frontiers and to build a new industry. The president, once in the middle of this mass of energy, had begun to step back, take a longer view, and think about organization rather than about products and technology. He saw a need to preserve the energy and the initiative while finding an unobtrusive way to coordinate the efforts of these people. Otherwise, by running so fast in uncoordinated directions they might run into one another. But the solution had to be one without the constraint that would put them under a bureaucratic yoke. If that were to occur, the spark might go out, and many talented individuals would leave the company.

As usual, the development of the statement of management philosophy was the first step. The group approached this task in a very intellectual and abstract manner, preferring to discuss the basic theories of economics and sociology underlying these ideas. They took great pleasure in working out their own synthesis of the concepts and did indeed develop their own theory of organization. Through this they understood, in the abstract, why the development of a clear and consistent philosophy should work in their situation.

The company grew so rapidly that no one worried about getting the next promotion or raise. Everyone saw the rewards that lay ahead for all if the company continued to prosper. The key concern was to keep efforts sufficiently coordinated to handle the fast growth. The initial meeting of three days, where the ideas of Theory Z were discussed and the interview results presented, was followed by a series of meetings among subgroups including all of the executive group. Within eight months after my first visit, the statement of philosophy had been agreed upon and the executives were busy presenting these ideas to discussion groups of managers, engineers, and production workers throughout the company.

Working quite independently, some of the managers created new plant-wide bonuses to reward groups of production employees for exceptional performance. Others began to develop quality control circles in their plants, where employees on company time discussed production problems and offered advice and recommendations to their supervisors. A major program underway to develop a piece-rate system was reevaluated and abandoned due to its probable effect on cooperative attitudes. Perhaps the single most important step, however, involved the core group of executives, none very experienced at managing a large, complex firm, who used their considerable intellectual and analytical skills to develop an understanding of organization and a theory of management. They became able to discuss problems of organization using a common language within an analytical framework, just as they could discuss problems of technology in their common language of science. The managers discussed organizational issues with the founders, also scientists, who attended the seminars as well. Whereas more intuitive approaches to management appeal to some, an explicitly analytical approach was necessary for this group.

THE RESULT

In financial terms, the result provided no change in the company's growth, profitability, or reputation for technology and reliability. This company continued to lead its industry in all of those categories. It is one of the very few promising new companies that has managed to grow into the "*Fortune* 500" size.

In more personal terms, the changes were vast. The biggest had to do with the openness between members of the executive group. They perhaps would have eventually solved their organizational problems on their own, but they might not have done so as quickly or as effectively had they not developed openness. The process of interviewing and feeding back impressions of the corporate culture brought out into the open a number of embarrassing mistakes, disagreements, and personal quirks. This group of scientists had no systematic way of thinking about human behavior, and thus felt uncomfortable addressing it. Within this framework, however, they understood the importance of trust. Vice-presidents were able to say to the president, "You may not be aware of it, but your aggressive style makes me feel that you don't trust my judgement. I get the feeling that you insist on twice-weekly reports because you think that I'll fall asleep at the switch unless I know that you're checking up on me. I wish you'd cut that out." This kind of sentiment was raised from the category of "politics and mushy feelings" to the category of an organizational phenomenon worthy of discussion and of action.

Case History Three: The Problem of Succession

The transition of Theory Z in this third case history was but a small piece of a larger project. The discussion focuses on the problem faced by the chief executive officer in preparing the company for his retirement. Most every organization faces this problem at some time. The company, a service rather than a manufacturing business, operates across the United States and in some foreign countries. After some setbacks, it has gained the reputation of being a leader in its industry.

THE STIMULUS FOR CHANGE

For five years I had worked with various executives of this company in one capacity or another. The chairman and I had developed both trust and respect for each other. The company, after a long history of leadership in the field, suffered a series of reverses, causing many talented managers to leave and the profitability to sink very low. Frantic for an answer, the company plucked a relatively inexperienced manager out of the ranks, installed him as president, and later made him chairman and chief executive officer. During his tenure as leader, he completely transformed and restored vitality, profitability, and growth. As a result, the chairman possesses a degree of individual and personal power within the firm that is rare. Under his leadership in the past ten years, the average manager has enjoyed triple the income and more exciting and fulfilling work. Few would challenge the judgement or the leadership of the chairman.

The chairman foresaw his retirement coming within several years and began to plan for it. Aware of the firm's success under his guidance, he wanted to prepare another equally strong person to succeed him. In a company headed by an exceptional leader, however, obvious candidates for the job were few. At a general meeting of the managers of the firm, I reflected on the character of the firm as I had seen it develop. I offered a comparison of the company's nature to the Type Z organization, noting differences from the Type Z in some important respects. The next morning, the chairman asked me to join him for lunch on my next visit to delve further into some of my general comments.

THE ACTION

During my meeting with the chairman, I reviewed my extensive notes. My analysis led to one clear conclusion: the firm had apparently been close to a Type Z during its earliest years. After a damaging period of emphasis on short-run goals begun at the top, the company reached its ebb. More recently, this company had been working hard to renew its Type Z properties. The firm lived by an extensive and thoroughly discussed statement of management philosophy. One strategy deemphasized the size of individual bonuses to promote long-run views. Some small operations, fundamentally incompatible with the firm's underlying culture, were sold. Key managers moving across divisions promoted integration and took on many other developmental steps. In short, top managers were

now able to work cooperatively in a collegial manner. I
suggested they did not need a strong leader. Perhaps, I argued, a
leader of modest skill would succeed if supported by a collegium
of top managers who shared collective interests in a consensual
way. Certainly the company could do without a chief executive.
But a Type Z company capable of cooperative management
does not need a great individual leader. Perhaps, I argued, a
leader of modest skill and ability would succeed if supported by
a collegial team of subordinates.

I failed completely to convince him of my argument. At his
suggestion, I dined alone with his president to develop another
view of my ideas. In the end, both men convinced me that even a
thoroughly integrated Type Z company needs a strong leader.
Indeed, a Type Z company can dangerously close itself to
change and to the outside world in a culture of its own. With a
strong leader balanced against an equally strong management
team, new directions can more readily be discussed, argued, and
considered.

These two leaders agreed that their top management group
could cooperate and had the incentives to take the long run,
corporate view. I encouraged the creation of a new executive
council to permit top managers to practice working together on
key policy issues and to develop trust in each other through a
more intimate relationship. The chairman and the president
instituted these changes, creating a unified group of managers
directly below who could plan together, share views and, of
course, collectively challenge the ideas of the chairman and of
the president.

This experience, more than any other, brought home to me
the importance of integrity. The chairman's integrity was never
in doubt. It was my own that I questioned. The academic rarely
has the opportunity to see rather abstract ideas translated into
reality. A request for advice is flattering. There is a great
tendency to challenge whatever exists, to push for change just to
see whether change can be produced and whether the advice will
be taken. This tendency is a fundamentally dishonest one,
pushing for power and influence at the expense of the best
interests of the organization.

Chief executive officers, unlike other managers, rarely are
presented with easy choices. Typically, the issues that come
before them are so vague and so important that reasonable

people after extensive analysis make opposite recommendations, which is why executives are asked to decide. They learn, first of all, to judge the intent and the integrity of the giver of advice. They develop finely-honed skills at discovering the underlying purpose and the honesty of their advisors. I felt clearly that my analysis was unquestioned, but that my intent was being carefully scrutinized. In this "hardball" league, the decisions are weighty and the mistakes costly. It is not a place for the uncertain or the querulous and, above all, not a place for the selfish or the dishonest.

THE RESULT

The new executive structure is now in place and beginning to function. It is too early to tell whether this system will achieve a collegium of management at the top. The early signs indicate that it will. The members of the top management group are noticeably more open with one another, and the chairman and the president like this change. My relationship with the company continues and the date of my next dinner with the chairman appears on my calendar.

Case History Four: Theory Z in the Office and the Plant

One plant of a large, multi-plant company and the office associated with it make up this example. The Theory Z process began many levels above this plant, and the case described here occurred the third year after the change had begun at higher levels.

THE STIMULUS FOR CHANGE

This plant was one of the worst in the company, plagued with a history of labor conflict, chronically high absenteeism and turnover, and poor quality and productivity. A new plant manager had arrived, a person who had been deeply involved in the Theory Z development of the larger corporation. His explicit purpose at the plant was implementing Theory Z in hopes of improving conditions. Before his arrival, the outgoing manager had announced a change from a one-shift to a two-shift operation, so that some of the present employees, along with new hires, would soon have to report for work for a night shift. This announcement produced an outcry among the employees and threats of a strike.

THE ACTION

The new plant manager began by explaining the situation clearly and completely to the first-ever meeting of all employees, held on company time. He brought them to reality, pointing out the likelihood that competitors would erode their business. He reviewed a study showing the demands of customers, and then emphasized the necessity that the plant produce a profit to justify continued jobs and future investments. The employees had been, as usual, held in a state of ignorance, unaware of the competitive realities facing them. They did not understand the corporate hierarchy, the accounting system that measured their performance, or the information system that regulated their stream of work. Evaluating and improving their own efficiency was beyond them, since they were simply carrying out tasks. They had no sense of being an integrated part of a larger system, no sense of the why's of their work lives.

The new manager next retreated with his team of plant managers, conducting training in the elements of the philosophy, explaining the relationship of the plant to the rest of the company, and practicing interpersonal skills. He encouraged skepticism, practiced openness, and trust began to develop. The foremen, confused about the meaning of participation, asked if they could no longer discipline workers who smoked marijuana on the job or who reported for work inebriated. Who would bear the criticism if the plant got out of control, if they failed to meet their quotas and schedules? What would happen if they loaned two workers to another supervisor to complete a critical task, but caused them to fall below their own targets? They told the new plant manager he'd never last.

As the foremen debated each issue, they realized that the new methods did not throw out all of the controls and measurements and leave nothing in their place. Instead, it meant leaving the present systems in place, and building around them a new attitude, a new approach to management. In time, the old ways would become obsolete and could be phased out. Workers needing reprimands could still be confronted. Those who failed to exert effort were to be released. The point of participation is that everyone, each worker and manager, must bear his or her full share of the burden. All share an equal responsibility to satisfy the customer by producing quality items.

As for the production targets assigned daily, all supervisors would from now on meet as a group with their manager to set weekly targets. The managers as a group would meet to review the overall performance of each supervisor, taking into account the assistance that one supervisor gave to another section. Each would circulate among the different supervisory jobs in the plant, getting to learn all of the functions and the people. Some would be asked to take on supervisory jobs in the office, in order to improve coordination between the office and the plant. In addition, they could expect to see some office personnel, whom they distrusted, taking over jobs in the plant.

As for the conversion to shift work, the plant manager assembled another meeting of all employees, taking a precious twenty minutes out of a pressure-filled and tightly-constrained work day, to announce a series of discussions to resolve the issue. Obviously no one wanted to work at night, but the manager, understanding the need to satisfy customers' needs, would jointly seek a solution with workers. At these meetings over the ensuing weeks, the workers came to understand the problem and arrived at a creative solution. Instead of going to two separate shifts of eight hours each, they recommended running one shift from five in the morning until one in the afternoon, with the second shift running from ten in the morning until six in the evening. The two shifts would overlap from ten until one in the afternoon, but the doubling of manpower during the period would work fine. The job schedule would be arranged so that work on both shifts could be accomplished without anyone standing idle. The employees much preferred this plan and implemented it with enthusiasm.

THE RESULT

Within one year after the arrival of the new manager, the plant ran more efficiently than ever. Absenteeism and turnover were down, efficiency and quality were up, and the shift system was in place and running. Not all of the managers, foremen, or workers liked this new style, however, and not all of them supported it. An organization does not have to be perfect to bring about significant improvements in function.

Case History Five: a General Motors Plant

Among all United States companies, none has undertaken a more thorough and serious approach to participation at the plant level than General Motors. The company has had some spectacular success. The Buick Final Assembly plant, once the poorest performer among all of the corporation's assembly plants, introduced a participative approach to management. Two years later, this assembly plant was tops in the corporation in quality and in productivity. Some developments at General Motors, documented in great detail, give a more complete picture of the process of organizational advancement than is available in any other example.

In recent years GM has suffered from Japanese automobile competition, as has the United States automobile industry generally. This decline hit GM despite the fact that it is the lowest-cost producer of automobiles in the United States and the largest producer of automobiles in the world. Although not privy to special information about GM, I can easily surmise how it arrived at its current dilemma. GM practices many of the properties of the Type Z organization. Alfred P. Sloan left behind him a legacy of cooperation, of promotion from within, and of openness among the management. Over the years, however, GM has become increasingly insular, making the company relatively immune to the outside world, as is the case with some Type Z companies. GM hires a large fraction of its professional and engineering employees from a radius of one hundred miles around Detroit. Until recent years, many were graduates of the General Motors Institute. The company has since reduced the size of the Institute and has searched more widely for new employees, but the great body of current managers are from a homogeneous background, and nearly all are lifetime employees of the company.

Another key reason explains the failure of United States automakers to build small cars years ago. Traditionally the automobile industry pays very large bonuses to top executives. Five years ago, when decisions to build small cars should have been made, a typical vice-president at an automobile company earned a base salary of $100,000 with a bonus of up to $300,000, based on the profitability of the corporation and of his division. These large bonuses supposedly protected the shareholders during down-turns in business. If the company failed to earn a profit, then no bonuses were paid, and thus the executives shared in the misery. The toal compensation, although certainly high at $400,000, was needed to keep top managers from transferring to higher paying companies. The problem was not with the total size of the compensation package, but with the incentive effects of the bonus. Whereas base pay does not fluctuate very much from year to year, a bonus is based entirely on the past year's profitability. Although the bonus is actually paid to the executive over a period of years rather than in one lump, the recipient remains acutely aware of how much money goes into the bonus pot each year. As long as the American consumer desired a big, gas-guzzling automobile, the automakers could maximize short-term profits by investing ten million dollars in expanding plant capacity to build more big cars. If instead the company invested that money in developing and testing small cars that people might not buy for three to five years, then this year's profits and bonus would suffer. Consequently, the companies systematically gave their leaders a strong incentive to maximize profits now by building big cars. Of course, that short-run profit maximization has led to long-run losses.

Despite this misadventure, the fact remains that General Motors retains many of the positive features of the Type Z organization. More importantly, the company has provided us, the public, with a key example of a successful and productive approach to the implementation of participative approaches at the plant level. To this final example we now turn.

THE STIMULUS FOR CHANGE

Ann Arbor, Michigan, is the home of the University of Michigan. Like many university centers, it is home not only to students and professors, but also to many corporate executives who prefer life in such a community to the country club settings of the more typical executive enclaves. Academics and executives in such a community will mix together socially and intellectually. One such mixture developed in the form of a dinner group that included social scientists and automobile executives and met monthly during the mid-1960s for food, company, and challenging discussion.

Two group members are of special interest. One was Rensis Likert, a maverick social scientist, founder of the Institute for

Social Research, and a leading proponent of the idea that social science research is useless unless applied to the problems of business and society. Likert had developed the idea that business organizations typically are of four different kinds, varying from "System I" organizations which operate on a top-down approach in which managers distrust workers and vice versa, to the opposite "System IV" organizations, in which managers and workers trust one another and cooperate in a participative mode of running the business. Through many years of dedicated research, Likert and his colleagues had demonstrated that being tough is not good business. His studies showed that the participative "System IV" companies, like Type Z organizations, were more profitable and had emotionally healthier employees than did the autocratic "System I" companies. In addition, he found that very few people preferred "System I," although many businesses were of this type.

A second member of this dinner group was Edward N. Cole, president of General Motors. Cole stood at the top of the largest, richest industrial firm in the world. Rather than commanding those hundreds of thousands of managers and workers under him to work hard and produce, Cole understood that he could only lead these people with their willingness to be led. He doubted the validity of the tradition that the boss should make the decisions and then give commands to workers, suspecting that, because no boss could know all of the details of each job, the workers themselves should have a lot to say about these decisions. The dilemma that faced him must have seemed enormous. The great burst of efficiency that had brought the automobile within the means of every American, which had fueled the American way of living and had made the automobile business the mainstay of the United States economy, had long since faded. Continued advances in engineering, in plant design, in more efficient equipment no longer produced significant drops in the price of an automobile. Instead, each additional improvement in manufacturing methods produced a smaller and smaller improvement in productivity. Cole saw that radical change was necessary, that the revitalization of the American automobile industry depended on a new understanding of people and of management as a process of organizing human beings. The automobile industry had sunk to such a low level of cooperation with its own employees that, in self-defense, the employees had created powerful labor unions which had adopted a hostile, adversarial position toward their own managers. It seemed highly unlikely that these unions would be willing to work at creating a cooperative relationship or that these managers would be ready to trust their workers. Some executives argued that the only long-run solution was to automate the workplace so completely that the number of workers could be greatly decreased.

Alfred P. Sloan, the man most often recognized for setting General Motors on the road to success, left many legacies behind. One of those, accepted by managers at all levels of General Motors even today, is the belief that the company must prepare for and seek change. Perhaps this readiness for change produced the chemistry between Cole and Likert. Cole spent many months talking with Likert, reading his studies, considering the possibility that General Motors might attempt to change from a top-down to a participative form of management. If the company were to attempt such a change, would discipline evaporate? Would coordination disappear? Would profitability be forgotten?

THE ACTION

On August 13, 1980, the members of the Academy of Management, a group of more than two thousand professors in the United States business schools, met at their annual convention in Detroit. Dr. Delmar "Dutch" Landen, director of Organizational Research and Development at General Motors, addressed the group: "Participative management is not a threat to a company, it is simply common sense. When a plant manager tells me that participative management means that he will have to give up his proper managerial prerogatives, I ask him just how the hell much managerial prerogative he has when his employees are marching around his front gate in a picket line."

At this time Dutch Landen managed a corporate staff of nearly thirty and a field staff of nearly four hundred, all of them engaged in the process of converting General Motors in the directions first envisioned by Likert and Cole. None of this would have been possible without the parallel willingness of union leaders to seek a new kind of relationship with management. Even today many union leaders and managers are skeptical of the participative approach, perhaps because it violates their cherished and proven values. Yet, both managers and union leaders acknowledge the need for change as new organizational methods yield more job security, higher produc tivity, and better working conditions

But before he brought Landen onto the scene at General Motors, Cole asked Likert to undertake some studies of a few automobile plants. Cole, interested but skeptical, wanted to test whether or not his more profitable plants in fact had the participative "System IV" characteristics that Likert predicted and whether his less profitable plants had the autocratic "System I" type. These early studies confirmed Likert's predictions and intensified the interest of GM's top managers, although doubt and even hostility toward these new ideas abounded.

At a meeting in 1970 with Landen and Steve Fuller, a former Harvard Business School professor who had joined GM as director of personnel, a decision was made to enlarge the small corporate staff of organizational specialists to further investigate the possibilities. Landen, who directed this fledgling group, went out of his way to hire bright Ph.D.s who understood the theory and the method of organizational change and development, and then went equally out of his way to persuade his young staff that they had to discard the trappings of their profession in order to be accepted as members of the GM culture. Until accepted, Landen told them they could not influence anyone. In short, they represented a foreign and potentially disruptive point of view. Because the "iron pushers" were antagonistic toward their body of theory, they had to demonstrate trustworthiness, which meant showing that their motives were to be helpful.

This staff continued research within the corporation to determine, as fully as possible, whether the early results of the Likert studies would hold up in the other plants. In the process, many managers came into contact with the new ideas, had the opportunity to express their enthusiasm or skepticism and saw these methods put to a test. No one was asked to make a change in his plant on the blind faith that good things would come of the effort. Instead, the principles of participative management went through the most thorough kind of scrutiny.

Meanwhile, high level company officials developed a new set

of ties with leaders of the UAW. Union leaders, expressing doubts about participative management, feared that if the company won back the employee loyalty, the weakened union would be helpless to defend its members against future abuses. Others simply felt management was obligated to make the decisions and take the ulcers, while union members did only the work. Ultimately, the union leaders, sensing that the old tradition of hostility was not going to be appropriate for the decades ahead, willingly considered new possibilities while reserving judgement. From these discussions came the GM-UAW National Committee to Improve the Quality of Work Life, in 1973. This committee concentrated first on developing union-management trust by helping numbers learn to understand some of the subtleties of the other side's position by developing some social intimacy. This committee clearly never attempted to circumvent the collective bargaining process; all of the paraphernalia of the old adversarial system was still in place and working. Meanwhile, however, this new form was beginning to create a new working relationship between management and labor.

Interestingly what was largely perceived by GM as a productivity issue was expressed in the title of the committee as having the goal not of increased productivity, but of better "Quality of Working Life." As one union leader observed, reminding the audience that the UAW leaders are elected by the membership, "higher productivity is a lousy platform to run on." If in fact higher productivity, sought by GM, was fundamentally at odds with higher quality of working life, sought by the UAW, then the attempt would have failed. Its success gives evidence that the two objectives are not at odds. The public-at-large may still suspect the motives of GM to be fundamentally selfish; and they may suspect the UAW to be basically self-serving. They are right, of course, since the only interest is self-interest. To describe each side as selfish, however, is not to say that they must be short-sighted or incapable of subtlety. In this case, while the outside world may remain cynical, the world within GM and UAW is discovering once again that the long-run interests of both sides depend on learning to trust one another.

On April 12, 1978, GM held a remarkable conference: The Executive Conference on Quality of Work Life.[1] Although the study of participative management and how to produce change had been going on for ten years, this was the first large-scale attempt to convey the new direction to a body of managers. In opening the conference, the GM vice-president and general manager of the Pontiac Motor Division described a seminar where he and fifteen other executives along with sixteen UAW leaders had each presented personal views on the characteristics of the best and worst organizations they had ever known. The descriptions by union and management often converged, as the vice-president summed up:

> The characteristics of the best organizations tend to bring out the best in people. Note that all of the characteristics deal with human relationships. No mention is made of technology, economic considerations, or the product. The entire focus is on human qualities — how and why people work well together. . . . In conclusion, all people are at their best when they are an essential member of an organization that challenges the human spirit, that inspires personal growth and development, that gets things done and that symbolizes and stands for only the highest standards of ethical and moral conduct. That is what quality of work life is all about. That is why we are here today.

Sounds suspicious? It shouldn't. This commitment, not a selfless devotion to social welfare, is based on a firm and tested understanding that the goals of workers and managers converge so that both can support the other without fear of being cheated. In fact, when General Motors studied the working conditions not of union members but of production supervisors in twenty-three assembly plants, they found that the plants scoring highest in "quality of working life" were also highest in the company's monitored quality index, in customer satisfaction with body workmanship, and lowest in grievances (supervisors who are allowed participation apparently turn around and include their workers as well), lowest in absenteeism, and rated in the top half with respect to efficiency.[2]

Thus had the change at GM begun at the top. Over a period of twelve years, a process of testing, of proving, and of gaining the understanding of a broad group of top and then of middle managers ensued. This understanding had now extended down to the level of supervisors in plants.

UNLEARNING OLD WAYS

Throughout, the one theme arising repeatedly at all levels at GM and at all Type Z companies is the opposition between profits for the company and consideration for the workers. Every manager who has successfully brought about a change has developed a personal philosophy on this point. Perhaps the key element of this philosophy is a coming to grips with the apparent conflict between humanitarian and commercial goals. Whatever it is, managers in United States companies, so universally accustomed to a short-run view of performance, have been forced to look at people and profits as opposites. In the short run, an investment in employee training will reduce output; in the short run, an unrealistic level of pressure on employees will increase output; and in a short-run oriented firm, of course, a manager who fails in the short run will not be around to see the long run.

When these same managers begin to look carefully at their own organizations and at their approaches to managing people, however, they begin to see just what is called for: investment in training employees, long-run development of working relationships, consideration for the social and emotional needs and the dignity of employees, and participation of employees in decision making. Yet what that same manager had been taught about maximizing the short run is exactly the opposite. Thus the other dilemma: the apparent opposition between making a profit (defined as short-run performance) versus encouraging employees to become more productive (in the long run). Every company and every manager who undertakes such a change appears to go through these same agonies. Those who succeed at the change have likely succeeded also at developing a philosophical position to justify caring for the welfare of employees in a profit-making firm. To a Japanese manager, who does not carry the burden of this short-run orientation, the dilemma of the American manager is a puzzle. The Japanese see a natural and symbiotic relationship between employee welfare and corporate earnings, since both are viewed from a long-run perspective.

The long run was slowly taking hold at GM. In 1978 GM executives had more to report: the spectacular level of participation of the shop workers continues to draw widespread attention from industry, unions, academics, and the press.

Basically, the principles they adopted all hinged on a long-range view of GM's new Packard Division plant in Brookhaven, Mississippi:

o *Trust in Relationships.* Without trust, any human relationship will inevitably degenerate into conflict. With trust, anything is possible.
o *Involvement.* Decision making at the lowest level, where the facts are. What people help create, they support.
o *Communication.* People want to know as much as possible about their work environment, and not knowing hurts. It hurts their pride, insults their intelligence, arouses their fears, and results in counterproductivity.
o *Higher Expectations.* A wise man once said, "Set high goals, for they have the magic to stir men's blood." Pride is the product of accomplishing challenging objectives.

These could just be words and nothing more. These four basic principles seem at once so desirable and so at odds with our public perception of steel-pushing, people-crushing automakers that we cannot help but feel cynicism over their sincerity and wonderment that they could have been uttered at all. But another interpretation emerges when we put aside old, stereotypic assumptions about the way corporations run. These statements are the enthusiastic, zealous announcements of managers liberated from managerial duplicity and made into whole, integrated people. Managers, after all, come from the same broad society and culture as do workers, sociologists, and ministers. They harbor the same underlying values for equality, humanity, and the good of all. It can be a tortuous experience for an idealistic young person to discover, after fifteen years working up the managerial ranks, that Calvinist beliefs provide no solace. Too often managers see bad decisions knowingly made in favor of some short-run goal. Too often managers see another manager under pressure take unfair advantage of his employees. What a moral relief it must be to join, after this, a group of managers who believe that doing good and earning a profit are, after all, compatible goals. It is hardly surprising that a person who has had such an experience will proclaim this new truth with the enthusiasm and the simplicity of a child.

RETOOLING THE NUTS AND BOLTS

The reality that followed from the philosophy at Brookhaven's Packard Division was anything but child's play. It is a fine example of the systematic application of these principles in a nearly unrestricted way. In August 1975 a task force — with no restrictions — met to design a socio-technical system for the Brookhaven plant. The following is an excerpt from the task force report:

> The task force studied various management styles, visited other plants, and analyzed human behavior in a variety of work situations. From this background, it developed a basic philosophy about people and the principles on which a management style could be designed. It centered on improving quality of working life and effectiveness through involvement. The task force spent hundreds of hours detailing the steps involved in making a harness. Our analysis enabled us to group the tasks required to build a harness into whole jobs. Jobs a team of people could do. Jobs with meaning. Jobs with responsibility. Jobs that required involvement of team members. The combination of philosophy and team structure allowed us to develop a socio-technical model that included:
>
> o Overall philosophy
> o Team design
> o Team responsibility
> o Selection procedures
> o Compensation programs
> o Plant layout and facility design
> o Start up planning data

The task force completed its job. The decision to use all, part or none of the results would be up to the Brookhaven management group. At Packard, a task force only recommends, the plant management team decides and implements.

In January of 1977, the new plant's management team was in place, had decided to accept the recommended socio-technical design, and the first hourly employees were hired. These new employees, all referred by the Mississippi State Employment Service, were screened not only for technical skills but for interpersonal skills as well. All were required to complete a 30-hour junior college training program in technical, economic, and interpersonal subjects. The plant had a complement of 474 people, of whom forty-two were salaried: forty-one percent were minority, forty-five percent female, over fifty were United States military veterans, and seven were significantly handicapped. Their ages ranged from eighteen to fifty-five, with a mean of thirty.

The plant manager described the organization as follows:

The team is the fundamental plant group. It is the basis of our quality of working life and employee involvement. The teams include from eight to twenty people. Each team is responsible for all activities related to its function, including quality control, die setting and maintenance. Initially, teams had little involvement outside of learning the task required. As each team developed, more responsibility was added. The following are some of the current activities which represent employee involvement beyond more traditional systems:

- o Selection of their team leader
- o Job assignment within teams
- o Performance evaluation and control
- o Absenteeism control
- o Time and attendance records
- o Calculations of internal efficiencies
- o Scheduling part number changeovers
- o Budget forecast and control of plant related accounts
- o Scrap control
- o Job knowledge evaluation for pay raises

We see this list on involvement significantly expanding as individuals and teams improve their competence and confidence.

In addition to these groups, each team elected a representative to plant-wide committees that dealt with issues of broader concern. One of these issues concerned the development of standards for evaluating individual work skills with higher levels of skill carrying wage increases. A plant-wide worker committee prepared recommendations favorably received by the management. Other issues concerned changes in day-to-day work arrangements:

- No time clocks
- No shop rules
- Ample meeting rooms
- One parking lot, entrance, and dining room
- The minimization of status symbols
- Plant-wide quarterly meetings
- Regular communications programs at work and to the homes
- Direct employees in "production meetings"
- Freedom to have meetings when the need is there
- Expectations to be the best plant in General Motors

"This atmosphere is different from GM plants," the plant manager reported. "Yet the majority of our top management group was raised in the traditional atmosphere. What is their quality of working life? Last year's formal QWL Survey indicated it was pretty good, ninety-plus percent."

Veterans of movements in job design, work humanization, and other developmental attempts of earlier decades will recognize many of the items in the list above. In the past decades many companies have used employee newsletters, communication meetings, suggestion boxes, and all manner of trappings intended to give employees a feeling of value. In reality, however, the programs often only created that impression. Out of the appropriate organizational context, these embellishments are no more than a sham soon abandoned as a "giveaway program" that failed to produce a rise in productivity. What happened at Brookhaven, however, was quite different.

THE RESULT

"With all this talk about involvement, we must also mention the plant's commitment to meet the demands of the business," the manager pointed out. "In the first half of the 1978 model year, some quantitative results for our eighth through thirteenth months of operation are:

o Excellent quality with the lowest cost of quality per budget labor dollar in the division
o Delivery reliability of ninety-nine percent with no chargeable premium transportation
o A safety record that is the best in the Corporation for our first reporting period
o Overtime controlled to less than two percent for both hourly and salaried
o Casual absenteeism of 2.8 percent
o Significant operating savings vs. budget
o Routed labor improvements vs. budget of nineteen percent
o $1,800,000 in completed cost improvement projects
o Ninety-six percent and higher labor efficiency since January"

At the end of 1980, GM had underway approximately 160 organizational change projects similar to Brookhaven's. Virtually all of these included union-represented employees and were taking place with the joint support and involvement of the UAW. The current openness of the United Auto Workers to the prospect of change is a critical feature of these successful changes.

Some Final Comments

In a real sense, a participative approach to management asks all workers to give more. They are not being asked to carry heavier loads nor to exert themselves more physically. The productivity gains come from improved coordination rather than from increased physical effort. However, these improvements in coordination come only if all employees willingly engage in analysis, planning, and decision making. Although these responsibilities displace other tasks, since the employees take time away from production to attend meetings, in another sense these new roles represent a net increase of employee contribution — more commitment and more emotional and mental energy. Without question employees leave work relatively more exhausted at the end of a day but more fulfilled and excited about work. Having asked for more of the whole person's involvement in the success of the enterprise, the firm must be willing to give back more, to maintain an equitable balance. In a Scanlon Plan company, the payment comes in the direct form of additional cash payments.[3] At Hewlett-Packard a Type Z company, the payment, also direct, is in the form of a bonus paid to all employees. At GM, the UAW prefers that no direct bonus payments be made, taking the position instead that, "Let's work together to make our company more competitive. Don't you worry about paying us enough. We'll get ours at the bargaining table."

Considering all of these examples together, one is struck by their diversity of approach but also by a few underlying similarities. First, an individual who enjoys freedom of operation typically initiates the changes. This person may be a new manager with an unspoken grace period from superiors and subordinates for a wide latitude of behavior, or a secure manager who has earned the right to introduce variant ideas into the organization. Second, the organization itself is typically in a healthy state when it begins the change. The process of going from A to Z constitutes an investment that will pay future returns. Companies in serious financial trouble do not typically have access to resources that can be devoted to such long-run investments. Thus most companies making the transition are profitable. Such companies also tend to have managers who, as a consequence of the corporate success, feel more secure as individuals. Such individuals will tend toward introspectiveness and will more willingly share power. Third, the leader who initiates the changes often sees some distant warning that signals the need to take action now to forestall future trouble. A major electronics firm has recently embarked on a major organizational change. Currently it has large order backlogs and high profits, but two recent market surveys indicate that newly introduced Japanese products have superior characteristics and quality at a lower price. Also the technology developed by this Japanese company is one that the United States firms have not yet mastered. Although those Japanese firms today hold less than one percent of the United States market, the market studies sparked a thoroughgoing corporate effort into improving productivity and quality.

Finally, I have been personally struck with what can only be described as the strong moral character of these leaders of change. Each of them has had a deep and complex understanding of obligations to family, to stockholders, to employees, and to customers. Each has a clear sense of right and wrong. Other leaders may see with equal clarity the need for change but be unable to gain support. The process of going from A to Z is one that presents employees with a heightened sense of uncertainty and of personal risk. There is the chance that one will be inadequate to the demands of participation, that the new openness will lead to painful criticism, that others will take advantage of egalitarian relationships. Given these pitfalls, perhaps the average employee will follow only when led by a person who has sufficient personal integrity to be counted on as honest and reliable. Without an idea of what lies ahead, employees look to a person who acts with confidence.

And what of the other companies that don't succeed at implementing Theory Z? When the long process of conversion fails, it disrupts morale to the point of lower productivity. Of all the Z companies I know, only one aborted its attempt to put Theory Z to work. I suspect that all of the Z approaches offered in this case were presented to management and to workers as an "experiment" only. No one believed in its longevity with the company. Everyone gave it a try, as they had tried other changes, waiting for it to be proven a mistake and then forgotten.

I say "everybody," but the other problem in this situation arose because the change did not begin at the top. The company leaders adopted a wait-and-see attitude, and then in what seemed a self-fulfilling prophecy, scrapped the incipient changes. No matter who initiates Theory Z changes, there must be support at the top. Otherwise, failure is inevitable.

The price of failure is immense, but the profits of success in adopting Theory Z are far greater. These successful Z companies and others like them have forged a response to the Japanese challenge. They have understood that the real challenge from Japan is not to undercut their prices, not to re-automate our plants, nor to erect trade barriers. Neither is it to see whether we can mimic the art of Japanese management. The challenge is to understand and to acknowledge a distinctively American approach to management, to realize that it has stayed the same for two hundred years, and to apply our ingenuity to the development of new organizational and managerial solutions.

8

A Z CULTURE

TRADITION and climate make up a company's culture. More than that, culture implies a company's values, such as aggressiveness, defensiveness, or nimbleness — values that set a pattern for activities, opinions, and actions. Managers instill that pattern in employees by their example and pass it down to succeeding generations of workers. A Theory Z culture has a distinct set of such values, among them long-term employment, trust, and close personal relationships. No area or facet of a Z company is untouched by that culture, from its strategies to its personnel; even its products are shaped by those values. Of all its values, commitment of a Z culture to its people — its workers — is the most important. In fact, the humanizing elements of a Type Z culture extend beyond the walls of the corporation. This chapter reports on one Z company which I studied in detail over a period of three years, and on a company of Type A which I studied in an identical manner.

A Theory Z culture assumes that any worker's life is a whole, not a Jekyll-Hyde personality, half machine from nine to five and half human in the hours preceding and following. Theory Z suggests that humanized working conditions not only increase productivity and profits to the company but also the self-esteem for employees. An increased sense of ease makes everyone function better as people. Up to now American managers have assumed that technology makes for increased productivity. What Theory Z calls for instead is a redirection of attention to *human* relations in the corporate world.

Consider the old adage that a job is more than just a job. For many citizens of industrial nations, our occupation defines the major part of our lives. It determines how we spend our waking hours, where in the world we live, as well as in what kind of neighborhood. Our occupation influences our interests and pastimes and the kinds of illnesses we develop. Certainly, it determines how we will spend retirement years, in what financial comfort and with what constraints.

The sociologist Emile Durkheim pointed out that, in a mobile society, it is one's occupation alone which can remain constant throughout life — even *as all else changes*. If this occupation takes place entirely within one organization (as in Type Z companies), then the hope of moral integration with the larger social order and of solidarity with one's community can be more fully realized. Paradoxically, however, most bureaucracies respond to increasing mobility not with Theory Z, but in just the opposite fashion. As mobility increases, individuals tend to regard their current employer in a very short-run fashion, and such a person will be distant, uncommitted, often hostile, and even litigious. How is a firm to respond to such employees? Often companies create specialized and formalized jobs and working conditions, becoming more inflexible, more contractual, and more distant from their employees. In this manner the bureaucratic organization adapts to protect itself from an anomic society. Such is the miracle of bureaucracy: It can take thousands of people, each a complete stranger with no intention of staying very long, and out of that collection coordinate efforts and actually produce a product! Now, however, the employee is not only fully justified in distrusting the firm, he or she is also left in a state of high anomie, totally without moral support, alone in society and in life.

In precisely this setting, the Type Z organization succeeds largely because its culture offers employees a stable social setting in which to get their bearings and draw support to cope with and to build the other parts of their lives. And even while some Type Z firms may develop in a paternalistic manner and become smothering and all-encompassing, they will not necessarily do so. In fact, traditional social institutions may have become so under-developed that they cannot satisfy our personal needs. Expecting primary bonds of family and/or friends to fulfill us personally may be unrealistic.

Consider one current explanation for the currently high rates of divorce in the United States. Throughout the history of the monogamous, one-spouse relationship, every male or female enjoyed, in addition to a marital relationship, friendship with people of the same sex from whom they could draw support and complain to during the ups and downs of life. Only within the past few decades, and principally in the West, isolated living situations make it necessary for young couples to completely meet one another's needs, a very unrealistic situation. With one partner from Chicago, the other from Atlanta, they live now in a north Dallas apartment complex with a monthly turnover of twenty percent. They have few true neighbors, no club or church affiliations, and no kin nor childhood friends nearby. At the end of each day he vents his tensions and frustrations on her, because he has no one else to share them with. She, after a day of work, likewise puts all of her burdens on him. As a social mechanism, marriage was never intended to carry that heavy a load unaided—and it cannot. The only resolution for the abuse of their one primary bond is to sever it, to divorce. That, of course, leaves each of them entirely alone. Our astonishing high rates of alcohol abuse, drug abuse, child abuse, and suicide reflect this alienation.

Individuals almost invariably attribute the failure of a marriage to a weakness in one of the partners or to a misfit between them. Yet in how many instances can two individuals be perfectly fitted to one another? Is not a stable marriage one capable of providing that which is asked of the relationship? Partners with other sources of nurturing can bring more warmth, more support to the marital relationship rather than having only to take from it. The answer lies in the social structure in which that relationship develops.

Far from being a usurper of social relations, the Type Z corporation, based on the industrial clan, can be a positive force for the strengthening and developing of other societal bonds. As studies of Type Z culture have demonstrated, those people with an integrated and supportive working environment tend also to be more successful in maintaining outside social relationships.

One might imagine that in Japan, people would suffer from a sort of "primary overload," with primary bonds both at work and in the community. Sociologists who specialize in the study of family structures have noted, however, that the Japanese nuclear family is unique among industrial nations.[1] As soon as the male enters seriously into a career, he drops most of his communal ties and participates almost exclusively in his work-related groups. Meanwhile, the women and children, who have typically known one another for many years, develop their own society quite independent of the men. Not uncommonly, a group of women and their children will go on a holiday together without their husbands. This bifurcation of the nuclear family avoids the very real possibility of primary overload. This social device may have little appeal to some Westerners, but we do not want to be too quick to condemn it. Some sociologists point out that marriage as partnership is a relatively recent invention. In the history of civilized society, Americans rather than the Japanese deviate in their interpretation of marriage.

A Z company, by contrast, can balance social relationships with productivity, because the two relate closely anyway: a society and an economy represent two facets of one nation. If the social corpus fails to operate smoothly, then the economic body is affected. An economic organization is not a purely economic creation; it is simultaneously a social creation. Like any social system, a work organization involves a subtle form of coordination between individuals. Each person and each group within an organization is indeed like an organ in the body. If the coordinating mechanisms between the eyes and the hands are disrupted, then harder work by either the eyes or the hands will fail to improve their joint productivity. Industry does not need managers or workers to toil more assiduously. Instead the mechanisms of coordination between them must be more attuned to subtlety of relations that are essential to their joint productivity.

A Place for Criticism and Honesty

At company Z each division and department meets at least quarterly, with a major meeting held annually. At many of these annual meetings, a short play follows business. The actors in these plays are the top managers of the corporation and of the division. Over the years, some norms have developed to guide these skits. Each skit is written by one or two individuals, typically not the top managers, who serve as volunteers on their own time. The story revolves around some aspect of the division's business, usually a successful event of major importance. No one who has a role can see the script beforehand. The point of all this, I had been told, was to deflate the egos of the most important, the most powerful, and the most successful.

The theme may cause some mild embarrassment but with a real sting, enough to demonstrate that no one is too high to be brought back to earth, that, in the end, all are equals. These company skits are very private affairs, and though I had held candid talks with most of the managers, they still hesitated to let me see any of these skits.

My moment finally came after dinner on the second day of a four-day meeting in the woods. The sixty managers involved were engaged in relaxed conversation when Robert Levinson, a veteran manager, took the small stage. He announced the evening's entertainment and asked each player to step forward as he called their names. Each of perhaps fifteen managers received a script with parts clearly marked. My name was one of those called. Nothing, I thought, like participant-observer to push science forward!

The plot involved the introduction of a new product, some difficulties that had developed, and the ineptitude of certain key managers in overseeing this process. The lines called for much sharp criticism of some of the actors, all of whom were among the most powerful and high-ranking in the company. Each barb was met with gales of laughter and wild applause. On many occasions, actors referred menacingly to what would happen when "Big John" arrived to straighten things out. "Big John" clearly referred to the founder of the company, who was seated in the audience. As the plot developed, a major organization error had been committed by Ralph. Ralph, subjected to a great deal of criticism and harrassment by the other actors, was warned about Big John's wrath. Ralph was the highest-ranking corporate officer on the stage. He was the man to whom virtually all the others in the room (except for Big John) reported and was, in addition, the man who had, from the first, supported and sponsored my research in Company Z. Indeed, Ralph had allowed me access to the company after my three previous attempts to gain entree had been rebuffed by company officials. Clearly, I owed him a great deal.

Finally, the entrance of Big John was announced, and on I came greeted by much laughter and applause. As the least central person in the room, I ironically portrayed the most central. I was introduced into the skit with three sharp, verbal jabs, each quite unexpected. The first involved a reference to a recent, little-known setback in my career that had caused a great deal of pain to me and my family. Second was a disparaging comment about my Los Angeles home — something having to do with kosher burritos served with Teriyaki sauce, that sort of thing. Third was a pointed reference to the fact that, although I am an academic, I engage in organizational consulting, implying that I was not only selling, but selling out my commitment to science in favor of Mammon. In the midst of the hilarity and the applause, I was experiencing a complex mixture of emotions. More than anything else, I felt naked before these people. I was not a professor, not a consultant, not a scholar. Instead, I was a human being whose aspirations, fears, and weaknesses were in plain view. However, I also felt safe, even in that nakedness. I felt in that room, in the reactions of the people, the intent to understand, to comfort, and to accept me, even with all of my deep and obvious imperfections. I can only describe the experience as a moment of communion, of a feeling of unity and wholeness of the sort that Rosebeth Kanter observed in utopian communes.

It fell to me, as the Big John impostor, to fire Ralph, my friend and supporter. In firing Ralph, I let fly a string of criticisms of both his performance and abilities, each based on a kernel of truth but each blown up to obviously unreal proportions. Ralph, a participant in many such skits in the past, was truly touched by this play acting. He was hurt, embarrassed, and made vulnerable. If only for a fleeting moment, his pain clearly showed on his face. While this was play-acting, the play criticism could not be so unreal as to pass safely beyond the inner person. Each actor knew he would suffer some momentary but real embarrassment. This willingness to subject one's self to this experience gave proof to the audience, some subordinates, of an essential humanity, an acceptance of an egalitarian idea.

In the end the real Big John took the stage and set everything right. He fired me, restored Ralph to his rightful position, and displayed the kind of wisdom and evenhandedness that everyone expected and wanted, in order to provide a happy ending. In a way, Big John had also been subjected to some criticism, but only distantly. My impersonation of him had called for some unreasonable acts which, by implication, were samples of things for which the founder might be criticized. However, the real Big John clearly occupied a unique and special role in the proceedings. He and he alone appeared superhuman, possessed of qualities of foresight, fairness, and business acumen. In a sense, the real Big John represented the underlying philosophy of the

company, the embodiment of the values and beliefs towards
which all managers looked for guidance. Everyone in the room
knew that Big John was a wealthy man many times over; a man
whose company was sought after by the rich and the powerful all
over the world. His impact was communicated simply by his
presence in that room. That he would take the time to be with
this group of managers, to listen to plans and problems that he
had heard many times over, to choose their company over his
many alternatives, this alone clearly signalled to them their
importance to him and to the firm. In addition, his presence
clearly reminded them that their own participation with subordinates many levels below them would have similar meaning.
No one in company Z is above criticism.

After the play was over, everyone participated in a sing-along.
One of the company's veteran managers, a recently retired man
known and loved by all, had joined the group for that evening.
He sat on the stage with his guitar and sang two or three songs.
Then he invited the managers from each foreign country
represented to take the stage and sing one of their native songs.
The voices were clearly amateur, the performers were universally
embarrassed, but all were warmly received and loudly cheered.
When I, representing the "foreign country" of Los Angeles, was
invited to the stage, I was welcomed with a warmth of applause
that healed all remaining bruises from my part in the play. A
young manager seated next to me, who had never before
attended one of these meetings, looked at me with amazement. I
asked his reactions, and he could only shake his head in
wonderment. He had heard many times that Company Z was
unique, he had seen the difference in the way that they operated,
but this experience was beyond his imagination. I can only
describe it as a secular communion, a coming together and an
expression of unity that gives to each participant clear evidence
of the commitment to integrated, cooperative action.[2]

Mutual trust was conveyed throughout the structure of the
evening. The author of the script worked entirely without the
intervention of his co-workers or superiors. In most companies,
a skit or clever show might be developed by middle-level
managers or staffers, but it would certainly be subject to at least
the general and probably the specific approval of higher-ups. I
cannot imagine most companies being capable of actually going
through with a skit that made fun of a top executive without the
prior approval of the exact wording of the skit by top managers.

In Company Z, where the top management trusts middle management to take on such a delicate task, it is no surprise that they equally trust middle managers to make daily business decisions without central control and scrutiny. At the same time, how many middle managers, given the opportunity, would choose to write such a script? How many would trust their superiors to accept sharp criticisms and ridicule and not carry out some future plan of revenge? At Company Z, these skits have been taking place for more than twenty years.

The subject of the play was the poor performance and subsequent firing of key managers. In fact, that is the evil spirit to be exorcised at Company Z, and the moral of the play was that any manager who takes a short-run view of performance (as I did in my part) is the one who is subject to dismissal (as the top executive dismissed me in the end). The play's subtleties of construction must be appreciated. Rather than relying only upon examples immediately familiar to even the newest of the managers, the plot played upon subtle themes, leaving newer employees with the clear impression that it takes time to become fully part of this clan. It was also a warning: There is no room for large egos or overly sensitive types in this Z company. Large egos are "popped" with openness and humor through the skits and jokes.

The unmistakable sense of intimacy of the evening seemed to depend upon the trust between managers in that group. Intimacy involves a readiness to expose our weaknesses to others, or rather, a willingness to reveal ourselves in a manner so complete that others may find weaknesses there. The evening illustrated that we all inevitably have weaknesses that will be discovered, but each person is accepted in spite of them. The knowledge that nothing need be concealed brings on a profound sense of relief and of openness as well as a willingness to work hard, since contributions will be found out just as surely as mistakes. This, in part, is how a Z culture works.

Trusts, Friendships, and Working Together

Without a doubt Z people have unique ways of working together. Intimacy and trust are cornerstones of the culture both in and out of the business setting. "I have some very deep friendships with people at Z," one manager told me, "but not many are purely social. Although company social functions with spouses and friends are relatively few, about once every two weeks we have someone from Z over to the house, but it's more of a passing parade, not deep friendship. Company socializing seems to be a tradition. My wife enjoys Z people and views my social relationships with them as joyous because we spend so much time together! Our founder, on the other hand, says, 'what's nice about Company Z is the chance to accomplish objectives with friends.' It's obvious at business meetings with dinner that we like each other's company. It's characteristic of the whole company. Twenty to thirty of the top managers in our group will rent some houses at the ocean twice a year for a planning meeting. This way you develop personal relationships with the people you work with. It takes an informal atmosphere to do this: have lunch, play volleyball, stroll down the beach with someone, then have more meetings, then cocktails and dinner and poker. Joke, b.s., sit around. You develop relationships and learn to trust the other people. You learn about them in a way you couldn't across a desk."

Another manager agreed: "The single worst act at Company Z is untrustworthiness. I have fired two people for that kind of game-playing. You will find a very low tolerance for game-playing. The amount of pressure to keep you from behaving that way is immense. A supervisor trying to make his group look successful by blaming others, by maneuvering or withholding support to cause another group not to succeed is absolutely the worst sin." I asked him how this ideal works in a business sense. "The trust that exists here makes implementing a decision far easier, because others tend to accept the idea that a decision probably was made for the right reason, even though they may not see it. Rarely are a person's motives questioned, but rationale, yes," he said.

"I, myself, am a very conflict oriented person," he continued. "I take a devil's advocate position. If that doesn't demolish an argument, I accept it. All kinds of personal styles operate here That doesn't mean disagreement on issues is lacking. Sooner or later, if you deal from goodwill, you can learn from one another and resolve the issue. First get at the reasons for a disagreement. Compromises are few in this company; people end up agreeing on the same position. The Japanese management style fascinates me. The Z way is carried to the extreme but there are startling similarities with our organization. For example, we usually make decisions by consensus. If no solution is apparent, we think, 'he must know something I don't, or we wouldn't still disagree.' Fortunately the frustration level in this company is very low."

Beyond day-to-day decisions, trust marks the company's success in the long run. People must accept involvement in a program of broadening career paths, for instance. As one Z manager explained, "Everybody at the top levels started in technical jobs. Rotation through functions happens, but not through some conscious plan. There is a conscious program to get young people for a short time to experience another area: for example, an engineering designer goes to production. But once he gets further along, it's a shame to do that. With skills to be a good section manager in a lab, it's a shame to put him in production just to broaden him. Exposure to other areas comes because of the way decisions are made. You can learn about someone else's job without being in it. That's where trust matters. There are no job secrets, no secret rituals at department X. That's due to our open atmosphere. People have to know people and have people know them, so experienced people have difficulty succeeding here. Also, if they've worked elsewhere they tend to be a little manipulative."

Trust is a way of working together in a Z culture — a way of communicating to people that they matter as people, not as parts. Trust, I have seen, is another side of egalitarianism. As another Z manager told me, "Here at Company Z we all work for the same goals. We try to maintain such a philosophy overseas. We grow internally and we grow slowly. We start small, not with a big flourish. We spend much time with new people in getting them into the Company Z philosophy. I know it sounds corny, but I think what I am talking about here is the basis of what most of us believe. Our philosophy is unique, for example, in Penang, Malaysia. We do not lay off people during a manufacturing slump. We feel our employees are our most important resource. Consequently, we often incur substantial cost in carrying surplus labor. In Malaysia, our attrition rate is four to five percent, whereas the attrition rate of other companies there is twenty to thirty percent.

"It is fun to work at Company Z because we all work together. We all work for common goals and objectives. I often hear reports that Company Z employees always seem happy and enjoy their work. This seems too good to be true to those that listen to such reports. It seems that employees of many other companies bitch and moan about their work. Basic to the company Z philosophy is the notion that if you enjoy what you are doing, there is a good chance you will do a good job. It is a very complementary thing. High performance and job satisfaction do go together. These ideas are very compatible "

Teaming Up

In non-managerial ranks, too, such interpersonal work relationships make Type Z companies succeed both as human social systems and as economic producers. Given its high premium on working together, it comes as no surprise that our Type Z company is characterized by many cohesive and semi-autonomous work groups even though a Z company seldom undertakes any explicit attempts at team building. Instead, it first creates a culture to foster interpersonal subtlety and intimacy, and these conditions encourage cohesive work groups Individuals who are accustomed to depending upon one another, who have a long-term commitment to their working relationships, and who work well together will form cohesive groups and are naturally more adept at tackling problems they all must face. These groups have just as much autonomy as any individual in the morally integrated industrial clan, which is a great deal compared to bureaucratic organizations. Indeed, one can expect to find a number of "unnecessary" groups in an industrial clan, groups formed by individuals for the pure pleasure of the relationships; groups through which the individual members express their ability to coordinate with one another.

In most cultures, membership in groups is thought to be confining, and compromise is thought of as a loss of personal freedom and of individual expression. At a recent meeting of the American Sociological Association, a young anthropologist from the University of California expressed the opposite view. This woman had completed a study of the behavior of certain African religious groups that spoke in tongues. Each group engaged in a highly stylized pattern of ceremony that specified the role of every individual. The religious ceremony moved through a series of set steps from which it never wavered over the years, and the motions and participation of each participant was equally prescribed. American social scientists had long thought that this form of highly patterned religious participation failed

to produce emotional involvement and that the rigidly circum-
scribed parts left no room for true individual interpretation of
meaning. In fact, this research with its striking videotapes
clearly demonstrated that the participants were immersed in the
ceremony, often going into trances and speaking in tongues, both
right on cue. But that participation, while highly patterned and
leaving no room for individual taste, was undoubtedly deeply
felt by all. The interpretation of this remarkable study was as
follows: Religious experience involves the expression of
thoughts and of feelings so deep, so complex, and so subtle that
often no words can effectively communicate them. Even when
words exist, the public display of intimate feelings, often
embarassing, is thus avoided. Participation in a ritualized
religious ceremony frees individuals from the potential awk-
wardness of individual behaviors. This ceremonial form sym-
bolically represented thoughts and emotions of the sort that
cannot be put forth in words. Far from restricting individuality,
the ritual permitted complete expression of the deepest emotions.

Type Z organizations do not commonly have managers
speaking in tongues, although it may sometimes seem that we
have difficulty understanding them. They do, however, have
collective means of expression that stem from their underlying
cohesiveness. The formation of groups may well be the result
rather than the cause of organizational health.

Management by Walking Around

The way the managers and teams of personnel work together
is via a system of "Management by Walking Around." "Often
we move the desk of a top manager to the center of a problem
area, so he is right in the middle of the action," said one Z
manager. "New employees are exposed to Company Z's objectives during formal orientation periods of about five days, but
the real workings and philosophies of the company are learned
on the job. Sometimes new people don't fit in right away, but
they are pointed in the right direction. Sometimes sales meetings
get scrappy between marketing and sales people. For example,
one division has twenty-six product lines with eight pieces of
geography for a sales area. In such an instance everybody meets
to negotiate quotas and sales territory. Such a system relies
heavily on trust. Such trust rests on a foundation of long
association and truthful cost information. But most of all it's

important to move people around to different divisions and different experiences to keep managers walking around. We often move a manager to an apparently lower level job to give him new exposure. In this way the manager gets the flavor of the different divisions and their unique problems. It is a humbling experience to practice managerial skills in a variety of situations, with a variety of types of people."

Management by Walking Around (MBWA) conveys the necessity of this hands-on, direct participation of managers, not distant order-giving. It pokes fun at Company Z's own extensive use of Management by Objectives as well as the main source of managerial talent, the holders of the degree Master of Business Administration. "MBWA is our approach, not MBA" is often heard.

These managers give us a feeling for the texture, the flesh and blood that comes to life in Type Z company. The top management is clearly dedicated not to brainwashing employees but to setting objectives that permit every individual to satisfy their own self-interest while simultaneously serving the corporate interest. They seek an integrated social structure.

Valuing People Who Value Their Products

What does all this emphasis on people mean for the lifeline of any company — the products it produces? In a Z culture the insistence on the long run requires that its clients and customers continue to appreciate their products and services over many years. And sometimes, even efficiency apparently comes second in value in what a Z company produces.

As one manager told me: "Company Z sees profit as the premium a customer pays for the company's part in solving their problems. Therefore, the customer decides whether or not you've succeeded. You may do some very ingenious things and nobody buys it — it's not a contribution. Therefore, we do value pricing, not cost-plus pricing. The customer pays you a premium for what you've done. If you've done very well, the rewards will be very high.

"Another, different definition that I believe some companies use is that profit is the difference between price and cost. That says you can do two things: raise prices or cut costs. Both amount to gouging the customer. A lot of people at Company Z feel our approach to profits is very moral; they hold to it. In a sense, the customer gives us a 'tip' for what we do. The better we do, the bigger the tip."

With value paramount, emphasis on efficiency — at least as others define it — takes a back seat. At Company Z, not even the manufacturing competence is measured carefully. As they told me, "That's because we don't succeed by being efficient, we succeed by putting out new things that people want use of. We've cut the price on our new product by a factor of four over the past three years by developing new technology. If you're looking at cost changes of that magnitude, you don't worry about three percent efficiency."

According to Z traditions, efficiency means being professional, not saving on cost. "We have three thousand different products," the manager went on. "In some production areas half of the products didn't exist two months ago! You never have a chance to really refine the process, because somebody always changes either the technology or the product. We don't want economies of scale requiring an efficiency orientation and our production lines aren't interested in efficiency. Remember our traditions and our values. They are internally compatible and consistent with our products."

The Chicken or the Egg

Interestingly, not all Z cultures are pieced together in the step-by-step process that Z companies are. In fact, most successful Theory Z companies have developed their cultures slowly under the leadership of one or a handful of owner-managers. In the case of the Type Z company that I studied in depth, the question arose whether the culture had developed after the company had matured, or whether it had begun in that manner. A careful study of historical records revealed many sources published during the company's earliest days, which indicated an early distinctive culture maintained as it grew and prospered. It is also my impression that the other companies of this type also began as Type Z organizations. While it may be the case that a Type A company can, with time, make a successful conversion to this form, the long history of distinctive corporate cultures suggests a systematic link between the incentives and style of the owner and the development of the clan form. When the firm is effectively controlled by its founder, that person need not justify decisions to anyone. If some of the critical long-run decisions are subtle, then the owner may base decisions on "intuition" or an inherent but inexpressible sense of the long run. If, on the other hand, the firm is owned by a large number of shareholders, each of whom owns stock in many firms, then quite a different situation occurs. In such a case, none of the owners of the firm is close enough to it to have a sensitive awareness for the intricacies of the business. Lacking intimacy, the owners fail to appreciate subtlety and thus have no basis for trusting the judgment of their professional managers. The managers, knowing that their job security and future advancement will be based on the outcomes of decisions with clear-cut, short-term outcomes, shy away from tenuous, long-term decisions. Thus a concentrated form of ownership or control may be a necessary condition for the development of Type Z organizations.

A distinctive corporate culture develops only with time. As one company Z manager told me, "Almost all of the people we have are working with the idea that this company will be their career. Our policies make sense, and most people come on board when they understand them. We just finished putting two hundred managers through an intensive training program, and we're about to put nine hundred more through. We feel strongly about teaching them our outlook. Not only does it take time and a variety of experience to communicate the cultural intricacies to new managers, it also takes their desire to learn. A new employee who anticipates a lifelong career in a company is more likely to be interested in learning its subtleties.

Supportive Z Environments

A Z company may require a special kind of environment. Those few Type Z organizations that currently exist are anomalous, and each current Type Z organization, therefore, must have developed in a unique niche that provided a setting hospitable to this form. At least three settings act in this manner. First are the *company towns,* like Kodak, and Proctor & Gamble. These companies center much of their employment in a small- or medium-sized town. In such surroundings, employees naturally develop a web of wholistic relations. The network of ties here binds co-workers together in their religious, neighborhood, and civic roles. However, it's also the kind of network that can become overbearing, especially when the company hierarchy is transmitted to community life, so that instead of a status reversal in community life, which produces a more egalitarian corporate climate, we can end up with just the opposite — a community shackled by the same hierarchy that characterizes corporate life. A plantation-style, paternalistic organization, quite different from the Type Z with its egalitarian atmosphere, then arises. However, not all company towns will grow in this manner; some will develop into Type Z organizations that respect individual privacy. In such a case, it's hard to say whether the company culture has overtaken the town or the town culture has overtaken the company, but in either case the result is the same: a company whose employees are joined together in a rich network of primary bonds.

The second setting congenial to the Type Z culture is distinctly represented by the United States military and by some large industrial firms. These organizations move their employees so often that they never have a chance to settle down and to put down roots in a community. Studies have shown that such families "move in" to a community much more quickly than do families unaccustomed to moving. They know their stay is short, and they respond by plunging actively into community and church activities. Nonetheless, a response of this sort provides only a partial solution, since such families cannot replace completely the social supports others enjoy. Often, they adapt by developing a homogeneous culture within the work organization. As families move from city to city, they count upon having a familiar social framework that directly involves families in the social structure of the work organization. Thus the "Colonel's wife" has a specified role in the social structure of the army base, one that greets her with a familiar and comforting role as she moves from one place to another. Again, the cost of this solution is that the hierarchy of the organization may invade all other spheres of life in a relatively complete manner, placing all of one's social existence into an inflexible network of hierarchical relationships. This is the cost of having stable surroundings to prevent a life disoriented and anomic in the extreme. As a result, homogeneous array of settings arose so that to an outsider an army base, whether in West Germany, in Illinois, or in Hawaii, has the familiar look, feel, and smell of Oklahoma.

The third environment amenable to Theory Z is that of Hewlett-Packard, or of Texas Instruments, or of companies in sunbelt locales. In California, as in Texas, it seems as if everyone is from someplace else. Few have familiar friends, family, or social ties. Encounter groups, support groups, small groups of all sorts flourished in California in the past decade. These groups had a common property: each seemed to be a place where one could make friends. Yet many of these groups have died because of artificiality, not in the intent or openness of their participants, but in the sense they did not occur in the normal path of one's life. To participate in some of these groups, one had to pay a fee and travel to Carmel for the weekend. The relative inaccessibility of these settings kept them from becoming a dominant form for the creation of integrated social life. Within the context of day-to-day work activities, however, lonesome and unaffiliated individuals naturally sought more than just a job. At their place of employment, they could develop a sense of belonging, an attachment of some depth and stability to other human beings. Most employers in this setting actively encouraged such socializing at work, few recognized that work organizations are social organisms that exist as part and parcel of their surroundings, and did not stand in the way of this development.

The Significance of Living in a Z Culture

While working with newly converted Z companies, I tried to determine whether people living in a Z culture were different from people breathing the A air. Assuming some differences did exist, I built into my survey questionnaires very careful mechanisms that would prevent me from slanting the results.[3] Nevertheless, almost all of my hypotheses were confirmed. The Type A and Type Z people were in every respect quite different.

For example, the employees at Company Z typically have been there longer and expect to remain there longer in the future than their counterparts at Company A. Company A replaces twenty-five percent of its vice-presidents each year and has done so for at least the past twenty years without much variation, while Company Z replaces only four percent of its vice-presidents each year, primarily through retirements. Lower level employees at Company Z assume that the company will not lay them off and do not often quit on their own, while Company A employees expect either to be laid off or to quit in the near future.

At all levels Company Z employees have been promoted more

slowly and have worked in more different kinds of jobs than
have their Company A counterparts. Company Z employees
report that they feel their company has a distinctive philosophy
using subtle and implicit forms of control, whereas Company A
employees feel no such distinctiveness or subtlety. With respect
to decision making, the vice-presidents at both companies
report a high level of participation, but lower level employees at
Company Z report high participation, while their counterparts
at Company A report little involvement.

I had expected that the values of collectivism at the companies
would *not* differ. I had regarded short-run individualism as
being a deeply-rooted cultural value that would be equally
strong among all Americans. To my great surprise, the data
show that Company Z employees express significantly more
collectivism than do Company A employees. This result suggested that perhaps Company Z was the sort of paternalistic
place that attracts people who do not want to control their own
lives, who prefer to be part of a larger whole that will both look
after them and control them. Were this so, then clearly the Type
Z would be a special case of limited appeal, not something that
could be widely applied within American industry. But when I
interviewed employees who had been with the Z companies for
one month or less, I found these new employees did *not* differ
from new employees at other companies on individualism or on
any other characteristic. In fact, any differences that exist
between employees at Z and other companies appear largely to
have developed after entry and as a consequence of being in one
or the other corporate culture for a period of time. The
individuals are equally aggressive and independent-minded in
both companies, but in Company Z they believe in collective
responsibility and action far more than do Company A people.

What about the sense of wholism, the intermixing of work life
with family and communal life on the one hand; and on the
other, the breadth of relationships among co-workers? With
respect to the intermixing of personal and work life, the A and Z
companies did not differ. Employees at both prefer to keep work
and family separate; in neither case do they feel pressure to
participate in a great deal of company-based social activity such
as dinner or cocktail parties. In terms of breadth of contact,
however, Type Z employees develop more and broader types of
relations with co-workers than do Type A employees. In
Company Z, employees know more about each other, talk

about a greater variety of subjects, and engage in a wider range of work-related activities than at Company *A*.

As for the effects of these differences, the employees at Company *Z* manifest much better emotional well-being than their counterparts at Company *A*. Company *Z* employees show significantly less anomie and hostility than do Company *A* employees. The spouses of Company *Z* employees report a more satisfying family life and marital relationships than do the spouses of Company *A* employees, although the employees themselves report no differences on these dimensions. This result suggests that Company *Z* employees have healthier work relations and thus take home a more positive frame of mind. This emotional state, largely irrelevant to one who works at a company, has a large impact on an employee's family. In addition to these social and emotional effects, it is important to note that Company *Z* and Company *A* began in business at about the same time, grew at similar rates, and are both among the 1,000 largest industrial firms in the United States. Over the past five years, Company *Z* has been far more successful than Company *A*, providing more jobs, earning more profits, and growing at a higher rate. Both socially and economically, Company *Z* can be said to have been more successful than Company *A*.

In addition to these results, our research produced some interesting differences of an unexpected sort. These had to do with how our research proceeded in each case. At Company *Z* everyone asked agreed to an interview. All interviews began on time or not more than ten minutes past the appointed time. At Company *A* the president refused to be interviewed, but we did interview the chairman of the board as well as all other corporate officers. At Company *A* the interviews began on the average thirty minutes late, and a start of forty-five minutes after the appointed time was not unusual. Whereas the interviewees at Company *Z* gave the impression of being calm, organized, and in control, the Company *A* subjects appeared to be rushed, harried, and barely on top of things.

But perhaps the major differences were brought out by the Company *A* managers themselves. One example: "I have single-handedly fired more people in this industry than everyone else put together. And do you know what? The ones that I've fired thank me for it today. They were square pegs in round holes." Or, as another Company *A* manager said, echoing the voices of many of his colleagues, "There's no relationship between my work life and my family life. My deal with my wife is that 8 AM Monday to 10 PM Friday is for work, and she doesn't bother me. Keep my clothes clean, and if you happen to see me, feed me, otherwise don't worry. Weekends are for my family. I may go to a social function for the company once or twice a year, but we don't socialize with company people. We have our own social life outside the company. I work almost every night and put in a lot of time. When the deadlines come, they get whatever it takes. In my field the pressures come with deadly regularity. I've always been opposed to too much connection between social and work life, because I've seen too many times when a decision was or wasn't made for non-business reasons. That's one reason I don't want to be president of this place."

Continuing on, this Type A manager has some other observations to share. "The toughness can lead to competition between people. I see it all the time. If I see two guys who can't work together, I call them in and say, 'If you can't work together, I don't need either of you.' That usually takes care of it. What I mean about toughness is that after you've been banged for eight months of disasters you don't give up, which is very easy to do. You fix it again. Guys who don't quit, that's toughness. Successful ones never do quit, they always do their best. Maybe that's a commentary on life.

"Team playing depends on the top guy, it's an attitude, the way you behave. You just have to send out clear signals or others won't play the game. If they can't do that they go find another job.

"Division managers and their staffs are basically measured on what they produce. If he's in trouble because the market dried on him, he'll get help and understanding; or at least I hope he would. It's great to be a successful division manager, you have salary incentives, stock options, prestige, you can do anything you want. It's a lot of fun. It's stature in the company to be able to control your own destiny. But if you start to get in trouble, the corporate staff comes down to help you make your decisions and put controls on you. The guys hate that, other people dabbling in their business. What makes a division manager run more than anything else is wanting to keep the other people out of his hair."

Perhaps the most astonishing difference of all is this. All of the executives interviewed at Company Z are still there, with the exception of one executive who had been brought in from the outside and who has since resigned. Of all the executives interviewed at Company *A*, approximately two-thirds have resigned since the conclusion of the interviews. One of them took his own life. Not all *A* companies suffer so much by comparison with *Z* companies. But the differences are almost always apparent.

CONCLUSION

THE SURVIVAL OF BUSINESS *AMERICANUS*

GENERAL Motors, Ford, Chrysler, Hewlett-Packard, General Electric, Westinghouse, IBM, Texas Instruments, Intel, Tektronix, Pillsbury, Honeywell, Lockheed, Eli Lilly, Baxter-Travenol, Syntex, Fairchild Camera and Instrument, Toro, International Harvester, Brunswick, and a group of six rabbis in Los Angeles. What they all have in common, of course, is that all studied the Japanese form of organization. All have undertaken attempts, big and small, to move from *A* to *Z*, to develop their own clans. All within the past few years.

An organization need not be large to have problems of social integration. The six rabbis, for example, are engaged in running a social service agency in which they employ a number of social workers who are not rabbis. Thus two distinctive cultures must be integrated. Their need to rotate jobs, to develop an explicitly and commonly accepted philosophy, to develop skill at participative decision making is no less than the need for the marketing and manufacturing groups at a multi-billion dollar firm to get together. Or consider a small, family-dominated savings and loan with one hundred employees that has grown to the point where it is largely run by non-family members. Management philosophy, once taken for granted between family members, must now be made explicit if the organization is to survive. Consider an art museum that must coordinate curatorial and business staffs, or a hospital with medical and business personnel. Each has a complex network of relationships too subtle and complex to be specified in advance through bureaucratic procedures. With the development of goal congruence and trust, the organization can operate successfully.

The "normal science" of management is long since in need of a new paradigm. We need to exclaim, "The Emperor has no clothes!" Americans believe massive capital investments are necessary for efficient production of automobiles, yet Japanese automakers produce low-cost, high-quality products in companies that a few years ago were a fraction of the size of the smallest American automakers. We believe that large factories promote efficiency, but the Japanese want the smallest plants possible, so they can adapt plant design to keep up with new technologies every few years. To us high quality comes from more testing and not from workers producing higher quality, but the Japanese believe that high quality comes from inviting workers to continually refine the design and the manufacturing process.

Americans believe that decision making by consensus will produce camels when we want horses, but the Brookhaven plant of GM has achieved superlative levels of quality and efficiency through participation. We believe that specialization leads to productivity, but Company Z achieves higher productivity than Company A with lower specialization. We believe that creativity stems from individual maverick genius, but the most creative, innovative of our high technology companies have been the first to explore Type Z organization. We believe that the typical United States rates of twenty-six percent annual turnover and of eight percent average absenteeism are an irreducible minimum, but annual turnover among European firms averages twelve percent and among Japanese firms six percent, with lower absenteeism rates as well. We believe that, fundamentally, only high pay and rapid promotion will spur the most talented to achieve, while Company Z and Brookhaven have both found that commitment and participation are far more powerful in conflict over the proper division of profits. Here Scanlon Plan companies succeed at creating higher profits by sharing the additional wealth among both parties.

The monarch must be reclothed. Perhaps we have been the victims of an extended period of superstitious learning, which must now be unlearned. For more than one hundred years, our nation has surged forward under the momentum of the industrial revolution. If we take it as inevitable that the advent of factory production, of low-cost transportation and communication, and a few other innovations would bring a great increase in wealth in our nation, then the scene was set for superstitious learning. In essence, once these basic innovations were in place, our economy was destined to grow.[4] No matter how well or how poorly we organized and managed our commercial enterprises, no matter what we did or failed to do, there would be growth, wealth, and success of an economic sort. In this setting, whatever beliefs developed about management were bound to be supported by success. Having "learned" how to manage successfully, we have continued to perfect this approach. Only now, when most of the benefit of these innovations has been exhausted, are we forced to see that our paradigm of management never did contribute anything to that success.

Fortunately, deviants exist in every age. In ecological language, those deviants are the source of variation that make possible the continued adaptation and survival of the population. In this case, the population of United States commercial organizations concerns us. Within this population, the Type A has for years been the dominant type. Nonetheless, the Type Z deviants did exist. Now, with the need for change apparent, many other organizations in that population are learning from those deviants. As in any competitive natural environment, what will follow will be a process of natural selection. If the Type Z indeed has superior competitive characteristics, then it will get the best people, produce the best goods and services at competitive prices, and survive. The others will be selected against by nature and will fail.

Organizations are not entirely like biological organisms, however. Ecological theories typically pay little attention to the microscopic properties of individual members of a population, since those individuals, once created, cannot change form. Only through intergenerational change can a population of organisms change its dominant properties. Organizations, however, are themselves aggregations of more fundamental individual units. Thus, while we are concerned with the survival of the genus, Business *Americanus,* in fact each of its members is, in turn, a population of individuals. The underlying properties of those individuals cannot be changed in major ways. They will continue to be self-interested. Organizations cannot reform their employees. What remains, therefore, is for organizations to change their internal social structure in a manner which simultaneously satisfies competitive needs for a new, more fully integrated form, and the needs of individual employees for the satisfaction of their individual self-interest. It may be that the Type Z organization, the industrial clan, approximates this new form.

APPENDIX ONE

COMPANY Z PHILOSOPHIES

HEWLETT-PACKARD

Statement of Corporate Objectives

The achievements of an organization are the result of the combined efforts of each individual in the organization working toward common objectives. These objectives should be realistic, should be clearly understood by everyone in the organization, and should reflect the organization's basic character and personality.

If the organization is to fulfill its objectives, it should strive to meet certain other fundamental requirements:

FIRST, the most capable people available should be selected for each assignment within the organization. Moreover, these people should have the opportunity — through continuing programs of training and education — to upgrade their skills and capabilities. This is especially important in a technical business where the rate of progress is rapid. Techniques that are good today will be outdated in the future, and people throughout the organization should continually be looking for new and better ways to do their work.

SECOND, enthusiasm should exist at all levels. People in important management positions should not only be enthusiastic themselves, they should be selected for their ability to engender enthusiasm among their associates. There can be no place, especially among the people charged with management responsibility, for half-hearted interest or half-hearted effort.

THIRD, even though an organization is made up of people fully meeting the first two requirements, all levels should work in unison toward common objectives and avoid working at cross purposes if the ultimate in efficiency and achievement is to be obtained.

It has been our policy at Hewlett-Packard not to have a tight military-type organization, but rather, to have overall objectives which are clearly stated and agreed to, and to give people the freedom to work toward those goals in ways they determine best for their own areas of responsibility.

Our Hewlett-Packard objectives were initially published in 1957. Since then they have been modified from time to time, reflecting the changing nature of our business and social environment. This booklet represents the latest updating of our objectives. We hope you find them informative and useful.

DAVID PACKARD
Chairman of the Board

WILLIAM HEWLETT
President and Chief Executive Officer

1. Profit

OBJECTIVE: To achieve sufficient profit to finance our company growth and to provide the resources we need to achieve our other corporate objectives.

In our economic system, the profit we generate from our operations is the ultimate source of the funds we need to prosper and grow. It is the one absolutely essential measure of our corporate performance over the long term. Only if we continue to meet our profit objective can we achieve our other corporate objectives.

Our long-standing policy has been to reinvest most of our profits and to depend on this reinvestment, plus funds from employee stock purchases and other cash flow items, to finance our growth. This can be achieved if our return on net worth is roughly equal to our sales growth rate. We must strive to reach this goal every year without limiting our efforts to attain our other objectives.

Profits vary from year to year, reflecting changing economic conditions and varying demands for our products. Our needs for capital also vary, and we depend on short-term bank loans to meet those needs when profits or other cash sources are inadequate. However, loans are costly and must be repaid; thus, our objective is to rely on reinvested profits as our main source of capital.

Meeting our profit objective requires that we design and develop each and every product so that it is considered a good value by our customers, yet is priced to include an adequate profit. Maintaining this competitiveness in the marketplace also requires that we perform our manufacturing, marketing and administrative functions as economically as possible.

Profit is not something that can be put off until tomorrow; it must be achieved today. It means that myriad jobs be done correctly and efficiently. The day-to-day performance of each individual adds to — or subtracts from — our profit. Profit is the responsibility of all.

2. Customers

OBJECTIVE: To provide products and services of the greatest possible value to our customers, thereby gaining and holding their respect and loyalty.

The success and prosperity of our company will be assured only if we offer our customers superior products that fill real needs and provide lasting value, and that are supported by a wide variety of useful services, both before and after sale.

Our responsibility to the customer begins with product development. Products must be designed to provide superior performance and long, trouble-free service. Once in production, these products must be manufactured at a reasonable cost and with superior workmanship.

A prime objective of our marketing departments is to see that the finished product is backed by prompt, efficient service. Moreover, good communication should be maintained with the customer and among various HP sales teams.

Because of our broad and growing line of products, very often several sales teams will be working with a single customer. Each of these teams has a high degree of technical knowledge and sales skill. There must be considerable cooperation among teams to assure that the products recommended best fulfill the customer's overall, long-term needs.

HP customers must feel that they are dealing with one

company with common policies and services, and that our company is genuinely interested in arriving at proper, effective solutions to their problems. Confusion and competition among sales teams must be avoided by a clear assignment of sales responsibilities, plus sound judgment by HP sales people in understanding customer needs and HP objectives.

3. Fields of Interest

OBJECTIVE: To enter new fields only when the ideas we have, together with our technical, manufacturing, and marketing skills, assure that we can make a needed and profitable contribution to the field.

The original Hewlett-Packard products were electronic measuring instruments. Today our product line has expanded to include instruments for chemical and biomedical measurement and analysis, computers to automate measurement and to process the data, as well as electronic calculators and complete computer systems. Thus our growth has led to a continuing expansion of our fields of interest. To a large extent, diversification has come from applying our resources and skills to fields technically related to our traditional ones.

The key to HP's prospective involvement in new fields is *contribution*. This means providing customers with something new and needed, not just another brand of something they can already buy. To meet this objective we must continually generate new ideas for better kinds of products. It is essential that before final decision is made to enter a new field, full consideration be given to the associated problems of manufacturing and marketing these products.

4. Growth

OBJECTIVE: To let our growth be limited only by our profits and our ability to develop and produce technical products that satisfy real customer needs.

How large should a company become? Some people feel that when it has reached a certain size there is no point in letting it grow further. Others feel that bigness is an objective in itself. We do not believe that large size is important for its own sake; however, for at least two basic reasons, continuous growth is essential for us to achieve our other objectives.

In the first place, we serve a rapidly growing and expanding segment of our technological society. To remain static would be to lose ground. We cannot maintain a position of strength and leadership in our field without growth.

In the second place, growth is important in order to attract and hold high caliber people. These individuals will align their future only with a company that offers them considerable opportunity for personal progress. Opportunities are greater and more challenging in a growing company.

5. Our People

OBJECTIVE: To help HP people share in the company's success, which they make possible; to provide job security based on their performance; to recognize their individual achievements; and to insure the personal satisfaction that comes from a sense of accomplishment in their work.

We are proud of the people we have in our organization, their performance, and their attitude toward their jobs and toward the company. The company has been built around the individual, the personal dignity of each, and the recognition of personal achievements.

We feel that general policies and the attitude of managers toward their people are more important than specific details of the personnel program. Personnel relations will be good only if people have faith in the motives and integrity of their supervisors and of the company. Personnel relations will be poor if they do not.

The opportunity to share in the success of the company is evidenced by our above-average wage and salary level, our profit-sharing and stock purchase plans, and by other company benefits.

The objective of job security is illustrated by our policy of avoiding large ups and downs in our production schedules, which would require hiring people for short periods of time and laying them off later. We are interested that each employee carry a full load and be eager to remain with and grow with the company. This does not mean we are committed to an absolute tenure status, nor do we recognize seniority except where other factors are reasonably comparable.

In a growing company there are apt to be more opportunities for advancement than there are qualified people to fill them. This is true at Hewlett-Packard; opportunities are plentiful and it is up to the individual, through personal growth and development, to take advantage of them.

We want people to enjoy their work at HP, and to be proud of their accomplishments. This means we must make sure that each person receives the recognition he or she needs and deserves. In the final analysis, people at all levels determine the character and strength of our company.

6. Management

OBJECTIVE: To foster initiative and creativity by allowing the individual great freedom of action in attaining well-defined objectives.

In discussing HP operating policies, we often refer to the concept of "management by objective." By this we mean that insofar as possible each individual at each level in the organization should make his or her own plans to achieve company objectives and goals. After receiving supervisory approval, each individual should be given a wide degree of freedom to work within the limitations imposed by these plans, and by our general corporate policies. Finally, each person's performance should be judged on the basis of how well these individually established goals have been achieved.

The successful practice of "management by objective" is a two-way street. Management must be sure that each individual understands the immediate objectives, as well as corporate goals and policies. Thus a primary HP management responsibility is communication and mutual understanding. Conversely, employees must take sufficient interest in their work to want to plan it, to propose new solutions to old problems, to stick their necks out when they have something to contribute. "Management by objective," as opposed to management by directive, offers opportunity for individual freedom and contribution; it also imposes an obligation for everyone to exercise initiative and enthusiasm.

In this atmosphere it is particularly important that the strength of the whole company is kept in mind and that cooperation between individuals and between operating units is vital to our profitable growth.

It is important for everyone to realize there are some policies which must be established and strictly maintained on a corporate-wide basis. We welcome recommendations on these corporate-wide policies from all levels but we expect adherence to them at all times.

7. Citizenship

OBJECTIVE: To honor our obligations to society by being an economic, intellectual, and social asset to each nation and each community in which we operate.

All of us should strive to improve the environment in which we live. As a corporation operating in many different communities throughout the world, we must assure ourselves that each of these communities is better for our presence. This means building plants and offices that are attractive and in harmony with the community; it means solving instead of contributing to the problems of traffic and pollution; it means contributing both money and time to community projects.

Each community has its particular set of social problems. Our company must help to solve these problems. As a major step in this direction, we must strive to provide worthwhile employment opportunities for people of widely different backgrounds. Among other things, this requires positive action to seek out and employ members of disadvantaged groups; and to encourage and guide their progress toward full participation at all position levels.

As citizens of their community, there is much that HP people can and should do to improve it — either working as individuals or through such groups as churches, schools, civic, or charitable organizations. At a national level, it is essential that the company be a good corporate citizen of each country in which it operates. Moreover our employees, as individuals, should be encouraged to contribute their support to the solution of national problems.

The betterment of our society is not a job to be left to a few; it is a responsibility to be shared by all.

DAYTON-HUDSON CORPORATION

Statement of Philosophy

Strategic Mission and Direction

Dayton-Hudson Corporation is a diversified retailing company whose business is to serve the American consumer through the retailing of fashion-oriented quality merchandise.

Serving the consumer over time requires skilled and motivated employees, healthy communities in which to operate and maximum long-range profit. We are committed to meaningful and comprehensive employee development, to serving the business, social and cultural needs of our communities, and to achieving levels of profitability equivalent to the leading firms in industry.

Thus, Dayton-Hudson Corporation serves four major constituencies: consumers, employees, shareholders, and communities. The common denominator in serving these constituencies is profit — our reward for serving society well. Long-range profit is thus our major responsibility so that we can continue to serve our constituencies in the future.

Corporate Purposes

The corporation has specific purposes with regard to serving each of its four constituencies. These purposes and associated key objectives are as follows:

A. To serve as the consumers' purchasing agent in fulfilling their needs and expectations for merchandise and services.

1. To offer dominant assortments of quality and fashion merchandise.
2. To offer merchandise which represents true value to consumers.
3. To support merchandising activities with appropriate levels of service, creative yet informative advertising, and well-maintained stores.
4. To occupy preeminent competitive positions in each market we serve and within the merchandise lines we carry.
5. To maintain the highest levels of honesty, integrity and responsiveness in meeting merchandise and service needs of our customers.

B. To contribute to the personal and professional development of our employees.

1. To provide opportunity for all employees — regardless of age, race, color, sex, religion or national origin — to develop their full potential through education, training and work experience.
2. To provide employees opportunity to advance in position and responsibility consistent with proven performance.
3. To provide an atmosphere which encourages employee initiative and input and which fosters trust, creativity and economic security.
4. To support the concept of superior compensation for superior performance.

C. To provide an attractive financial return to our shareholders.

1. To be a premier investment as measured against the best in the retail industry and industry in general.
2. To provide shareholders with consistent growth in dividends per share as current income.
3. To provide shareholders with growth in share value over time, consistent with growth in earnings — ranking in the industry's top quartile in terms of Price Earnings multiple, Return on Investment and Return on Equity.
4. To achieve the following standards of financial performance.

ROE
EPS Growth

D. To serve the communities in which we operate.

  1. To demonstrate exemplary corporate citizenship in the conduct of our business and in the relationship of the corporation and its employees to all their constituencies.
  2. To observe the highest legal, ethical and moral standards.
  3. To work cooperatively with business, civic, and governmental agencies to improve the environments in which we operate.
  4. To contribute annually 5% of federally taxable income to improve the quality of life in communities of which we are a part.

Corporate Objective

Our primary objective is to be premier in every facet of our business. We aspire to be recognized as premier in fulfilling our obligations to all four constituencies — customers, employees, shareholders and communities. Further, we strive to be innovative and at the forefront of the retail industry in its continuing evolution.

Achievement of this objective assumes attaining premier status as a retail investment. While profit is our reward for serving society well, it is also a requisite for continuing to serve society at all. Thus, the task is to manage the corporation so that it is recognized as a premier investment in the retail field.

Merchandising Philosophy

The aim of each of our operating companies is to serve its customers better than any comparable retailing organization in its markets. Each strives to achieve a specific customer-orientation and a clear customer perception of its merchandise and service offering. Inherent in this philosophy are four key elements:

A. DOMINANCE

means both merchandise dominance and market preeminence. Specifically, we strive for a merchandise offer that assures consumers our stores have the best selection of the items they seek. Furthermore, we strive to be the leading retailer in those markets and merchandise lines in which we elect to compete.

Implicit in a decision to enter a market is the long-term financial commitment to achieve preeminence in that market.

B. QUALITY

is the essence of all of our operations. It is expressed most importantly in merchandise, but the concept of quality applies equally well to the corporation's management team, to its facilities and its locations. Our customers should perceive us as a quality business operated by quality people selling quality merchandise and providing quality services.

C. FASHION

is at the heart of our business. Fashion is change — change with direction. Newness and change can be predicted, however, through Trend Merchandising. Our aim is for each company to be the fashion leader within its markets. Regardless of the specific merchandise category, our companies will lead customers to that which is new and exciting in the marketplace.

D. VALUE

is more than price alone; it is giving the customer a favorable return on investment.

For the merchandise itself, value means quality at a price. Our companies seek to provide maximum value to customers by acting aggressively as their buying agent — in purchasing quality goods and negotiating for the best possible price. Our companies seek to keep cost structures and operating expenses lean — recognizing that such costs are inevitably reflected in consumer prices.

Further, we are sensitive to the expanded meaning of the term value: customer time spent locating products or waiting for service, energy costs incurred in a shopping trip, serviceability of durable goods, and the psychic and emotional value of the shopping experience itself.

Real Estate Philosophy

The corporation recognizes that long-range success is as dependent on a sound real estate strategy as on a merchandise strategy. The hallmark of the corporation is the successful melding of the two. The concept of dominance, quality, and fashion applies as much to locations and facilities as to merchandise. We aim, therefore, to have quality stores that bespeak fashion and good taste. We seek premier locations, building our stores and our facilities for the future.

Management Philosophy

The management philosophy of the Dayton-Hudson Corporation is a balance of operating autonomy and flexibility on the one hand, and corporate input and direction, on the other hand.

TO THIS END:

A. The corporation will:

1. Set standards for ROI and earnings growth
2. Approve strategic plans
3. Allocate capital
4. Approve goals
5. Monitor, measure, and audit results
6. Reward performance
7. Allocate management resources

B. The operating companies will be accorded the freedom and responsibility:

1. To manage their own business
2. To develop strategic plans and goals which will optimize their growth
3. To develop an organization which can assure consistency of results and optimum growth
4. To operate their businesses consistent with the corporation's Statement of Philosophy

C. The corporate staff will provide only those services which:

1. Are essential to the protection of the corporation
2. Are needed for the growth of the corporation
3. Are wanted by operating companies, and which provide a significant advantage in quality or cost

D. The corporation will insist on:

1. Uniform accounting practices by type of business

2. Prompt disclosure of operating results
3. A systematic approach to training and developing people
4. Adherence to appropriately high standards of business conduct and civic responsibility, in accordance with the corporation's Statement of Philosophy

Growth Philosophy

The stability and quality of the corporation's financial performance will be developed through the profitable execution of our existing businesses, as well as the acquisition or development of new businesses. Our growth priorities, in order, are as follows:

1. Development of the profitable market preeminence of existing companies in existing markets, through new store development or new strategies within existing stores

2. Expansion of our companies to feasible new markets

3. Acquisition of other retailing companies that are strategically and financially compatible with Dayton Hudson

4. Internal development of new retailing strategies

Capital allocations to fund the expansion of existing operating companies will be based on each company's return on investment, in relationship to its ROI objective and consistency in earnings growth, and on its management capability to perform up to forecasts contained in capital requests.

Expansion via acquisition or new venture will occur when the opportunity promises an acceptable rate of long-term growth and profitability, an acceptable degree of risk, and compatibility with the corporation's long-term strategy.

Ethical Standards and Business Conduct

The policy of the corporation is to maintain a consistently high standard of business conduct, ethics and social responsibility. Individual employees are expected to demonstrate high levels of integrity and objectivity, uncmcumbered by conflicting interests in all decisions and actions affecting the corporation.
Corporate policies governing the business conduct of em-

ployees will serve as a minimum standard of performance.
Premier status requires exemplary behavior and attitudes —
conduct befitting premier employees.

ROCKWELL INTERNATIONAL

Automotive Operations Culture Analysis "What was, What Is and What It Should Be"

Background

o Transportation Markets of the eighties and nineties are Undergoing Rapid Change.

- More Complex
- Tougher Domestic and Foreign Competition
- Aggressive Competitive Pricing.

o Government Regulation is Increasingly Affecting Our Management, Decision Making, and Business Flexibility.

- Industrial ransom
- De-Regulation
- EEO
- Fuel Economy

o Our Employees at all Levels of the Organization are Undergoing Changes in Make-Up and Values.

- Better Educated
- Pressing for Job Security
- Need to be Convinced Rather than Commanded
- Increasing Female and Minority Representation
- Want to be Heard
- Ownership Desires
- Shared Decision Making

o In Order to Maximize Our Ability to Handle Rapidly Changing Market, Government, and People Complexities, We Must Continue to Modify and Develop Our Culture

- Beliefs
- Traditions
- Values
- Management Systems

In a Manner which will provide the Overall Framework to Approach the eighties and nineties.

o The Development, Implementation and Communication of Our Culture will Provide a Key Ingredient in Promulgating an Environment Characterized by:

- Innovation
- Prudent Risk Taking
- Value Congruence
- Progressive Management Styles

Culture profile

Culture Category	Where We Were Mid-70's	What We've Done	Where We Are 1 3 5 7 10 X	Future Direction
Short vs. Long Term Environment	Short Term Focus— Monthly, Quarterly, and Annual PBT Were Central Issues.	Improved Strategic Planning Process	Organization Still Perceives Many Mixed Signals	Need Better Balance Between Short and Long
		Recruited Planning Talent	Futures People Eliminated from Headcount	Reinforcement from Top Management that Long Term Focus Is Key to Business and Individual Growth
		Acquisitions in Non-Core Businesses	College Recruiting Vastly Reduced	(Outside) Study Is Good Example. Many Thought We Would not Proceed
		Introduction of Quarterly Business Reviews	Quarterly Reviews Heavily Weighed with a Short Term Operational Review	Increase R & D Focus
		Promotions of Non-Manufacturing Executives	Engineering Still Focused on Sustaining	Create a True Marketing Department and Hire the Required People
		Commitment to New Facilities	No Discernible Movement to Creating a Real Marketing Organization	Generate Management Commitment to Bring in People Needed for Future Growth
			Little Perceived Response to Competitive Challenges	Get Strategic Planning to Become a Daily Process. Short Term Decisions Made Under Umbrella of Long Term

Culture profile

Culture Category	Where We Were Mid-70's	What We've Done	Where We Are 1 3 5 7 10	Future Direction
Organization Communication	Grew an Organization Which Spent Little Time Communicating With Its Employees On	Implemented Communications System Only at New, Non-Union Business Units	Little Progress Accomplished	Emerging Values of Employees Will Necessitate Development of Open Communication Channels with Which to
	Goals Values Business Issues		At Most Locations Have No Continuous Mechanism for	Develop Mutually Beneficial Values and Understandings
			Communicating Down	Hear the Needs, Fears, Concerns of Employee Groups
			Hearing Up	Take Advantage of the Ideas and Knowledge Base of All Employees

Culture profile

Culture Category	Where We Were Mid-70's	What We've Done	Where We Are 1 3 5 7 10 X	Future Direction
Information Sharing	Information Was Closely Guarded	Started to Get Functional Division Heads Together to Discuss Mutual Problems	Lack of Systematic Approach to Gather and Share Information Between Divisions	Need to Create Critical Data and Informational Bases
	Not Shared Across Divisions	Monthly Marketing Meetings	Fear Still Persists of Transmitting Up "Downer" Information	Stress Honesty and Trust as Related to Good and Bad News
	Often Not Shared Up	Top Management Verbals on Wanting Straight "Scoop"	Honesty in AOP Development Still Has a Long Way To Go	Create Right Forums to Share Information Among Divisions and Between Line and Staff
	Keep Bad News Private in Hope of Fixing It		Presentations Viewed as "Pitches"	
	"Sandbagging" of Good News			

Culture profile

Culture Category	Where We Were Mid-70's	What We've Done	Where We Are 1 3 5 7 10 X	Future Direction
Individual Orientation	Development of Decentralized Divisions Created a Territorial Attitude	Created Some Systems for an Overview	Lack of Understanding and Sharing of Overall Goals and Direction	Need to Promote an Understanding, Support and Ownership of Common Goals at All Levels of the Organization
		Business Planning		
	Decisions at the Plant or Division Level Made in a Vacuum	Key Management Placements	Rewards System Geared to Individual Business Segments	Establish Systems and Organizations to Develop Critical Wide Threads
				Key Customer Strategies
	Poor Working Relationships Between Staff & Line	Established Forums Through Executive Seminars to Have General Managers Interact on a Common Basis	This Has Both Positive and Negative Effect	Geographic Strategies
		(Outside) Study Vividly Points Up Shared Issues	Ideas Generated in (Outside) Study Calling for an Overview on Individual Unit Decisions Need to Be Sold	Take a Systematic Look at the Value Added Features of Staff Review Systems
		Approach to Layoff Was a Demonstration of Shared Problems	Line View of Staffs Is Negative in Many Instances	Eliminate or Change Process Where Evident Lack of Value Added .

Culture profile

Culture Category	Where We Were Mid-70's	What We've Done	Where We Are 1 3 5 7 10 X	Future Direction
Job Security	Individual Job Security Has Not Been Viewed as a Company Goal. Especially: With Production Employees With Salaried Employees at Visible Levels Such as Plant Manager	Salaried Layoffs Have Been Done in a Systematic Basis to Avoid Favoritism and Legal Implications	Mid-Point Rating Scale Is a Result of Healthy Business Climates Over the Past Decade Doesn't Result from a Built-In Management Concern Plants Are Run with Little Management Thought as to Employee Security Issues Salaried Employees Who Cannot Succeed at a Given Level Are Normally Not Provided Opportunity to Function at a Lower or Different Level Automatic Recognition Issues Are Based on Job Security Fears	Need to Develop an Internal Understanding that Job Security Is an Emerging and Vital Issue to All Employee Levels Look at Management Production Planning Systems Which Can Minimize Layoff Cycles Over the Long Run Develop Employee Attitudes Which Make Them Feel an Intricate Part of the Organization in Order to: Obtain Their Assistance on Improving Productivity Without Fearing Loss of Jobs

213

INTEL

Informal Culture

I. Technology/Business

o An Intel Corporate objective is to be and be recognized as the best, the leaders, #1, in both technology and business. If as a corporation we achieve this objective, then it will clearly reflect positively upon us as individuals. It is assumed that it is not possible to be an outstanding success as an individual if the Corporation is mediocre or average. Our ego is strongly tied into this aspect of our culture.

o *Innovativeness, creativity* are stressed in our technology, products, and approach to the business (e.g., our approach to management training if not unique, is uncommon). In some cases this leads to high exposure to failure, but upside is high.

o The Corporation in general has a *high technology orientation,* and tends to be run by a bunch of "engineers". We have focussed less on the support aspects of our business until recent times, where we now have goals to achieve the same degree of excellence in these areas as we have in purely technical areas.

o A *bottom line emphasis* prevails throughout the Corporation, and as a result most actions are viewed relative to their impact on the bottom line. This occasionally results in conflict as exemplified by the "intensity" of the participants in wafer start allocation meetings during periods of factory capacity limitations.

o We are sensitive to our *image with our customers and the business community.* Commitments to customers

214

are considered sacred and we are upset with ourselves when we do not meet our commitments. We strive to demonstrate to the business world on a continuing basis that we are credible in describing the state of the corporation, and that we are well organized and in complete control of all things that determine the numbers.

II. Management Style

○ Intel is a company of individuals, each with his/her own personality and characteristics. And while this is true of the management team, over the course of the last ten years, certain general characteristics of the management style have emerged that have allowed us to achieve our corporate objectives.

○ *Management is self critical.* The leaders must be capable of recognizing and accepting their mistakes and to learn from them.

○ *Open (constructive) confrontation is encouraged* at all levels of the Corporation, and is viewed as a method of problem solving, conflict resolution. Hiding problems is not acceptable. Covert political activity is strongly discouraged.

○ *Decision by consensus* is the rule. Decisions once made are supported. Position in the organization is not the basis for quality of ideas. Decisions are encouraged to be made at the lowest possible level in the organization.

○ A *"highly communicative"/"open" management* is part of the style. There are an incredible number of meetings (defined as "two-way teaching" sessions). Problems are discussed in open forum, decisions are made in open forum and so on. Managers at all levels in the corporation are accessible.

○ A high degree of *Organizational Skills and Discipline* are demanded. Consistent with our business objectives, management is expected to be organized in its approach, and a high degree of planning is required. Performance to commitments are closely monitored and viewed as a key indicator of an individual's overall performance.

o *Management must be ethical.* Decisions and actions must be consistently beyond question from an ethics standpoint. Management, by telling the truth, treating all employees equitably, has established credibility that it is ethical.

o *Management faces up to difficult decisions,* whether they are business decisions (e.g., Microma), organizational, or individual.

o The responsibility for *individual development* rests with the direct line manager. To behave in an ethical manner here means that time and effort will be put into the professional development of subordinates.

III. Work Ethic/Environment

o It is a general objective of Intel to line up individual work assignments with career objectives. Further, we seek to create an environment that allows the employee to enjoy his/her work while achieving his/her goals.

o We strive to provide an *opportunity for rapid development.* A necessity for this is a strong commitment to training.

o Intel is a *results oriented* company. The focus is on *substance* vs. form, *quality* vs. quantity.

o We believe in the principle that *hard work, high productivity* is something to be proud of. A high degree of discipline is to be expected and admired.

o The concept of assumed responsibility is accepted. (If a task needs to be done, assume you have the responsibility to get it done.)

o *Commitments are long term;* if career problems occur at some point, reassignment is a better alternative than termination.

o We desire to have *all employees involved and participative* in their relationship with Intel. We want the employees to care about their company. To aid in achieving this end, we stress good communications and attempt to organize the company in smallest possible groups to allow a sense of identity and closeness.

o There is an expectation of *ethical behavior* on the part of all employees.

IV. Intel Teams

○ Teams are an integral part of the Intel work/ethic environment. Team performance is critical to the accomplishment of Intel objectives.

○ Teams at Intel come in a variety of forms. There are (essentially) formally defined teams in many organizations of the Company (e.g., the Field Sales Force, Fab IV, etc.). There are special teams that are formed to solve major problems, many of which are inter-divisional in nature. We frequently call this type of team a "task force."

Although the above teams are important, probably most important to Intel are the "invisible" teams, not formally defined, not specially formed, that rise to the occasion to solve team problems that occur on a continuing basis during normal operations. It is only through the efforts of these invisible teams that Intel achieves its aggressive objectives.

○ *Team objectives* take *precedent* over *individual objectives*. The principle is applied in day to day operations and is fundamental. If changes in job assignments or organizational structure are necessary, they are made in a manner to optimize team results, rather than to maintain individual career paths.

○ There is much emphasis on "*managing interfaces*". We operate in the world of matrix management and "multi bosses". In many situations responsibilities are ill defined and it is critical that the principle of assumed responsibility is applied. The alternative is to build large overhead operations, with much duplication of talents, to cover such situations.

ELI LILLY CO.

Basic Personnel
Policies

Complying with requests that have been made, the following indicates some of my thoughts relative to the fundamental principles that should be followed in taking care of the personnel policies of the company. These are ideas which, doubtless, will not be found in any printed form. They have been distilled through the last thirty-nine years from experience in dealing with people; consequently, they may be faulty to a large extent. However, experience with them will indicate whether or not they should and can stand the test of time or should be replaced by other, more modern methods of handling people.

These are not particularly arranged in their order of importance or in the order in which they should be considered. They should be considered merely as some rambling thoughts that have deposited themselves in my mind and which I have been asked to reduce to writing.

1. Fairness

The company must always be considered fair by the employee. Even though an employee may not consider his immediate supervisor fair or his associates fair, everything must be done to see that the employee knows by his own experience and the experience of others that the company is always fair with its employees.

If such an understanding can be brought about, then it gives the individuals carrying out the personnel policies of the company a very good standing and will help eliminate many of the individuals the line supervision wants to discharge. Experience has indicated in many instances of this kind that, if the individuals concerned are given to understand exactly the situation as to what caused the difficulty with their associates or supervision and are given another opportunity, then they either fire themselves or prove the charges made against them were false. In either event, the people in the personnel department handling the situation have done a good job, because the employees feel they had fair and just consideration.

An individual with the least understanding of people can fire anybody if he has the authority, but it takes a confident individual with much tolerance, consideration, and understanding of human beings to help an unfortunate employee to overcome a situation and develop that employee to a point where he will be a satisfied, happy, and contented employee. Such individuals really are worth working with.

2. Discharges

Over the years we have had a philosophy that no person with supervisory responsibility was forced to keep someone under his supervision whom he did not want, whatever the reason might be. That means that a department head can indicate that he does not want a particular individual and that individual must be removed from that particular department. The same is true of a manager, division director, vice president, or an executive vice president.

The only individuals who can separate a person from the company are those in the personnel department. This, I think, is a fundamentally sound philosophy, because if it is understood by the employees then they know their cases will have proper and complete consideration and they will receive fair treatment, if the philosophy indicated in Item #1 is understood.

This philosophy on discharges also helps the line supervision, because they know they must have a just and reasonable cause for recommending the separation of an individual and, just because they don't like Bill Jones or Sadie Smith, they can't have that particular person separated from the company.

3. Outside Conduct

There is always a question of conduct when there are two or more people associated together. Many years ago we tried to develop a policy which, I believe, has worked out quite well — that being that it is none of our concern what an individual does on the outside as long as the action does not interfere with the individual's work here or with his associates in the business.

This may seem like a rather loose sort of a program to follow but, after all, it is hard to find anyone in the organization who can decide what is right and what is wrong for each and every individual employee. I was never able to do it and I think the employees appreciate the fact that we understand and realize that from time to time they may slip from the straight and narrow way, but we are not going to pass judgment on them. If we were to follow that sort of plan, who in the organization would there be to pass judgment on the last man?

4. Decision by Supervision

As happens when there are around a thousand people in supervisory positions, some of them make wrong decisions affecting employees — some of which are beneficial to the employees and some of which are not. However, supervision must be backed up by the company in connection with the decisions made, if at all possible. Otherwise, supervision would lose its standing and the employees would be running to every Tom, Dick, and Harry for a revision of the decision made by the immediate supervisors on the job.

The following of such a policy indicates that people in the supervisory positions must be properly trained and they must understand how they are to handle people, otherwise a most unfortunate situation would result.

Every once in a while some supervisor will make a decision that may cost the company money to back up, but that sort of a plan must be followed. In this way the employee can never be given the opportunity of saying that the company went back on its word and, of course, the company's word is the supervisor's word.

5. Know Everyone

This is something that becomes more and more difficult to do as the operations increase in size and the number of employees increase. At one time it was a simple thing for the people in the personnel end of the organization to know every employee. However, the same principle must apply and plans must be developed to make this possible.

It would seem that the top people in the personnel department should appear before groups of employees as often as it is possible, taking advantage of the opportunities offered by the Introductory School, Information Course, Supervisory Institute, etc. Not the least among the opportunities for knowing people and having people know you are the social activities of the organization in the employee activities groups.

If the employees, through contacts of one kind or another, have the impression that the individual at the head of the personnel department of the organization is a "good fellow", then I think the employees will feel more comfortable about coming to that individual for consideration than if they do not know the individual who is responsible for the personnel department.

In other words, the employees feel they want a friend in court and they want to know who that friend is and as much about that individual as they can in order to appraise the service he is capable of rendering for them. If this appraisal is satisfactory, then you have good personnel relations throughout the organization. If the appraisal is unsatisfactory, then the person should be removed, because, after all, it is the appraisal of the people in the personnel department by the employees that either makes or breaks personnel work in a company.

6. Responsibility

In this organization we have been very fortunate in having the only four presidents of the company bear the Lilly name.

The Lilly family is held in high regard not only by the employees, but by the citizens of Indianapolis and by other individuals who have had an opportunity to know them. This is, indeed, very helpful from a personnel point of view.

Whenever anything advantageous to the employees has been

put into effect, we have always felt that this information should be given to the employees over the signature of the president, because it furthers the belief in the minds of the employees that he is a fine fellow and is interested in their welfare.

Conversely, if anything of a different nature is necessary, then this must of necessity be sent out to the employees over the signature of the top personnel individual. If that individual has enough contacts throughout the organization and has the proper acceptance by the employees, they will accept the decision feeling that if it were not right and fair the individual at the head of the personnel activity would not have signed it.

The acceptance of the various things presented to our employees, I think, has been one of the most satisfactory things that we have around here. I think it is based on the definite knowledge by the employees that things presented to the employees are for the employee's good or they would not have been presented. This is a wonderful feeling to have exist and, as long as it exists, I do not think we will have any labor difficulties of any kind. However, the situation could change very, very quickly. If just once someone in whom the employees have confidence would mislead them or not be fair or truthful with them, then the work that has been done during all the previous years can disappear like a snowball in the proverbial hot place.

The above information has been developed on request, so if it is not what you think it ought to be, or if you feel it is of no value, it can be permanently disposed of as you see fit.

E. BECK

2/19/53

APPENDIX TWO

THE Q-C CIRCLE

One of the most intriguing lessons of the art of Japanese management — and one that is close in spirit to Theory Z — is the Quality Control Circle or Q-C Circle. In fact, many American managers who have visited Japan have been struck by the effectiveness of these circles and are determined to implement similar techniques in their own companies at home.

The explanation for the circles' popularity lies in their unique function. What they do is share with management the responsibility for locating and solving problems of coordination and productivity. The circles, in other words, notice all the little things that go wrong in an organization — and then put up the flag. For that reason, the Q-C Circles, which were developed in Japan, are a useful method for achieving high quality, improved productivity and increased employee morale — all at a relatively low cost. So popular are they here right now that they are in danger of becoming the management fad of the eighties, replacing such previous fads as "Zero-Based Budgeting" and "Management by Objectives." Nevertheless, whatever their current popularity, the Q-C Circle has claims to greater longevity: For those companies that make a commitment to adapting the underlying principles of the Q-C Circle — and not just their ideals — the circles provide a way to improve an organization at all levels.

In Japan the results are spectacular. As of December, 1979, there were more than one hundred thousand Q-C Circles officially registered with the "Q-C Circle Headquarters of the Union of Japanese Scientists and Engineers." This figure does not include any of the estimated one million additional unregistered circles. According to Mr. Joji Arai, director of the Washington, D.C., office of the Japan Productivity Center, the average Q-C Circle in Japan produces each year fifty to sixty implemented suggestions per worker. The current record is held by one company that averaged *ninety-nine implemented suggestions per worker* for a single year. Imagine the mass involvement of all workers at all levels. It adds up to thousands of work improvement suggestions and ideas that contribute substantially to the productivity of the Japanese firm. These improvements, however, do not come without cost. Mr. Arai also reports that the average Japanese employee, during his or her first ten years of employment, receives approximately 500 days of training, including classroom instruction and on-the-job training.

How do the circles work so well? In Japan a Q-C Circle typically consists of from two to ten employees who are permanently assigned to that circle. All employees (temporary, part-time, and employees at all levels) are encouraged to participate. Each circle's employees form a natural working group in which everyone's work is related in some way. In the larger scheme, individual circles are related to one another through "Q-C Circle" — temporary federations of a number of Q-C Circles within a plant, formed for the purpose of working on one specific project. The task of each Q-C Circle, headed by a foreman, is to study any problems of production or service that fall within the scope of its work. In most cases, a circle undertakes a study project that can be solved within about three months, and which should take no longer than six months. Then, in each November — which is designated National Q-C Circle Month — conventions are held, study of the circle's efforts is undertaken, and recognition is offered.

Ordinarily, each circle meets for an hour or two each week, sometimes on company-paid time, sometimes on the employees' time, to discuss their project. A typical project may involve a problem in quality which one or more circle members have identified. Perhaps they will suggest that the problem is a serious one, and will discuss it with other members of the circle, including the foreman. The group may then begin a systematic study of the problem, collecting statistics on its type and nature, perhaps even counting the number of defects per part at each of the stages in the production process covered by members of the circle. At the end of the study period of perhaps six weeks, members meet again to analyze the data, drawing charts and graphs to determine the problem's source: Is it a defective design being supplied by engineering, a mis-designed part coming from suppliers, a machine improperly set up, or a lack of coordination among members of the circle? Once the problem is identified, circle members then suggest steps that should be taken to correct it. If those steps can be undertaken entirely by members of the circle, they will implement their suggestion. If the problem is a more general one, then members may call upon the formation of a Q-C team to seek out the plant-wide source of the problem; or they may make a recommendation to upper levels of management on what the solution should be. Ultimately, a solution is identified and implemented. The results of the study are published in the plant newsletter; recognition for successful implementation is given to that circle; and, if it is a particularly innovative or important solution, it will be nominated for a company, industry, or even national award. The company will report to its employees the collective impact of all the implemented suggestions, so that everyone will see the relationship between their successful work and the profits of the company and the size of their bonuses.

Q-C Circles have been succeeding in Japan for a long time. They were begun after World War II, in January of 1949. Eighteen months later, Dr. W. E. Deming, an American professor of statistics, was invited to teach in the first "Eight-Day Quality Control Seminar," which was organized by the Union of Japanese Scientists and Engineers. The impetus for the seminar was the Union's belief that industry's long-standing separation of study and analysis from work routines was ineffective. The engineers felt they could not possibly investigate all the problems of quality and productivity within a plant, and so were determined to provide a framework within which workers could share those tasks. Dr. Deming provided the workers with training in statistical techniques that could be used to identify problems of quality and productivity. These techniques, which had been developed by industrial engineers in the United States, formed the underlying analytical tools still used by Q-C Circle.

While there is no particular magic in the statistical techniques themselves — they have been widely used in the United States for more than 100 years — what is different is the determination of the Japanese to invest in teaching these techniques to production-level employees, and then to delegate to these employees the power and authority to influence changes in the organization of work, in order to bring about improvements in quality and productivity. It was this sharing of power with lower-level employees and the investment in training these employees that marked Japan's innovation.

The importance of the statistical techniques in Japan was so great that in June of 1951 the "Deming Prize" was instituted to recognize outstanding achievements by Q-C Circles in Japan. The American influence was strengthened in 1954 when Dr. J. M. Juran, a United States professor, was invited to teach in the "Quality Control Management Seminar," also organized by the Union of Japanese Scientists and Engineers. But statistics alone were not the crucial element in the circles' success. The combination of the measurement techniques contributed by Deming and by Juran plus the Japanese attention to the human side of organization has produced the phenomenon of the Q-C Circle as we know it.

As the Japanese emphasize, the success of their Q-C Circles depends not solely on technique but on exactly this underlying human aspect of their productive aims. As the Union has put it, the fundamental purposes of the Q- C Circle are to:

- o "Contribute to the improvement and development of the enterprise.
- o Respect humanity and build a happy, bright workshop which is meaningful to work in.
- o Display human capabilities fully and eventually draw out infinite possibilities."

Clearly, there is quite a distance between the attention to statistical techniques on the one hand, and the grand vision embodied in these general purposes on the other. In the successful implementation of the Q-C Circle, it is essential that *both* qualities be fully implemented. The danger in the United States appears to be that many companies make use of the statistical techniques, while regarding the general purposes as nothing more than meaningless homilies to be largely ignored.

When the human and the statistical are thoughtfully combined, the scope of Q-C Circle is nearly limitless. According to the Union of Japanese Scientists and Engineers handbook, "Q-C Circles are usually introduced into production workshops.

However, the circle has already expanded beyond the production floor, for example, to offices, sales departments, warehouses, banks, insurance companies and so on. There are Q-C Circles involving both a parent company and its affiliates or subcontractors that work closely together in the day-to-day operation. Many of these circles have successfully improved their operations, as well as communications between them." In some cases, cooperation even extends between competitors: "Q-C Circles of rival companies hold exchange meetings, for instance in such areas as the iron and steel and shipbuilding industries. Exchanges of this nature may or may not be possible, depending on the philosophy of top management and the historical background of a cooperative relationship." Because ninety-four percent of Japanese children attend senior high school or technical high school, the vast majority of Q-C Circle members are at least high school graduates. In fact, in many technical high schools, there is an increasing demand for the study of techniques and concepts required for Q-C Circles activities, in addition to the study of conventional technical and engineering disciplines.

But perhaps the greatest contribution of the Q-C Circles in Japan concerns the treatment of the individual worker, as the handbook points out:

> No matter how much factories are mechanized, so far as there are people still working there, they should be treated as human individuals. But this aspect is seriously neglected these days. Those companies that do not give due consideration to humanity will lose their best people sooner or later. There was ample evidence of this in such countries as the United States in the past twenty years or so. There can be no excuse for disregarding individual personality, slighting a man's ability, regarding people as machinery and discriminating against them.
>
> . . . People spend much of their lifetime at their working place. It would be much more desirable to work in a pleasant place where humanity is paid due respect and where people feel their work has some real meaning. That is what Q-C Circle aims to achieve. . . . A mechanized factory still requires control by a workshop of people. As people are driven by a desire to study more, they acquire an ability far beyond their previous expectations.

It is doubtful whether the mechanism known as meritocracy, a system that rates people based on their current performance and already acquired ability, can draw out their hidden ability.

Unfortunately, many American companies seem to insist on the use of Q-C Circles simply by managerial fiat. The Japanese stress the impossibility of this approach. Instead, management must create positive conditions, and then the patience to allow effort and morale to grow naturally. The handbook goes on: "Circle activities should be so designed that morale is gradually elevated, or rather morale becomes elevated as a natural consequence of taking part in the activity. While it is an objective to create harmonious relations, the word 'create' should not be interpreted as doing something by force. Harmonious relations should bloom spontaneously as flowers do. It is a poor workshop where operators and foremen are considered to be part of the machinery and required to do a job specified by set standards. What constitutes a human being is the ability to think. A workshop should become a place where people can think and use their wisdom. It must be one of the objectives of Q-C Circle activities to develop this. Rather than disciplining operators to do the job strictly as they have been taught, is it not possible to make them think and ask questions whenever they face a problem? Why not allow them to improve or allow them to express their opinions or present information useful for improvement if the nature of improvement requires authorization and coordination above the workshop level?"

Again, there must be a sharing of rewards with employees, if the underlying concept of equal participation and sharing is to have meaning. "One of the strong desires of working people is to earn a better income. Q-C Circle objectives naturally include increasing income. The Theory goes that as a pie gets larger, so does the individual shares of that pie. Q-C Circle activities boost company profits and eventually increase income of those people who contributed through Q-C Circle activities to the increased earning power."

In a sense, the objective of the Q-C Circle is to permit every employee to be a planner and an engineer as well as a worker. "The function of engineers differs according to ability, status, customs, and their relations with the workshop. In the United States, for example, engineers formulate standards, while operators in the workshop implement the standards faithfully. The engineers' function is separated from that of the workshop and a gap exists between the two. It is true that Q-C Circle activities aim at freeing engineers from the workshop so that they can devote their time to more constructive work. So for best results measures must be taken to keep them in close contact with Q-C Circles."

The underlying messages are many, but they are not overwhelming. Perhaps the first message to the United States is that a firm can realize the full potential of its employees only if it both invests in their training and then shares with them the power to influence decisions. Without training, the invitation to participate in decision making will lead only to frustration and conflict. Without a sharing of decision-making power, an investment in training will be both frustrating and wasteful. That American firm that hopes to learn from the Japanese example need only do that which the Japanese themselves have done. Just as they have studied the United States industrial system and have blended together the best aspects of both, so we must do the same.

Of course, a successful implementation of the Q-C Circle in an American company can take place only if middle and upper levels of management truly understand the conditions necessary for the success of the program, and support them. This in turn means that the executive groups must offer the kinds of long-run and cooperative incentives without which cooperation at lower levels will not occur. Thus, the Q-C Circle cannot be understood in isolation, but only as one part of a larger and more complex organizational system — and such a system as Theory Z offers.

BIBLIOGRAPHY

Abegglen, James C. *The Japanese Factory: Aspects of Its Social Organization*. Glencoe, Ill.: The Free Press, 1958.

Argyris, Chris. *Integrating the Individual and the Organization*. New York: John Wiley & Sons, Inc., 1964.

Argyris, Chris, and Donald A. Schon. *Organizational Learning: A Theory of Action Perspective*. Reading, Mass.: Addison-Wesley, 1978.

Barnard, Chester I. *The Functions of the Executive (30th ed.)* Cambridge: Harvard University Press, 1968.

Blau, Peter M., and W. Richard Scott. *Formal Organizations*. San Francisco: Scott, Foresman, 1962.

Chandler, Alfred D., Jr. *Strategy and Structure*. Garden City, New York: Doubleday-Anchor, 1966.

Coke, Robert E. *Work, Mobility, and Participation*. Berkeley: University of California Press, 1979.

Dore, Ronald. *British Factory — Japanese Factory*. Berkeley: University of California Press, 1973.

Durkheim, Emile. *Suicide: A Study in Sociology*, trans. J. A. Spaulding and G. Simpson. New York: The Free Press, 1951.

Durkheim, Emile. *The Division of Labor in Society*, trans. G. Simpson. New York: The Free Press, 1933.

Etzioni, Amitai. "Organizational Control Structure." *Handbook of Organizations*, ed. J. G. March. Chicago: Rand McNally, 1965.

Goode, William J. *World Revolution and Family Patterns*. New York: The Free Press, 1963.

Gouldner, Alvin W. "The Norm of Reciprocity." *American Sociological Review*, Vol. 25 (1961).

Hannah, Michael T. and John H. Freeman. "The Population

Ecology of Organizations." *American Journal of Sociology,* Vol. 82 (March 1977).

Homans, George C. *The Human Group.* New York: Harcourt, Brace & World, Inc., 1950.

Johnson, Richard T., and W. G. Ouchi. "Made in America (Under Japanese Management)." *Harvard Business Review* (Sept.–Oct. 1974).

Kanter, Rosebeth Moss. *Commitment and Community.* Cambridge: Harvard University Press, 1972.

Kuhn, Thomas. *The Structure of Scientific Revolution.* Chicago: University of Chicago Press, 1962.

Light, Ivan H. *Ethnic Enterprise in America.* Berkeley: University of California Press, 1972.

Likert, Rensis. *The Human Organization: Its Management and Value.* New York: McGraw-Hill, 1967.

March, J. G. and H. A. Simon. *Organizations.* New York: John Wiley & Sons, Inc., 1968.

Marx, Karl. *Capital.* New York: Modern Library, 1936.

Mauss, Marcel. *The Gift: Forms and Functions of Exchange in Archaic Societies,* trans. Ian Cunnison. New York: W. W. Norton & Company, Inc., 1967.

McGregor, Douglas. *The Human Side of Enterprise.* New York: McGraw-Hill, 1960.

Nakane, Chie. *Japanese Society.* Middlesex, England: Penguin Books, 1973.

Ouchi, W. G. "A Conceptual Approach to the Design of Organizational Control Mechanisms." *Management Science* (August 1979).

———, "Markets, Bureaucracies, and Clans." *Administrative Science Quarterly* (March 1980).

———, and A. M. Jaeger. "Type Z Corporation: Stability in the Midst of Mobility." *Academy of Management Review* (April 1978).

———, and Jerry B. Johnson. "Types of Organizational Control and Their Relationship to Emotional Well-Being." *Administrative Science Quarterly.* Vol. 23 (June 1978).

Porras, Jerry I. and P. O. Berg. "The Impact of Organizational Development." *The Academy of Management Review* (April 1978).

Roberts, B. C., H. Okamoto, and G. C. Lodge. "Continuity and Change in the Industrial Relations Systems in Western

Europe, North America, and Japan." *Draft Report of the Trilateral Task Force on Industrial Relations to the Trilateral Commission* (May 1977).

Rohlen, Thomas P. *For Harmony and Strength: Japanese White-Collar Organization in Anthropological Perspective.* Berkeley: University of California Press, 1974.

Schein, Edgar H. *Process Consultation.* Reading, Mass.: Addison-Wesley, 1969.

Sloan, Alfred P., Jr. *My Years with General Motors.* Garden City, N.Y.: Doubleday, 1964.

Tonnies, Ferdinand. *Community and Society,* trans. C. P. Loomis. New York: Harper Torchbooks, 1957.

Walton, Richard. "The Diffusion of New Work Structures: Explaining Why Success Didn't Take." *Organizational Dynamics* (Winter 1975).

Weber, Max. *Economy and Society,* ed. G. Roth and C. Wittich. New York: Bedminster Press, 1968.

Williamson, Oliver E. *Markets and Hierarchies: Analysis and Antitrust Implications.* New York: The Free Press, 1975.

Williamson, Oliver E. "Transaction-Cost Economics: The Governance of Contractual Relations." *The Journal of Law and Economics* (October 1979).

FOOTNOTES

INTRODUCTION

1. See George C. Homans, *The Human Group* (New York: Harcourt, Brace & World, Inc., 1950).

CHAPTER TWO

1. For a thorough and practical discussion of participative methods of decision making and their use in industry, see Edgar H. Schein, *Process Consultation* (Reading, Mass.: Addison-Wesley, 1969).
2. See Thomas P. Rohlen, *For Harmony and Strength: Japanese White-Collar Organization in Anthropological Perspective* (Berkeley: University of California Press, 1974).
3. Sociologists and anthropologists have offered a great variety of views on the nature and extent of American influence during the post-war era on the structure of Japanese industry. The interpretation which I present here is not definitive, but it is representative.
4. See Amitai Etzioni, "Organizational Control Structure," *Handbook of Organizations,* ed. J. G. March (Chicago: Rand McNally, 1965).

CHAPTER THREE

1. For a recent and complete translation of Weber's point of view, see Max Weber, *Economy and Society*, ed. G. Roth and C. Wittich (New York: Bedminster Press, 1968). For an interpretation of Weber's ideas as they apply to American organizations, see Peter M. Blau and W. Richard Scott,

Formal Organizations (San Francisco: Scott, Foresman, 1962).

2. Anyone interested in a formal statement of the ecological view as it applies to organizations should see Michael T. Hannan and John H. Freeman, "The Population Ecology of Organizations," *American Journal of Sociology,* Vol. 82 (March 1977).

3. See Douglas McGregor, *The Human Side of Enterprise* (New York: McGraw-Hill, 1960).

CHAPTER FOUR

1. See Harold J. Leavitt, *Managerial Psychology,* 4th ed. (Chicago: University of Chicago Press, 1978).

2. See Edgar Schein, *Process Consultation* (Reading, Mass.: Addison-Wesley, 1969).

3. Chris Argyris's work has been among the most influential within the field of organizational research as well as within my own thinking. Although he is prolific, I refer here specifically to his landmark book *Integrating the Individual and the Organization* (New York: John Wiley & Sons, Inc., 1964).

4. See Rosebeth Moss Kanter, *Commitment and Community* (Cambridge: Harvard University Press, 1972).

5. Here and elsewhere in the book I refer to industrial clans. The meaning of *clan* I derive from the use by the sociologist Emile Durkheim. In this usage, a disorganized aggregation of individuals is a *horde*, the smallest organized unit is a *band*, and a clan is a group of bands. A clan is an intimate association of individuals who are connected to each other through a variety of ties. The members of a clan may or may not share blood relations. Here I refer to an intimate group of industrial workers who know one another well but who typically do not share blood relations.

6. See Ivan H. Light, *Ethnic Enterprise in America* (Berkeley: University of California Press, 1972).

7. See Marcel Mauss, *The Gift* (New York: W. W. Norton, 1967).

8. I have developed this work in collaboration with Jerry B. Johnson. For a complete description of the initial study, see W. G. Ouchi and Jerry B. Johnson, "Types of Organizational

Control and Their Relationship to Emotional Well-Being,"
Administrative Science Quarterly, Vol 23, (June 1978). We
were assisted in this work by Alan Wilkins, David Gibson,
Alice Kaplan, and Raymond Price, to whom I am grateful.

CHAPTER FIVE

1. See Richard Walton, "The Diffusion of New Work Structures: Explaining Why Success Didn't Take," *Organization
   Dynamics* (Winter 1975).
2. Research by Professor Richard Rumelt of UCLA and by
   Professor Alfred Chandler of Harvard University suggests
   that firms that undertake business far removed from their
   expertise tend to be less profitable than firms that grow in
   directions related to their expertise. It may be that these risky
   and unfamiliar ventures are undertaken by companies that
   have failed to invest in the development of their future
   technology and products, and therefore feel they must gamble
   on growth by striking out in unfamiliar directions.

CHAPTER SEVEN

1. See "1978 Executive Conference on Quality of Work Life,"
   Organizational Research and Development Department and
   Personnel Administration and Development Staff, General
   Motors Corporation, Detroit, Michigan, 1978. This is the
   source for the G.M. case history reported.
2. These and other G.M. details are from the Executive
   Conference report cited in the previous footnote.
3. The Scanlon Plan is described in detail in Chapter 5 in Step
   Three, which concerns incentives.

CHAPTER EIGHT

1. See William J. Goode, *World Revolution and Family
   Patterns* (New York: The Free Press, 1963).
2. Ouchi and Johnson, cited above, reports statistical data on a
   comparison between Company A and Company Z.
3. These concepts I developed in concert with Alfred M. Jaeger.
   An earlier statement of these ideas may be found in W. G.
   Ouchi and A. M. Jaeger, "Type Z Organization: Stability in

the Midst of Mobility," *Academy of Management Review* (April 1978). The data referred to here are reported in the Ouchi and Johnson article.

4. This argument has been thoroughly developed by Alfred D. Chandler, Jr., in *The Visible Hand* (Cambridge, Mass.: Harvard University Press, 1977).

INDEX